Icelandic pocket dictionary

English-Icelandic & Icelandic-English

John Shapiro

Icelandic pocket dictionary
by John Shapiro

First edition: March 2017

ENGLISH-ICELANDIC

A

aardvark • *n* jarðsvín *(n)*
abacus • *n* talnagrind *(f)*
abandon • *v* hætta, við, yfirgefa
abase • *v* auðmýkja, niðurlægja
abasement • *n* auðmýking *(f)*, lítillækkun *(f)*
abashed • *adj* vandræðalegur
abattoir • *n* sláturhús *(n)*
abbess • *n* abbadís *(f)*
abbot • *n* ábóti *(m)*
abbreviate • *v* skammstafa, stytta
abbreviation • *n* skammstöfun *(f)*, stytting *(f)*
abductor • *n* fráfærir
ablaut • *n* hljóðskipti
aborigine • *n* frumbyggi *(m)*
abortion • *n* fóstureyðing
abscess • *n* kýli *(n)*
absinthe • *n* malurtarbrennivín *(n)*
abundance • *n* gnægð *(f)*
academy • *n* akademía *(f)*
acceleration • *n* hröðun
accent • *n* áhersla *(f)*
accessory • *adj* fylgihlutur *(m)*, vitorðsmaður *(m)* • *n* fylgihlutir
accident • *n* slys *(n)*
account • *n* reikningur *(m)*
accountable • *adj* skýranlegur *(m)*
accountant • *n* endurskoðandi *(m)*
accusative • *n* þolfall *(n)* • *adj* ásaka, þolfall
acetone • *n* asetón *(n)*
acetylene • *n* kolvetnisgas *(n)*, logsuðugas *(n)*, asetýlen *(n)*
acid • *n* sýra *(f)* • *adj* súr, beiskur, meinhæðinn *(m)*, meinhæðin *(f)*, meinhæðið *(n)*
acidity • *n* sýrustig *(n)*
acme • *n* hápunktur *(m)*
acorn • *n* akarn *(n)*
acrostic • *n* gripla *(f)*
actinium • *n* aktín
activation • *n* virkjun
actor • *n* leikari *(m)*, leikkona *(f)*
actress • *n* leikkona *(f)*
actuator • *n* armstjóri *(m)*
acumen • *n* skerpa *(f)*, skarpskyggni *(f)*, skarpur skilningur *(m)*, skörp greind *(f)*, vit *(n)*
addend • *n* samleggjandi *(m)*, liður *(m)*
addicted • *adj* háður
addition • *n* viðbót *(f)*, samlagning *(f)*
address • *n* viðfang
adenine • *n* adenín *(n)*

adjectival • *adj* lýsingarorð *(n)*
adjective • *n* lýsingarorð *(n)*
adjustable • *adj* stillanlegur
admirable • *adj* aðdáanlegur
admiral • *n* aðmíráll *(m)*
admissible • *adj* leyfilegur *(m)*, heimill *(m)*
adore • *v* dýrka
adult • *n* fullorðinn *(m)*
adventure • *n* ævintýri
adverb • *n* atviksorð *(n)*
adversary • *n* andstæðingur *(m)*, óvinur *(m)*
advertisement • *n* auglýsing *(f)*
advice • *n* ráð *(n)*, ábending *(f)*
advise • *v* ráða
aerosol • *n* úðaefni *(n)*
aesthetic • *adj* sjónrænn *(m)*
aesthetics • *n* fagurfræði *(f)*
affidavit • *n* eiðsvarin yfirlýsing *(f)*, skrifleg yfirlýsing *(f)*, eiðfest yfirlýsing *(f)*
affix • *n* aðskeyti
after • *prep* eftir
afternoon • *n* síðdegi *(n)*, eftirmiðdagur *(m)*, seinnipartur *(m)*
again • *adv* aftur, á ný
agate • *n* agat
agave • *n* þyrnililjuætt *(f)*, eyðimerkurliljuætt *(f)*
age • *n* sjálfræðisaldri
agony • *n* kvöl *(n)*, þjáning *(f)*
agora • *n* samkomustaður *(m)*, markaðstorg *(n)*
agoraphobia • *n* víðáttufælni *(f)*, torgageigur *(m)*
agriculture • *n* landbúnaður *(m)*, jarðyrkja *(f)*
air • *v* lofta • *n* loft *(n)*
airfield • *n* flugvöllur *(m)*
airline • *n* flugfélag *(n)*
airplane • *n* flugvél *(f)*
airport • *n* flugvöllur, flughöfn *(f)*, flugstöð *(f)*
aitch • *n* há *((hau))*
ajar • *adv* í hálfa gátt, úr samræmi, í ósamræmi, úr takti
alalia • *n* málhelti *(n)*
alb • *n* alba *(f)*
albatross • *n* súlukóngur *(m)*
album • *n* albúm *(n)*
albumen • *n* eggjahvíta *(f)*, hvíta í eggi *(f)*
alchemist • *n* gullgerðarmaður *(m)*
alchemy • *n* gullgerðarlist *(f)*
alcohol • *n* áfengi *(n)*

alder • *n* elri
ale • *n* öl *(n)*
alfresco • *adv* undir berum himni, úti
alga • *n* þörungur *(m)*
algebra • *n* merkjamálsfræði
algorithm • *n* reiknirit, algrím *(n)*, reiknisögn *(f)*, algóriþmi *(m)*
alkaloid • *n* beiskjuefni *(n)*
alleged • *adj* meintur
allele • *n* samsæta *(f)*, genasamsæta *(f)*, tvenndargen *(n)*
allergen • *n* ofnæmisvaldur *(m)*, ofnæmisvaki *(m)*
alley • *n* sund *(n)*, húsasund *(n)*, öngstræti *(n)*
alliance • *n* bandalag *(n)*
alliteration • *n* stuðlun *(f)*, stafrím *(n)*
allspice • *n* allrahanda *(n)*, negulpipar *(m)*
almighty • *adj* almáttugur
almond • *n* mandla *(f)*, sætmandla *(f)*
alms • *n* ölmusa *(f)*
alpha • *n* alfa *(n)*
alphabet • *n* stafróf *(n)*, rittáknakerfi *(n)*
already • *adv* þegar
also • *adv* líka, einnig
altar • *n* altari *(n)*
altercation • *n* bræta *(f)*, rifrildi *(n)*, deila *(f)*, orðakast *(n)*, orðahnippingar, orðaskak *(n)*, orðasenna *(f)*
although • *conj* þó að, enda þótt
altostratus • *n* gráblika *(f)*
alveolar • *adj* tannbergsmæltur
always • *adv* alltaf
ambassador • *n* sendiherra *(m)*, ambassadör
amber • *n* raf *(n)*
ambient • *adj* umlykjandi *(m)*, allt um kring, umhverfi
ambiguous • *adj* óskýr
ambivalence • *n* tvíveðrungur *(m)*, tvíbendni *(f)*
ambulance • *n* sjúkrabíll *(m)*, sjúkrabifreið *(f)*
amen • *adv* amen
amends • *n* sárabætur, miskabætur
americium • *n* ameríkín
ampere • *n* amper
ampersand • *n* táknið, og-lykkja, tengilykkja, hlíðskipulykkja
amphetamine • *n* amfetamín *(n)*
amphibian • *n* froskdýr *(n)*
anagram • *n* raðhverfa *(f)*, orðarugl *(n)*, stafabrengl *(n)*, stafarugl *(n)*
analog • *adj* hliðrænt
analysis • *n* greining *(f)*, stærðfræðigreining *(f)*, stærðfræðileg greining *(f)*

analyze • *v* greina
anaphoric • *adj* endurvísandi *(m)*
anarchism • *n* stjórnleysisstefna
anarchy • *n* stjórnleysi *(n)*
anchor • *n* akkeri *(n)*
and • *conj* og
androgen • *n* karlhormón *(n)*, andrógen *(n)*
anecdotal • *adj* atvikssögulegur, anekdótískur
anecdote • *n* atvikssaga *(f)*, anekdóta *(f)*
anemia • *n* blóðleysi *(n)*, blóðskortur *(m)*
anemic • *adj* blóðlaus *(m)*
anemometer • *n* vindmælir *(m)*
anesthesiologist • *n* svæfingarlæknir *(m)*
aneuploid • *adj* ójafnlitna *(m)*
aneuploidy • *n* ójafnlitnun *(f)*
aneurysm • *n* slagæðargúlpur *(m)*, gúlpur *(m)*
anew • *adv* á nyju
angel • *n* engill *(m)*
angelica • *n* hvönn *(f)*
angle • *n* horn *(n)*, sjónarhorn *(n)*
angry • *adj* reiður
angular • *adj* hyrndur, skarphyrndur, horn, beinaber
animal • *n* dýr *(n)*, óargadýr *(n)* • *adj* dýrslegur
anime • *n* anime
anisotropic • *adj* misátta *(m)*, stefnuháður *(m)*, stefnuhneigður *(m)*
ankle • *n* ökkli *(n)*
annihilate • *v* tortíma
anniversary • *n* afmæli *(n)*, dánarafmæli *(n)*, ártíð *(f)*, dánardægur *(n)*, brúðkaupsafmæli *(n)*
annoy • *v* trufla
annoying • *v* truflandi
annular • *adj* hringlaga
answer • *n* svar *(n)*, ans *(n)* • *v* svara, ansa
ant • *n* maur *(n)*
antaphrodisiac • *n* lostakælir *(m)* • *adj* lostakælandi *(m)*, kynhvöt *(m)*
anteater • *n* mauraæta *(f)*
antecedent • *n* undanfari *(m)*, forliður *(f)* • *adj* undanfari *(m)*
anthill • *n* mauraþúfa *(f)*
anthology • *n* sýnisbók *(f)*, safnrit *(n)*
anthrax • *n* miltisbrandur
anthropology • *n* mannfræði *(f)*
antichrist • *n* Antíkristur *(m)*
antihistamine • *n* ofnæmislyf *(n)*, andhistamín *(n)*
antimony • *n* antímon
antineutron • *n* andnifteind *(f)*
antinomy • *n* gagnkvæði *(n)*
antiparticle • *n* andeind *(f)*

antipathy • *n* andúð (f), ógeð (n), óbeit (f)
antiproton • *n* andróteind (f)
antisocial • *adj* andfélagslegur
antonym • *n* andheiti (n), andrætt orð (n)
antonymy • *n* andræðni
anus • *n* endaþarmsop, bakrauf
anvil • *n* steðji (m)
anxiety • *n* kvíði (m), órói (m), áhyggja (f), angist (f)
apartment • *n* íbúð (f)
apathetic • *adj* áhugalaus
apathy • *n* áhugaleysi (n)
ape • *v* apa eftir • *n* api (m)
aphasia • *n* málstol (n)
aphid • *n* blaðlús (f)
aphorism • *n* kjarnyrði (n), spakmæli, orðskviður
aphrodisiac • *n* ástalyf (n), frygðarlyf (n), kynorkulyf (n), frygðarauki (m) • *adj* lostavekjandi (m), kynorkuaukandi (m), lostaörvandi (m)
apocope • *n* brottfall (n)
apocryphal • *adj* vafasamur að uppruna (m), vafasamur (m), af vafasömum uppruna, apókrýfur (m)
apologetic • *adj* afsakandi
apostate • *n* trúníðingur (m)
apostolic • *adj* postullegur
apostrophe • *n* úrfellingarmerki (n)
appear • *v* birta, birtast
appendectomy • *n* botnlanganám (n), botnlangaskurður (m)
appendicitis • *n* botnlangabólga (f)
appendix • *n* bókarauki (m), viðauki (m), botnlangi (m), botnlangatota (f)
appetite • *n* matarlyst
apple • *n* epli (n)
application • *n* forrit (n), tölvuforrit (n), umsókn (f)
approximation • *n* nálgun (f)
apricot • *n* apríkósa (f)
apron • *n* svunta (f)
aquavit • *n* ákavíti (n)
arboreal • *adj* trjábýll (m)
arcane • *adj* hulinn (m), dulinn (m)
archaic • *adj* gamaldags
archangel • *n* erkiengill (m)
archbishop • *n* erkibiskup (m)
archduke • *n* erkihertogi (m)
archenemy • *n* erkióvinur (m), erkifjandi (m)
archer • *n* bogmaður (m)
archipelago • *n* eyjaklasi
architect • *n* arkitekt (m)
architecture • *n* byggingarlist
area • *n* flatarmál (n)
areola • *n* vörtubaugur (m)

argent • *n* silfur
argon • *n* argon
argyle • *n* tíglamynstur (n)
arm • *n* handleggur, armur (m)
armadillo • *n* beltisdýr (n)
armistice • *n* vopnahlé (n)
armpit • *n* handarkriki (m)
army • *n* her (m)
arrangement • *n* röðun (f), skipan (f), uppsetning (f), uppröðun (f), uppstilling (f), ráðstöfun, samkomulag (n), útsetning (f)
array • *v* klæða • *n* fylki (n)
arrival • *n* koma (f)
arrondissement • *n* hverfi (n), sýsluhverfi (n)
arrow • *n* píla (f)
arsenic • *n* arsen
art • *n* list (f), kúnst (f)
arteriosclerosis • *n* æðakölkun (f)
artery • *n* slagæð (f)
arthropod • *n* liðdýr (n)
artichoke • *n* ætiþistill
article • *n* grein (f), greinir (m), gr. (m)
artiodactyl • *n* klaufdýr (n)
as • *conj* er, þá, þegar
ascertain • *v* ganga úr skugga um, fá fullvissu um, komast eftir, komast að
asepsis • *n* smitgát (f)
asexual • *adj* kynlaus (m)
asexuality • *n* ókynhneigð
ash • *n* aska (f), æ (n)
ashtray • *n* öskubakki (m)
ask • *v* spyrja, fregna
asparagus • *n* spergill (m), aspas (m)
aspen • *n* ösp (f)
ass • *n* asni (m), hálviti (m), fífl (n), rass
assailant • *n* árásarmaður (m)
assassin • *n* launmorðingi (m)
assault • *n* áhlaup (n)
assemble • *v* samansetja, flykkjast, smala
assembler • *n* smali
asshole • *n* rassgat (n), asni (m), fífl (n), hálfviti (m)
assist • *n* stoðsending (f)
assistance • *n* aðstoð (f), hjálp (f)
assistant • *n* aðstoðarmaður (m) • *adj* aðstoð
associative • *adj* tenginn (m), tengiastatine • *n* astat
asterisk • *n* stjörnumerki (n)
asteroid • *n* smástirni
astonishing • *adj* undraverður (m)
astonishment • *n* undrun (f)
astride • *adv* klofvega
astrology • *n* stjörnuspeki (f), stjörnuspáfræði (f)
astronaut • *n* geimfari (m)

astronomy • *n* stjörnufræði *(f)*
astrophysicist • *n* stjarneðlisfræðingur *(m)*
astrophysics • *n* stjarneðlisfræði *(f)*
astute • *adj* slyngur, kænn, séður
asymmetrical • *adj* missamhverfur *(m)*, mishverfur *(m)*
asymptote • *n* aðfella *(f)*, ósnertill *(m)*
asynchronous • *adj* ósamstilltur *(m)*
asystole • *n* sláttarstöðvun *(f)*, samdráttarleysi í hjarta *(n)*, rafleysa *(f)*
atheism • *n* trúleysi *(n)*, guðleysi *(n)*
atheist • *n* trúleysingi *(m)*, guðleysingi *(m)*, heiðingi *(m)*
atom • *n* frumeind *(f)*, atóm *(n)*
atrophy • *n* rýrnun *(m)*
attic • *n* háaloft *(n)*, þakhæð *(f)*, loft *(n)*, ris *(n)*, rishæð *(f)*, hanabjálki *(m)*
attorney • *n* lögfræðingur *(m)*, fulltrúi *(m)*, umboðsmaður *(m)*
auditor • *n* endurskoðandi *(m)*
aunt • *n* föðursystir *(f)*, móðursystir *(f)*
aural • *adj* eyrna-, heyrnar-
aurist • *n* eyrnalæknir *(m)*
aurora • *n* segulljós
austerity • *n* strangleiki *(m)*, harka *(f)*
author • *n* höfundur *(m)*, rithöfundur *(m)*

autism • *n* einhverfa *(f)*, sjálfhverfa *(f)*
autistic • *adj* sjálfhverfur *(m)*
autograph • *v* árita • *n* eiginhandaráritun *(f)*
automatic • *adj* sjálfvirkur *(m)*
automaton • *n* sjálfvirki *(m)*, vélmenni *(n)*
automobile • *n* bifreið *(f)*
autonomy • *n* sjálfræði *(n)*, sjálfsstjórn *(f)*
autumn • *n* haust *(n)* • *adj* haust-, haustlegur *(m)*
avalanche • *n* snjóflóð
avenue • *n* troð, breiðstræti *(n)*
avert • *v* snúa frá, snúa undan, beina frá, snúa sér undan, líta undan, afstýra, koma í veg fyrir
await • *v* bíða
away • *adj* fjarverandi, ekki við, í, frí
awkward • *adj* klunnalegur, vandræðalegur, pínlegur
awl • *n* alur *(m)*
axiom • *n* frumsenda *(f)*, frumsetning *(f)*
axis • *n* ás *(m)*, möndull
axle • *n* öxull *(m)*
azure • *n* fagurblár *(m)*, himinblár, heiðblár

B

baa • *v* jarma • *n* jarm *(n)* • *interj* mee
babble • *v* babla, masa, þvæla, mala, blaðra, vera með heimskuhjal, tala of mikið, kjafta frá, fleipra út úr sér, niða, hjala • *n* babl *(n)*, óskýrt tal *(n)*, heimskulegt þvaður *(n)*, mas *(n)*, niður *(m)*, vatnsniður *(m)*
baboon • *n* bavían *(m)*, bavíani *(m)*, hundapi *(m)*
baboonish • *adj* eins og bavían *(n)*, bavíana-
baby • *n* ungbarn *(n)*, ungabarn *(n)*, kornabarn *(n)*
babyhood • *n* frumbernska *(f)*, vítvoðungsaldur *(m)*
babyish • *adj* smábarnalegur, barnalegur, kjánalegur
babysitter • *n* barnapía
bachelor • *n* piparsveinn *(m)*, einhleyplingur *(m)*, ókvæntur maður *(m)*
bachelorhood • *n* einlífi *(n)*, einhleypni *(f)*, ókvæni *(n)*
bacillus • *n* staflaga baktería *(f)*, baktería *(f)*
back • *n* bak *(n)*, bakhlið *(f)*, afturhluti *(m)*

• *adv* til baka
backache • *n* bakverkur *(m)*
backbite • *v* baknaga, rægja, rógbera
backboard • *n* bakfjalir, spjald *(n)*
backbone • *n* hryggur *(m)*, uppistaða *(f)*, meginstoð *(f)*, skapfesta *(f)*, bein í nefinu *(n)*
backdrop • *n* bakhengi *(m)*, baktjald *(n)*, bakgrunnur *(m)*, baksvið *(n)*
backer • *n* stuðningsmaður *(m)*
backhand • *n* bakhandarhögg *(n)*, rithönd sem hallar til vinstri
backhanded • *adj* bakhandar-, gerður með handarbakinu *(m)*, klunnalegur *(m)*, klaufskur *(m)*, öfugsnúinn *(m)*, tvíræður *(m)*, vafasamur *(m)*, hallandi til vinstri
backpack • *v* ferðast fótgangandi með bakpoka • *n* bakpoki *(m)*
backside • *n* bakhlið *(n)*, bak *(n)*, rass *(m)*, rasskinnar, sitjandi *(m)*
backspin • *n* baksnúningur *(m)*
backstage • *n* baksvið *(n)* • *adj* leynilegur • *adv* leynilegur, baksviðs, að tjaldabaki, aftan til á leiksviði
backup • *n* öryggisafrit *(n)*, afrit *(n)* • *adj*

öryggis-
bacon • *n* flesk *(n)*, beikon *(n)*
bacteria • *n* gerlar, bakteríur
bactericide • *n* gerlabani *(m)*, bakteríueyðir *(m)*
bacteriophage • *n* bakteríuveira *(f)*, faga *(f)*, gerilveira *(f)*, gerilæta *(f)*
bad • *adj* vondur, slæmur, illur
badger • *n* greifingi *(m)*
badminton • *n* badminton *(n)*
bag • *v* sekkja, setja í poka, veiða
bagpipes • *n* sekkjapípa *(f)*
bail • *n* trygging *(f)*
bailiwick • *n* fógetaumdæmi *(n)*, þekkingarsvið *(n)*, starfssvið *(n)*, áhugasvið *(n)*, valdsvið *(n)*
bake • *v* baka, seyða
baker • *n* bakari *(m)*
bakery • *n* bakarí *(n)*
balcony • *n* svalir, altan
bald • *adj* sköllóttur *(m)*
ball • *n* bolti *(m)*, kúla, kjaftæði *(n)*, rugl *(n)*, kjarkur *(m)*
ballerina • *n* ballettdansmær *(f)*
ballet • *n* ballett *(m)*, listdans *(m)*, leikdans *(m)*
balloon • *n* blaðra *(f)*, loftbelgur *(m)*
baluster • *n* rimill *(m)*, pílári *(m)*, brjóstriðssúla *(f)*, speli *(m)*, spæll *(m)*
balustrade • *n* brjóstrið *(n)*, súlnabrjóstrið *(n)*, handrið *(n)*, rimlahandrið *(n)*, grindverk *(n)*, rimlagirðing *(f)*
ban • *v* banna
banana • *n* banani *(m)*, bjúgaldin *(n)*
bandage • *n* umbúðir
bandwidth • *n* bandbreidd *(f)*
bang • *v* banga • *n* bang, toppur *(m)*
banister • *n* handrið *(n)*, stigahandrið *(n)*, rimill *(m)*, pílári *(m)*, brjóstriðssúla *(f)*, speli *(m)*, spæll *(m)*
bank • *n* banki *(m)*, bankaútibú *(n)*, bakki *(m)*, árbakki *(m)*
bankrupt • *adj* gjaldþrota
bankruptcy • *n* gjaldþrot
banner • *n* borði *(m)*
bannister • *n* handrið *(n)*, stigahandrið *(n)*, rimill *(m)*, pílári *(m)*, brjóstriðssúla *(f)*, speli *(m)*, spæll *(m)*
banquet • *n* matarveisla *(f)*, stórveisla *(f)*, fjöldaveisla *(f)*
banter • *v* stríða • *n* stríðni *(f)*
baobab • *n* apabrauðstré
baptism • *n* skírn *(f)*
bar • *n* stöng *(f)*, bar *(m)*, krá *(f)*, ölstofa *(f)*, pöbb *(m)*, taktur *(m)*, slá *(f)*, bar *(n)*
barbarian • *n* barbari *(m)*
barber • *n* rakari *(m)*

barefoot • *adv* berfættur, berum fótum
barge • *n* prammi *(m)*
barium • *n* barín
bark • *v* gelta, geyja, gjamma, bofsa • *n* gelt *(n)*, gá *(f)*, hundgá *(f)*, gey *(n)*, gjamm *(n)*, bofs *(n)*, börkur *(m)*, barkur *(m)*
barley • *n* bygg *(m)*
barn • *n* hlaða *(f)*
baron • *n* barón *(m)*
baronet • *n* barónett *(m)*
barrel • *n* tunna *(f)*, hlaup *(n)*, byssuhlaup *(n)*, baula *(f)*
barrister • *n* málafærslumaður *(m)*
bartender • *n* barþjónn *(m)*
baryon • *n* þungeind *(f)*
basalt • *n* basalt
base • *n* herstöð *(f)*, bækistöðvar, höfuðstöðvar, stikkfrí, grunnflötur *(m)*, veldisstofn *(m)*
baseball • *n* hafnabolti *(m)*, hornabolti *(m)*
basement • *n* kjallari *(m)*
basket • *n* karfa
basketball • *n* körfubolti *(m)*, körfuknattleikur *(m)*
bassoon • *n* fagott *(n)*
bassoonist • *n* fagottleikari *(m)*
bat • *n* leðurblaka *(f)*, kylfa *(f)* • *v* slá
bath • *v* baða
bathe • *v* baða • *n* bað *(n)*
bathrobe • *n* sloppur *(m)*, baðsloppur *(m)*
bathroom • *n* baðherbergi *(n)*
bathtub • *n* baðkar *(n)*, baðker *(n)*
battery • *n* rafhlaða *(f)*, batterí *(n)*, rafgeymir *(m)*, líkamsmeiðingar
battle • *n* bardagi *(m)*, barátta *(f)*
battlefield • *n* vígvöllur *(m)*
baud • *n* bot *(n)*, baud *(n)*, biti
bay • *n* vík *(f)*, flói *(m)*, bugt *(f)*
bayonet • *n* byssustingur *(m)*
bazaar • *n* basar *(m)*, markaður *(m)*, torg *(n)*
be • *v* vera
beach • *n* strönd *(f)*
beak • *n* nef *(n)*, goggur *(m)*
beam • *n* bjálki *(m)*, geisli *(m)*
bean • *n* baun
bear • *n* björn *(m)*
beard • *n* skegg *(n)*
bearded • *adj* skeggjaður
bearer • *n* beri *(m)*, kistuberi *(m)*, handhafi *(m)*
beautiful • *adj* fallegur, fagur
beautify • *v* fegra
beauty • *n* fegurð *(f)*
beaver • *n* bjór *(m)*, bifur *(m)*
because • *adv* vegna • *conj* því, af því, því

að, af því að, vegna, vegna þess, vegna
þess að, út af því að
bed • *n* rúm *(n)*
bedroom • *n* svefnherbergi *(n)*
bee • *n* býfluga *(f)*, bý, bé *((byeh))*
beech • *n* beyki
beef • *n* nautakjöt *(n)*
beehive • *n* býkúpa *(f)*, býflugnabú *(n)*
beer • *n* bjór, öl, ölkrús, bjórkrús
beeswax • *n* bývax *(n)*
beetle • *n* bjalla *(f)*
beetroot • *n* rauðrófa, rauðbeða
befool • *v* hafa að fífli, blekkja, pretta,
gabba
before • *prep* áður, fyrr
beggar • *n* betlari *(m)*, beiningamaður *(m)*
begin • *v* byrja, hefjast
beginning • *n* byrjun *(f)*
behold • *v* sjá
being • *n* vera, tilvera
bell • *n* bjalla *(f)*, klukka *(f)*, símtal *(n)*
bellicose • *adj* herskár *(m)*, deilugjarn *(m)*,
bardagafús *(m)*, óeirinn *(m)*, errinn *(m)*
belligerent • *n* styrjaldaraðili *(m)*, deiluaðili *(m)* • *adj* herskár, ófriðsamur, deilugjarn
bellows • *n* físir *(m)*, físar, físibelgur *(m)*,
físibelgir
belly • *n* magi *(m)*, malli *(m)*
belt • *n* belti *(n)*
bench • *n* bekkur *(m)*
bend • *v* beygja
bendable • *adj* beygjanlegur
benevolence • *n* örlæti
benzene • *n* bensen *(n)*, bensól *(n)*
bequeath • *v* arfleiða
bereave • *v* svipta, ræna, svipta ástvinum
bereavement • *n* ástvinamissir *(m)*, einstæðingsskapur *(m)*
bereft • *adj* svipta, taka frá
beret • *n* alpahúfa *(f)*
berkelium • *n* berkelín
berry • *n* ber *(n)*
beryllium • *n* beryllín
best • *adj* bestur
betray • *v* svíkja
better • *adj* betri • *adv* betur
between • *prep* á milli
beverage • *n* drykkur *(m)*
bib • *n* smekkur *(m)*
bicameral • *adj* tveggja deilda, með þvær
þingdeildir
bicuspid • *n* forjaxl *(m)*, framjaxl *(m)*
bicycle • *n* reiðhjól *(n)*
bidirectional • *adj* tvíbeind
big • *adj* fullorðinn
bigram • *n* tvístæða *(f)*

bilabial • *adj* tvívaramæltur
bilateral • *adj* tvíhliða
bilberry • *n* aðalbláber *(n)*
bile • *n* gall *(n)*
bilingual • *adj* tvítyngdur
bill • *n* nef *(n)*, goggur *(m)*, frumvarp *(n)*,
reikningur, nóta *(f)*
binary • *adj* tvíunda-, tvístæður *(m)*
binaural • *adj* tvíheyrnar-, tvíeyrna-,
tvíhlustar-
bind • *v* binda
binoculars • *n* sjónauki
binomial • *n* tvíliða *(f)*, tvíliða stærð *(f)* •
adj tvíliðu-, tvíliða
biochemistry • *n* lífefnafræði
biologist • *n* líffræðingur *(m)*
biology • *n* líffræði *(f)*
bioluminescence • *n* lífljómun *(f)*
biopsy • *v* taka vefsýni • *n* vefsýnitaka *(f)*
biotite • *n* bíótít *(n)*
birch • *n* björk *(f)*, birki *(n)*, birkitré *(n)*
bird • *n* fugl *(m)*
birth • *n* fæðing *(f)*, hingaðburður *(m)*
birthday • *n* afmælisdagur *(m)*, fæðingardagur *(m)*
bisexuality • *n* tvíkynhneigð *(f)*
bishop • *n* biskup *(m)*
bismuth • *n* bismút
bison • *n* vísundur *(m)*
bit • *n* biti, tvíundatölustafur
bite • *v* bíta
bitmap • *n* bitakort *(n)*, punktamynd *(f)*,
punktafylki *(n)*
bitter • *adj* beiskur
bittersweet • *adj* ljúfsár *(m)*
black • *n* svartur • *adj* svartur
blackberry • *n* brómber *(n)*
blackbird • *n* svartþröstur
blackmail • *n* fjárkúgun *(f)*
blacksmith • *n* járnsmiður
blade • *n* blað *(n)*, egg *(f)*, sverð *(n)*
blaze • *n* eldsvoði *(m)*, bál *(n)*
bleat • *v* jarma • *n* jarmur *(m)*
bleed • *v* blæða
blender • *n* blandari *(m)*
bless • *v* blessa
blind • *adj* blindur *(m)*
blond • *n* ljóshærður *(m)*, ljóshærð *(f)*
blood • *n* blóð *(n)*
bloodbath • *n* blóðbað *(n)*
bloody • *adj* blóðug
blowhole • *n* blásturshola *(f)*, blástursop
(n)
blue • *n* blár • *adj* blár
blueberry • *n* bláber *(n)*
blush • *n* kinnalitur *(m)*
boar • *n* göltur *(m)*

boast • *n* mont (*n*), gort (*n*), sjálfshól (*n*)

boat • *v* fara á báti, flytja á báti • *n* bátur (*m*)

body • *n* líkami (*m*)

bodybuilding • *n* líkamsrækt (*f*), vaxtarrækt (*f*)

boffin • *n* vísindarannsóknarmaður (*m*)

bogey • *n* skolli (*m*)

bogus • *adj* óekta (*m*), falskur (*m*), svikinn (*m*)

bollard • *n* polli (*m*)

bolt • *n* slagbrandur (*m*)

bomb • *n* spengja (*f*), holkúla (*f*)

bombshell • *n* sprengja (*f*), sprengikúla (*f*), óvænt atvik (*n*), þruma úr heiðskíru lofti (*f*), stórviðburður (*m*), æsifréttaefni (*n*), æsifregn (*f*)

bone • *n* bein (*n*), beinhvítur (*m*)

bonfire • *n* bál (*n*), varðeldur (*m*)

bongo • *n* bongótromma (*f*)

bonnet • *n* vélarhlíf (*f*), húdd (*n*)

bonus • *n* bónus (*m*)

boo • *v* púa, púa út • *interj* bú, bö, ú

book • *n* bók (*f*)

bookend • *n* bókastoð (*f*)

booklet • *n* bæklingur (*m*)

bookshelf • *n* bókahylla

bookshop • *n* bókaverslun (*f*), bókabúð (*f*)

boot • *n* stígvél (*n*)

bootstrap • *v* ræsa, inna ræsiforrit, sjálfþýða • *n* stígvélahanki (*m*), ræsiforrit (*n*)

border • *n* landamæri

bore • *v* bora

boring • *adj* leiðinlegur

boron • *n* bór (*n*)

bosom • *n* barmur (*m*)

boss • *n* stjóri (*m*)

botanist • *n* grasafræðingur (*m*)

botany • *n* grasafræði (*f*)

bother • *v* ergja, angra • *n* vesen (*n*), mál (*n*), vandamál (*n*)

bottle • *n* flaska (*f*)

bottom • *n* botn (*m*)

bough • *n* trjágrein (*f*), grein (*f*)

bouillon • *n* kjötkraftur (*m*)

bouncing • *adj* hraustlegur, myndarlegur

bouquet • *n* blómvöndur (*m*), vínilmur (*m*)

bow • *v* strjúka, bogna, svigna, bugast, beygja, sveigja, hneigja sig • *n* bogi (*m*), slaufa (*f*), hneiging (*f*), bógur (*m*)

bowfin • *n* eðjufiskur (*m*), boguggi (*m*), leirgedda (*f*)

bowl • *n* skál

bowstring • *n* bogastrengur (*m*)

box • *n* kassi (*m*), box (*n*)

boy • *n* negri (*m*), strákur (*m*), drengur (*m*), piltur (*m*), sveinn (*m*)

boyfriend • *n* kærasti (*m*)

bra • *n* brjóstahaldari

bracelet • *n* armband (*n*)

brachiation • *n* armsveiflun (*f*)

braille • *n* blindraletur (*n*)

brain • *n* heili (*m*)

bramble • *n* brómber (*n*), bjarnarber (*n*)

branch • *n* grein (*f*)

brandish • *v* bregða, sveifla

bravado • *n* mannalæti (*n*), sýndarhugrekki (*n*)

brave • *adj* hugrakkur

bravery • *n* hugrekki (*n*)

brawl • *v* slást, berjast, fljúgast á • *n* áflog, bardagi (*m*), slagsmál

bray • *v* rymja • *n* rymur (*m*)

bread • *v* velta, brauðmylsna • *n* brauð (*n*), peningur (*m*)

breadcrumb • *n* brauðmylsna (*f*)

breakfast • *n* morgunmatur (*m*), morgunverður (*m*), dögurður (*m*), árbítur (*m*)

breast • *n* brjóst (*n*), bobblingur (*m*), bringa (*f*), brjóst (*f*)

breaststroke • *v* synda bringusund • *n* bringusund (*n*)

breathe • *v* anda

brewer • *n* bruggari (*m*)

brewery • *n* ölgerð (*f*), ölgerðarhús (*n*)

bribe • *v* múta • *n* múta (*f*)

brick • *n* múrsteinn (*m*), tígulsteinn (*m*), leirsteinn (*m*), byggingarklossar, byggingarkubbar, ágætis manneskja (*f*), perla af manni (*f*), fyrirtaks manneskja (*f*) • *adj* úr múrsteini

bride • *n* brúður (*f*)

bridegroom • *n* brúðgumi (*m*)

bridge • *n* brú (*f*), bridds (*n*)

briefcase • *n* skjalataska (*f*)

bright • *adj* bjartur, skær, skínandi, ljómandi, greindur, skarpur, greindarlegur, bjartur (*m*), björt (*f*), bjart (*n*), hýr, glaðlegur

brine • *n* pækill (*m*)

bring • *v* færa

brittle • *adj* brothætt

broccoli • *n* spergilkál (*n*)

brochure • *n* bæklingur (*m*)

bromine • *n* bróm

broom • *n* sópur (*m*), kústur (*m*)

broth • *n* seyði (*n*)

brothel • *n* hóruhús (*n*)

brother • *n* bróðir

brother-in-law • *n* mágur (*m*), svili (*m*)

brown • *n* brúnn (*n*) • *adj* brúnn

brownie • *n* súkkulaðikökum
brush • *n* pensill *(m)*, bursti *(m)*, hárbursti *(m)*, tannbursti *(m)*
brusque • *adj* þurr á manninn, þurr á manninn *(m)*, stuttur í spuna *(m)*, stuttaralegur *(m)*, hranalegur *(m)*, byrstur *(m)*, ruddalegur *(m)*
bubble • *n* kúla *(f)*
buck • *n* hafur *(m)*
bucket • *n* fata *(f)*
buckwheat • *n* bókhveiti *(n)*, bæki *(n)*
bucolic • *adj* sveitalegur *(m)*, sveita-, sveitalífs-, sveitasælu-, óheflaður *(m)*, grófgerður *(m)*, prests-, bóndalegur *(m)*
budgerigar • *n* gári *(m)*
buffalo • *n* buffall
buffer • *n* biðminni *(n)*
build • *v* byggja
building • *n* bygging *(f)*
built-in • *adj* innbyggður *(m)*
bull • *n* naut *(n)*
bulldozer • *n* jarðýta
bullet • *n* byssukúla *(f)*, kúla *(f)*, skot *(n)*
bullshit • *n* kjaftæði *(n)*, bull *(n)*, þvættingur *(m)*, lygari *(m)*
bullying • *n* einelti *(n)*
bulwark • *n* bolvirki *(n)*, bolverk *(n)*
bumblebee • *n* hunangsfluga
bungling • *n* hálfkák *(n)*
bunting • *n* flaggdúkur *(m)*, tittlingur *(m)*
buoy • *n* bauja *(f)*
burden • *n* byrði *(f)*, burður *(m)*
bureaucracy • *n* skrifræði, skrifstofuveldi
bureaucrat • *n* kerfiskarl *(m)*
burette • *n* búretta *(f)*

burial • *n* greftrun *(f)*
burly • *adj* þrekvaxinn
burn • *v* brenna
bus • *n* strætisvagn *(m)*, strætó *(m)*, langferðabíll *(m)*, rúta *(f)*
bush • *n* runni *(m)*
businessman • *n* kaupsýslumaður *(m)*
bust • *n* brjóstmynd *(f)*
busy • *adj* upptekinn
but • *conj* heldur, en
butane • *n* bútan *(n)*
butcher • *n* slátrari *(m)*
butt • *n* rass *(m)*, afturendi *(m)*, stubbur *(m)*, sígarettustubbur *(m)*
butter • *n* smjör *(n)*
buttercup • *n* sóley
butterfly • *n* fiðrildi
buttermilk • *n* áfir
buttock • *n* rasskinn *(f)*
button • *v* hneppa • *n* tala *(f)*, hnappur *(m)*, takki *(n)*, valhnappur *(m)*, takki *(m)*, barmmerki *(n)*
buttonhole • *n* hnappagat *(n)*, blóm í hnappagat *(n)*, blóm í barm *(n)*
butyric • *adj* smjör-
buy • *v* kaupa
buzzard • *n* músvákur *(m)*
buzzword • *n* tískuorð *(m)*
by • *prep* við, fyrir, eftir
by-product • *n* aukaafurð *(f)*
bye • *interj* bæ
byte • *n* bæti *(n)*, tölvustafur *(m)*
byword • *n* málsháttur, máltæki

C

cabbage • *n* hvítkál *(n)*
cacao • *n* kakó
cache • *n* skyndiminni *(n)*
cactus • *n* kaktus *(m)*
cadmium • *n* kadmín
caecum • *n* botnristill *(m)*
caffeine • *n* koffín *(n)*, kaffín *(n)*
caffeinism • *n* koffíneitrun *(f)*
cage • *n* búr *(n)*
cairn • *n* varða *(f)*
cake • *n* kaka *(f)*, stykki *(n)*
calamus • *n* kalmusrót *(f)*, fjöðurstafur *(m)*
calcite • *n* kalkspat *(n)*, kalsít *(n)*
calcium • *n* kalsín
calculator • *n* reiknivél *(f)*
calculus • *n* deilda- og heildareikningur

(m), diffur- og tegurreikningur *(m)*, örsmæðareikningur *(m)*, reiknivísi *(f)*, steinn *(m)*
calendar • *n* tímatal *(n)*, dagatal *(n)*
calf • *n* kálfur *(m)*
californium • *n* kalifornín
calipers • *n* rennimál *(n)*, skífmál *(n)*
calisthenics • *n* leikfimiæfing
call • *v* kalla, hrópa, hringja í, heimsækja, heilsa upp á • *n* símtal *(n)*, heimsókn *(f)*, kall *(n)*, hróp *(n)*
calligraphy • *n* skrautskrift *(n)*, skrautritun *(f)*
callous • *adj* kaldgeðja *(m)*, tilfinningalaus *(m)*, harðgeðja *(m)*, harðlyndur *(m)*, harðbrjósta *(m)*, fólskulegur *(m)*
callus • *n* sigg *(n)*

calque • *n* tökuþýðing *(f)*
calyx • *n* bikar *(m)*
camaraderie • *n* félagsandi *(m)*, góður kunningsskapur *(m)*, góð samskipti
camel • *n* úlfaldi *(m)*
camera • *n* myndavél *(f)*, upptökuvél *(f)*
camp • *v* tjalda, campa, kampa
campfire • *n* varðeldur *(m)*
camphor • *n* kamfóra *(f)*
camping • *n* útilega
can • *v* geta, mega • *n* dós *(f)*
canal • *n* skurður *(m)*
cancer • *n* krabbamein *(n)*, krabbi *(m)*
candle • *n* kerti *(n)*
candlelight • *n* kertaljós *(n)*
candlestick • *n* kertastjaki *(m)*
cannibal • *n* mannæta *(f)*
cannon • *n* fallbyssa *(f)*
cannonade • *n* stórskotahríð *(f)*
cantaloupe • *n* kantalúpmelóna *(f)*, cantaloup-melóna *(f)*
canteen • *n* mötuneyti *(n)*, matsalur *(m)*, hnífaparakassi *(m)*, mataráhöld hermanna, vatnsbrúsi *(m)*
canvasback • *n* dúkönd *(f)*
canyon • *n* gljúfur *(n)*
capacitor • *n* þéttir *(m)*, rafþéttir *(m)*, rafmagnsþéttir *(m)*
capelin • *n* loðna *(f)*
caper • *n* kapers
capercaillie • *n* þiður
capillarity • *n* hárpípukraftur *(m)*, hárpípuhrif *(n)*, hárpípuverkun *(f)*, sogpípukraftur *(m)*
capital • *n* höfuðborg
capitalism • *n* auðvaldsskipulag
capon • *n* geldhani
capricious • *adj* duttlungasamur *(m)*, mislyndur *(m)*, kenjóttur *(m)*, dyntóttur *(m)*, duttlungafullur *(m)*
capsaicin • *n* kapsaísín *(n)*, capsæsín *(n)*
capsize • *v* kollsigla
capsule • *n* hylki *(n)*
captain • *n* flugstjóri
car • *n* bíll *(m)*, bifreið *(f)*, vagn *(m)*
caramel • *n* karamella *(f)*
caravel • *n* karavella *(f)*
carbohydrate • *n* kolvetni *(n)*
carbon • *n* kolefni *(n)*, kolefnis pappír
carbonate • *n* karbónat *(n)*
card • *n* kortið *(m)*
cardia • *n* munnahluti maga *(m)*
cardiac • *adj* hjarta, munnamaga-
cardinal • *n* frumtala *(f)*, kardináli *(m)*, hárauður *(m)* • *adj* höfuð-, aðal-, megin-, grundvallar-, hárauður
care • *v* sama

carefree • *adj* áhyggjulaus, kátur
careless • *adj* áhyggjulaus, kátur *(m)*, kærulaus, hirðulaus
carnivore • *n* kjötæta *(f)*
carp • *n* vatnakarfi *(m)* • *v* finna að, gagnrýna, gagnrýna smugulega, vera með sparðatíning, kvarta
carpet • *n* teppi *(n)*
carrack • *n* karkari *(m)*
carriage • *n* vagn *(m)*
carrot • *n* gulrót *(f)*
carry • *v* bera
cartel • *n* einokunarhringur *(m)*
cartilage • *n* brjósk *(n)*
cartographer • *n* kortagerðarmaður *(m)*
carton • *n* ferna *(f)*
case • *n* fall *(n)*
cash • *n* reiðufé *(n)*
cassock • *n* hempa *(f)*
cast • *v* kasta, varpa, fleygja
castle • *v* hrókera • *n* kastali *(m)*, borg, virki
castling • *n* hrókering *(f)*
cat • *n* köttur *(m)*, kisa *(f)*
catalysis • *n* hvötun *(f)*
catalyst • *n* efnahvati *(m)*, hvati *(m)*
catalytic • *adj* hvetjandi *(m)*
catatonic • *adj* stjarfur *(m)*
category • *n* ríki *(n)*
caterpillar • *n* lirfa
catharsis • *n* geðhreinsun *(f)*
cathedral • *n* dómkirkja *(f)*
cathode • *n* bakskaut *(n)*, mínusskaut *(n)*, neiskaut *(n)*, neikvætt rafskaut *(n)*, katóða *(f)*
cauliflower • *n* blómkál *(n)*
cause • *v* valda • *n* orsök *(f)*, málstaður *(m)*
cave • *n* hellir *(m)*
ceiling • *n* loft *(n)*
celeriac • *n* seljurót *(f)*
celery • *n* sellerí *(n)*
cell • *n* klefi *(m)*, fangaklefi *(m)*, fruma *(f)*
cellar • *n* kjallari *(m)*
cello • *n* selló *(n)*, knéfiðla *(f)*
cellulose • *n* sellulósi *(m)*, beðmi *(n)*
census • *n* manntal *(n)*
cent • *n* sent *(n)*
center • *v* miðja • *n* miðja *(f)*, miðstöð *(f)*, miðpunktur *(m)*
centipede • *n* margfætlur
century • *n* öld *(f)*
ceremony • *n* athöfn
cerium • *n* serín
certain • *adj* viss *(m)*, öruggur *(m)*
certification • *n* vottun *(f)*
chaffinch • *n* bókfinka *(f)*

chain • *n* keðja *(f)*
chair • *n* stóll
chalazion • *n* augnaþrymill *(m)*
chalice • *n* kaleikur *(m)*
chalk • *n* krítarsteinn *(m)*, krít *(f)*
chamber • *n* klefi *(m)*
chameleon • *n* kameljón *(n)*, kamelljón
(n)
chamois • *n* gemsa *(f)*
champagne • *n* kampavín *(n)*
chancellor • *n* Kanslari
chandler • *n* kertasali *(m)*, kertagerðarmaður *(m)*, kaupmaður *(m)*, kaupsali *(m)*,
mangari *(m)*, kramari *(m)*
change • *v* breytast
chanterelle • *n* kantarella *(f)*
chaos • *n* ringulreið *(f)*
chapel • *n* kapella *(f)*
chapter • *n* kafli *(m)*
character • *n* persóna
charity • *n* góðgerðarstarfsemi *(f)*,
góðgerðarstofnun *(f)*
chase • *v* elta • *n* eftirför
chasuble • *n* hökull *(m)*
chauffeur • *n* bílstjóri *(m)*, einkabílstjóri
(m)
cheat • *v* svindla, halda framhjá • *n*
svindl *(n)*
checklist • *n* gátlisti *(m)*, gaumlisti *(m)*
cheek • *n* kinn
cheers • *interj* skál
cheese • *n* ostur *(m)*
cheetah • *n* blettatígur *(m)*
chef • *n* kokkur *(m)*, yfirmatsveinn *(m)*,
matreiðslumaður *(m)*, matsveinn *(m)*
chemistry • *n* efnafræði *(f)*
chemosynthesis • *n* efnatillífun *(f)*
cheque • *n* ávísun *(f)*, tékki *(m)*
cherry • *n* kirsuber *(n)*, kirsuberjatré *(n)*,
kirsuberjaviður *(m)*
cherub • *n* kerúb *(m)*
chervil • *n* kerfill *(m)*
chess • *n* skák *(n)*, skáktafl *(n)*
chest • *n* kista *(f)*, kommóða *(f)*, bringa *(f)*
chew • *v* tyggja
chicken • *n* hænsn, kjúklingur *(m)*
chickweed • *n* arfi *(m)*
child • *n* barn *(n)*, barn
childhood • *n* barnæska *(f)*
chimney • *n* reykháfur *(m)*, skorsteinn
(m), strompur *(m)*
chimpanzee • *n* simpansi *(m)*
chin • *n* haka *(f)*
chisel • *n* sporjárn *(n)*
chiton • *n* nökkvar
chlorine • *n* klór
chloroform • *n* klóróform *(n)*

chlorophyll • *n* blaðgræna, laufgræna,
klórófýl
chloroplast • *n* grænukorn *(n)*
chocolate • *n* súkkulaði
choice • *n* val *(n)*
choir • *n* kór *(m)*
cholecystitis • *n* gallblöðrubólga *(f)*
cholesterol • *n* kólesteról *(n)*
choose • *v* velja
chopstick • *n* matarprjónn *(m)*, prjónn
(m)
chordate • *n* seildýr *(n)*
chortle • *v* hneggja af hlátri, rýta af hlátri
chrism • *n* krisma *(n)*
chromatic • *adj* lit-, lita-
chromium • *n* króm
chromosome • *n* litningur *(m)*
chronology • *n* tímatalsfræði *(f)*, tímatal
(n), tímasetning *(f)*
church • *n* kirkja *(f)*, kirkjan, messa *(f)*,
guðsþjónusta *(f)*
churn • *v* strokka • *n* kirna *(f)*
chyme • *n* fæðumauk *(n)*
cigar • *n* vindill *(m)*
cigarette • *n* sígaretta *(f)*
cinema • *n* bíó *(n)*, kvikmyndahús *(n)*
cinnamon • *n* kaniltré *(n)*, kanill *(m)*,
kanell *(m)*
cipher • *n* dulritunaraðferð *(f)*, dulritaður
texti *(m)*, dulrit *(n)*
circa • *prep* um það bil, circa, sirka
circadian • *adj* dægur, sólarhringur
circle • *n* hringur
circuit • *n* rafrás *(f)*, straumrás *(f)*, rafstraumsrás *(f)*, lína *(f)*, rás *(f)*
circumcise • *v* umskera
circumcision • *n* umskurður *(m)*
circumference • *n* ummál *(n)*
circumstance • *n* kringumstæður
cirrostratus • *n* blika *(f)*, skýjablika *(f)*
cirrus • *n* klósigi, blikutrefjar, blikufjaðrir,
vatnsklær
citizen • *n* ríkisborgari *(m)*, borgari *(m)*,
íbúi
citizenship • *n* ríkisborgararéttur
city • *n* borg *(f)*
clad • *v* klæða, húða
clairvoyance • *n* skyggnigáfa
claque • *n* klapplið *(n)*
clarinet • *n* klarínetta *(f)*, klarínett *(n)*
class • *v* flokka • *n* flokkur *(m)*, bekkur
(m), árgangur *(m)*, farrými *(n)*, klasi *(m)*
clavicle • *n* viðbein *(n)*
claw • *n* kló *(f)*
clay • *n* leir *(m)*
clean • *v* þrífa, hreinsa • *adj* hreinn, auður
cleave • *v* kljúfa, láta klofna

clef • *n* lykill *(m)*
clement • *adj* miskunnsamur *(m)*, mildur *(m)*
clementine • *n* klementína *(f)*
clever • *adj* snjall
client • *n* viðskiptavinur *(m)*, kaupandi *(m)*, kúnni *(m)*, skjólstæðingur *(m)*, biðlari *(m)*
cliff • *n* klettur *(m)*, berg *(n)*, bjarg *(n)*, hamar *(m)*
climate • *n* loftslag
climatology • *n* veðurfarsfræði
climb • *v* klifra, klífa
clipboard • *n* skrifbretti *(n)*, klemmuspjald *(n)*
clipping • *n* úrklippa *(f)*
clitoris • *n* snípur *(m)*
cloak • *n* skikkja *(f)*, möntull *(m)*
clock • *n* klukka *(f)*, úr *(n)*
clockwork • *n* klukkuverk *(n)*, úrverk *(n)*, gangverk *(n)*
clog • *v* stífla • *n* klossi *(m)*, hnallur *(m)*, tréskór *(m)*, stífla *(f)*
closed • *adj* lokaður *(m)*
closet • *n* skápur
closure • *n* lokun *(f)*
clothe • *v* klæða
clothes • *n* föt
clothesline • *n* þvottasnúra *(f)*, snúra *(f)*
clothing • *n* klæðnaður *(m)*, fatnaður *(m)*
cloud • *n* ský *(n)*
cloudberry • *n* múltuber
cloudless • *adj* heiður, heiðskír
cloudy • *adj* skýjaður
clove • *n* negull *(m)*, geiri *(m)*
club • *n* lauf *(m)*
clutch • *n* kúpling, kúpling *(f)*
coal • *n* kol *(n)*
coalition • *n* bandalag *(n)*
coast • *n* strönd *(f)*
coaster • *n* strandferðaskip *(n)*
coat • *n* jakki *(m)*, frakki *(m)*
coaxial • *adj* samása
cobalt • *n* kóbalt
cobbler • *n* skósmiður *(m)*
cochlea • *n* kuðungur *(m)*
cock • *v* spenna • *n* karlfugl *(m)*
cock-a-doodle-doo • *interj* gaggalagó
cockchafer • *n* aldinbori
cockroach • *n* kakkalakki *(m)*
coconut • *n* kókoshneta *(f)*
cocoon • *n* lirfuhýði *(n)*, egghylki *(n)*
cod • *n* þorskur *(m)*
coenzyme • *n* kóensím *(n)*, hjálparhvati *(m)*, ensímbót *(f)*
coeval • *n* samaldri *(m)*, jafnaldri *(m)*, samtíðarmaður *(m)* • *adj* samaldra *(m)*, jafnaldra *(m)*

coffee • *n* kaffi *(n)*, kaffibrúnn *(m)* • *adj* kaffibrúnn
coffin • *v* kistuleggja • *n* líkkista *(f)*, kista *(f)*
cognac • *n* koníak *(n)*
cognate • *n* samstofna, orð • *adj* samstofna, skyldur
coil • *n* spírall *(m)*, verri *(m)*, spóla *(f)*
coin • *v* slá mynt, búa til • *n* mynt *(f)*
coke • *n* koks *(n)*
colander • *n* dörslag *(n)*
cold • *n* kvef *(n)* • *adj* kaldur, kaldlyndur
colic • *n* kveisa *(f)*, magakveisa *(f)*
collar • *n* kragi *(m)*
collinear • *adj* samlína, á sömu línu, samása
collision • *n* árekstur *(m)*
color • *v* lita, roðna • *n* litur *(m)*
colostrum • *n* broddmjólk *(f)*, broddur *(m)*
columbine • *n* vatnsberi, vatnsberar
coma • *n* dá *(n)*, svefndá *(n)*, dauðadá *(n)*
comb • *v* greiða, kemba
combat • *n* slagsmál
come • *v* koma, fá það
comet • *n* halastjarna *(f)*
coming • *n* koma *(f)*
comma • *n* komma *(f)*
commandment • *n* boðorð *(n)*
comment • *n* athugasemd *(f)*
commerce • *n* verslun *(f)*
committee • *n* nefnd *(f)*
communism • *n* kommúnismi
commutative • *adj* víxlinn *(m)*
companion • *n* félagi *(m)*, kumpáni *(m)*
company • *n* fyrirtæki *(n)*
comparative • *n* miðstig *(n)*
compass • *n* áttaviti *(m)*, kompás *(m)*
competitor • *n* keppandi *(m)*
compiler • *n* þýðandi *(m)*, vistþýðandi *(m)*, þýðingarforrit *(n)*
composer • *n* tónskáld *(m)*
composite • *adj* samsettur *(m)*, þættanlegur *(m)*
compress • *v* þjappa
compression • *n* þjöppun *(f)*
computer • *n* tölva *(f)*, rafheili *(m)*, rafreiknir *(m)*, rafeindareiknir *(m)*
comrade • *n* félagi
concatenation • *n* samskeyting *(f)*
conceal • *v* fela, hylja
concentric • *adj* sammiðja *(m)*
concept • *n* hugtak
conception • *n* getnaður *(m)*
concert • *n* tónleikar
concord • *n* samhugur *(m)*, samræmi *(n)*

concrete • *n* steinsteypa *(f)*, steypa *(f)*
concupiscence • *n* girnd *(f)*, losti *(m)*, fýsn *(f)*, frygð *(f)*
concur • *v* vera sammála, samsinna, hittast
concurrent • *adj* samskeiða *(m)*
condom • *n* smokkur
conductivity • *n* leiðni *(f)*
conductor • *n* leiðari *(m)*, leiðir *(m)*
cone • *n* keila *(f)*, köngull *(m)*
confederation • *n* sviss *(n)*
confidant • *n* trúnaðarmaður *(m)*, trúnaðarvinur *(m)*, rún, rúna *(f)*
confidential • *adj* leynilegur *(m)*, heimullegur *(m)*
confidentially • *adv* í trúnaði, undir fjögur augu
confirm • *v* ferma
confirmation • *n* ferming *(f)*
confiscate • *v* upptækur
conflagration • *n* eldsvoði *(m)*, bál *(n)*, stórbruni *(m)*
confound • *v* rugla, gera vont verra, bæta gráu ofan á svart, niðurlægja
congeal • *v* hlaupa
congenital • *adj* meðfæddur
conglomerate • *v* safna saman, steypa saman, hlaupa í kökk • *n* samsteypa *(f)*, fjölgreinafyrirtæki *(n)*, völuberg *(n)* • *adj* samsettur *(m)*, sundurleitur *(m)*
congratulations • *interj* til hamingju, gott hjá þér
congregation • *n* söfnuður *(m)*, mannsöfnuður *(m)*
congress • *n* þing *(n)*
congressman • *n* þingmaður *(m)*
congruence • *n* leifajafna *(f)*, samleifing *(f)*, samsnið *(n)*, aljöfnuður *(m)*
congruent • *adj* samleifa *(m)*, samsniða *(m)*, aljafn *(m)*, eins *(m)*
conical • *adj* keilulaga, kóniskur
conifer • *n* barrtré *(n)*
conjecture • *n* tilgáta *(f)*
conjugation • *n* samkoma *(f)*, sagnbeyging *(f)*, persónubeyging sagna *(f)*
conjunction • *n* samtenging *(f)*, ogun *(f)*
connective • *n* samtenging *(f)*, tenging *(f)*, tengill *(m)*
conquer • *v* sigra
conscientious • *adj* samviskusamur
conscientiousness • *n* samviskusemi *(f)*
conscription • *n* herkvaðning *(f)*
consecrate • *v* helga
consent • *v* samþykkja, fallast á • *n* samþykki *(n)*
consequence • *n* afleiðing *(f)*
conservatism • *n* íhald *(n)*

conservative • *n* íhaldssinni
consist • *v* samanstanda, af
consonant • *n* samhljóð *(n)*, samhljóði *(m)*
constellation • *n* stjörnumerki *(n)*
constitution • *n* stjórnarskrá *(f)*
constraint • *n* ófrelsi *(n)*
consul • *n* konsúll *(m)*, ræðismaður *(m)*
consulate • *n* ræðisskrifstofa *(f)*, konsúlat *(n)*
contact • *v* hafa samband • *n* snerting *(f)*, samband *(n)*, tengiliður *(m)*
contagious • *adj* smitandi
contemporary • *n* jafnaldri *(m)*, samtíðarmaður *(m)*
contempt • *n* fyrirlitning *(f)*, óvirðing *(f)*
conterminous • *adj* samlægur
contiguous • *adj* aðlægur, samlægur, samliggjandi
continent • *n* heimsálfa *(f)*
contrabassoon • *n* kontrafagott *(n)*
contract • *n* samningur *(m)* • *v* herpa
contradistinction • *n* til aðgreiningar frá, sem annars konar fyrirbæri en
contrail • *n* flugslóði *(m)*, flugvélarslóði *(m)*
contraindicate • *v* mæla gegn
controversial • *adj* umdeildur
controvertible • *adj* umdeilanlegur
convalescence • *n* afturbati *(m)*, bati *(m)*, afturbataskeið *(n)*
convenient • *adj* hentugur
convergence • *n* samleitni *(f)*
convergent • *adj* samleitinn
conversation • *n* samtal *(n)*
converse • *v* spjalla, tala saman • *n* andhverfing *(f)*
convolution • *n* földun *(f)*
convoy • *n* bílalest *(f)*
coo • *v* kurr, hjala ljúflega, hvísla blíðuorðum • *n* kurr *(n)*
cook • *v* elda • *n* kokkur
cookbook • *n* matreiðslubók *(f)*
cool • *adj* svalur
coolant • *n* kælivökvi *(m)*, kæliefni *(n)*
cooperation • *n* samvinna *(f)*, samstarf *(n)*
cope • *n* kápa *(f)*, kórkápa *(f)*, biskupskápa *(f)*
copper • *n* eir
copula • *n* tengisögn *(f)*
copyright • *n* höfundarréttur
cordial • *adj* hjartanlegur *(m)*, alúðlegur *(m)*
coreference • *n* samvísun *(f)*
corkscrew • *n* tappatogari *(m)*
cormorant • *n* skarfur *(m)*
corncob • *n* maískólfur *(m)*, kólfur *(m)*

corollary • *n* fylgisetning *(f)*
corpse • *n* lík *(n)*, hræ *(n)*, nár *(m)*
corpulent • *adj* feitur, feitlaginn
correct • *adj* rétt
corroborate • *v* styrkja
corrode • *v* æta
corruption • *n* spilling *(f)*
corset • *n* lífstykki *(n)*
corticosteroid • *n* barksteri *(m)*
corvette • *n* korvetta
cosine • *n* kósínus *(m)*
cosmologist • *n* heimsfræðingur *(m)*
cosmology • *n* heimsfræði *(f)*
cosmos • *n* alheimur *(m)*
couch • *n* sófi
cough • *v* hósta • *n* hósti *(m)*
coulomb • *n* kúlomb
council • *n* ráð *(n)*
count • *v* telja, skipta máli • *n* talning *(f)*, tala *(f)*, greifi *(m)*
countenance • *v* láta viðgangast • *n* andlit *(n)*
counter • *n* afgreiðsluborð *(n)*, búðarborð *(n)*, teljari *(m)*
counterfoil • *n* svunta *(f)*
countess • *n* greifafrú *(f)*, greifynja *(f)*, jarlsfrú *(f)*
country • *n* land, land *(n)*, ríki *(n)*
couple • *n* par *(n)*
courage • *n* hugrekki *(n)*, kjarkur *(m)*
course • *n* námskeið *(n)*
court • *n* dómstóll *(m)*
cousin • *n* frændi *(m)*, frænka *(f)*
cover • *v* þekja
covered • *adj* þakinn *(m)*
cow • *n* kýr *(f)*, belja *(f)*, nautgripur *(m)*
cowardice • *n* gunguskapur *(m)*, heigulsháttur *(m)*, ragmennska *(f)*, bleyði *(f)*
cowbell • *n* kúabjalla *(f)*
cowl • *n* munkahetta *(f)*, vélarhlíf *(f)*
coyote • *n* sléttuúlfur *(m)*
crab • *n* krabbi *(m)*
cracked • *adj* brotinn *(m)*, klikkaður *(m)*
cradle • *n* vagga *(f)*
crane • *n* trana *(f)*, krani *(m)*
craven • *n* heigull *(m)*, raggeit *(f)*, bleyða *(f)*
crawl • *v* skríða • *n* skriðsund *(n)*
cream • *v* rústa, bursta • *n* rjómi *(m)*, krem *(n)* • *adj* kremaður
crease • *n* brot *(n)*
create • *v* skapa
creed • *n* trúarjátning *(f)*
cress • *n* karsi *(m)*
cricket • *n* krybba *(f)*
crime • *n* glæpur *(m)*
criminal • *n* glæpamaður *(m)*

crinoid • *n* sælilja *(f)* • *adj* sælilja
crisis • *n* kreppa
criticise • *v* gagnrýna, setja út á
crochet • *v* hekla
crocodile • *n* krókódíll *(m)*
croft • *n* hjáleigubóndi *(m)*, smábóndi *(m)*
crook • *n* glæpamaður *(m)*, þorpari *(m)*, hirðingjastafur *(m)*
crosier • *n* biskupsstafur *(m)*, krókstafur *(m)*, bagall *(m)*
cross • *n* kross *(m)*
cross-eyed • *adj* rangeygður
crossbow • *n* lásbogi *(m)*
crosshead • *n* krosshaus *(m)*
crotch • *n* klof *(n)*
crotchet • *n* fjórðapartsnóta *(f)*, fjórðipartur *(m)*
crow • *n* kráka *(f)*, kúbein *(n)*, hanagal *(n)*
crowbar • *n* kúbein *(n)*
crowd • *n* þyrping
crown • *v* krýna • *n* króna *(f)*, krúna *(f)* • *adj* króróna
crucible • *n* deigla *(f)*, digull *(m)*
crucify • *v* krossfesta
cruel • *adj* grimmur *(m)*, vondur *(m)*
crunch • *v* bryðja
crustacean • *n* krabbadýr
crutch • *n* hækja *(f)*, stoð *(f)*, styrkur *(m)*
cry • *v* gráta
cryolite • *n* krýólít *(n)*
cryptography • *n* dulritunarfræði *(f)*
cryptomeria • *n* hindartré *(n)*, keisaraviður *(m)*
cube • *n* teningur *(m)*, kubbur *(m)*
cuckoo • *n* gaukur *(m)*
cucumber • *n* gúrka *(f)*, agúrka *(f)*
cue • *n* kú *((koo))*, stikkorð *(n)*, markorð *(n)*, kjuði *(m)*
cuirass • *n* bolbrynja *(f)*
culinary • *adj* matreiðslu
culture • *n* menning *(f)*
cum • *v* fá það
cumin • *n* broddkúmen *(n)*
cummerbund • *n* lindi *(m)*
cumulonimbus • *n* skúrasky *(n)*, þrumusky *(n)*, skúraflákar, útsynningsklakkar
cunt • *n* píka *(f)*, kunta *(f)*, tussa *(f)*
cup • *n* bolli *(m)*
curd • *n* ystingur *(m)*
curiosity • *n* forvitni *(f)*
curium • *n* kúrín *(m)*
curl • *n* lokkur *(m)*
curse • *v* bölva, blóta • *n* bölvun *(f)*
cursor • *n* bendill *(m)*, músarbendill *(m)*, bendir *(m)*
curtain • *n* gluggatjald *(n)*, gardína *(f)*,

leikhústjald (n), tjald (n)
cusk • n keila
custom • n siðvenja (f)
customer • n viðskiptavinur (m), kaupandi (m), skiptavinur (m)
cut • v skera, klippa, troða, skera niður, skrópa, skipta, draga • n skurður (m), afskurður (m), snið (n)
cutaneous • adj húð-
cute • adj sætur (m), snotur (m)

cuttlefish • n blekfiskur (m)
cybernetics • n stýrifræði
cycling • n hjólreiðum (m)
cyclops • n kýklópi (m), kýklópur (m)
cylindrical • adj sívalningslaga
cystitis • n blöðrubólga (f)
cytology • n frumufræði (f)
cytoplasm • n umfrymi (n)
cytosine • n sýtósín (n), sýtosín (n)

D

daddy • n pabbi
dagger • n rýtingur (m)
daily • adj daglegur (m)
dairy • n mjólkurbú (n), mjólkurbúð (f), mjólkurafurðir (f)
daisy • n fagurfífill (m)
dale • n dalur (m)
dam • n stífla (f)
damp • n raki (m)
dance • v dansa • n dans (m)
dancer • n dansari (m)
dandelion • n fífill (m)
dandruff • n flasa (f)
danger • n hætta (f)
dangerous • adj hættulegur
dark • adj dökkur, dimmur
dark-skinned • adj hörundsdökkur
darken • v dekkja, dökkna
darkness • n myrkur (n), dimma (f), nifl (n), ljósleysa (f)
darling • n elskan • adj kær (m), ástkær (m)
data • n gögn
date • n daðla (f), dagsetning (f), stefnumót (n)
dative • adj þágufall
daughter • n dóttir
daughter-in-law • n tengdadóttir (f)
dawn • v daga, birta af degi • n dögun (f), dagrenning (f), morgunsár (n), afturelding (f), sólarupprás (f), sólris (n), sólaruppkoma (n)
day • n dagur (m)
deacon • n djákni
dead • n dánu (n) • adj dauður, dáinn, látinn
deaf • adj daufur
dealer • n díler (m), eiturlyfjasali (m)
dear • adj kær, dýr (f), dýrt (n)
death • n dauði (m)
debilitate • v veikja
debtor • n skuldari (m)

debugger • n kembiforrit (n)
decadent • adj hnignandi, hrörnandi, spilltur, úrkynjaður
deceive • v blekkja
deception • n blekking (f)
decipher • v dulráða
deckhand • n háseti (m)
declension • n fallbeyging (f), beyging (f), beyging falla (f)
decorticate • v afhýða
decrepit • adj farlama, örvasa, hrumur
dee • n dé ((dyeh))
deed • n dáð (f)
deeply • adv djúpt
deer • n hjörtur, krónhjörtur, rádýr (n)
defamatory • adj ærumeiðandi
defeat • v sigra, vinna • n ósigur (m), tap (n)
defeatist • n uppgjafarsinni (m)
defend • v verja
defender • n varnarmaður (m)
defense • n vörn (f)
defenselessness • n varnarleysi (n)
defibrillator • n hjartastillir (m)
definiteness • n ákveðni (f)
deflower • v afmeyja
deification • n dýrkun (f)
delay • n töf (f)
deletion • n eyðing (f)
deliberately • adv viljandi, vísvitandi, af ásettu ráði, af yfirlögðu ráði, yfirvegað, rólega
delicious • adj bragðgóður, ljúffengur
delta • n delta (n)
delve • v rannsaka
demand • v heimta, krefja, útheimta
democracy • n lýðræði (n), lýðræði
demonstrative • adj ábending
denigration • n ófræging (f), mannorðsspjöll (n)
denim • n dením (n)
denominator • n nefnari (m)

dental • *adj* tönn, tannmæltur
denture • *n* falskar tennur
deodorant • *n* svitalyktareyðir *(m)*
deontology • *n* skyldufræði *(f)*
departure • *n* brottför *(f)*
depilatory • *n* háreyðingarvara *(f)* • *adj* háreyðing
deponent • *n* aflagssögn *(f)*, deponenssögn *(f)*
deposition • *n* hélun *(f)*
depression • *n* þunglyndi *(n)*, Kreppa *(f)*
derisive • *adj* háðslegur
dermatologist • *n* húðsjúkdómafræðingur *(m)*
dermatology • *n* húðsjúkdómafræði *(f)*
derring-do • *n* þrekvirki *(n)*
descendant • *n* afkomandi *(m)*, niðji *(m)*
describe • *v* lýsa
desecrate • *v* vanhelga
desert • *n* eyðimörk *(f)*
design • *v* hanna • *n* hönnun *(f)*
designation • *n* heiti
desire • *n* löngun *(f)*
desk • *n* skrifborð *(n)*
desktop • *n* borðtölva *(f)*, skjáborð *(n)*
despondent • *adj* krumpinn
dessert • *n* eftirréttur *(m)*
destination • *n* áfangastaður *(m)*
destiny • *n* örlög, hlutskipti *(n)*
destroy • *v* eyðileggja, rústa, skemma
destruction • *n* eyðilegging *(f)*
detail • *n* smáatriði *(n)*
determinant • *n* ákveða *(f)*
determine • *v* ákveða
deuce • *n* tvistur *(m)*
deuterium • *n* tvívetni *(n)*, þungt vetni *(n)*, þungavetni *(n)*
devil • *v* djöflast í, plága, þjá • *n* djöfull *(m)*, fjandi *(m)*, skratti *(m)*, ári *(m)*, fjári *(m)*, djöfullinn *(m)*, andskotinn *(m)*, fjandinn *(m)*, skrattinn *(m)*, kölski *(m)*, fjárinn *(m)*, satan *(m)*, andskoti *(m)*
dew • *n* dögg *(f)*
dialect • *n* mállýska *(f)*
dialogue • *n* samtal *(n)*
diamond • *n* demantur *(n)*
diaper • *n* bleia *(f)*, bleyja *(f)*
diarrhea • *n* niðurgangur *(m)*, drulla *(f)*
diary • *n* dagbók *(f)*
diatomic • *adj* tvíatóma
dibs • *n* pant
dick • *n* typpi *(n)*, drjóli *(m)*, göndull *(m)*
dictation • *n* upplestur *(m)*
dictator • *n* einræðiherra *(m)*
dictatorship • *n* einræði *(n)*
dictionary • *n* orðabók *(f)*
die • *v* deyja, drepast, andast, sálast, týna

lífinu, skylja við, látast, láta lífið, lognast út af, falla frá, fara yfrum, verða bráðkvaddur • *n* teningur *(m)*
differentiable • *adj* diffranlegur *(m)*, deildanlegur *(m)*
difficult • *adj* erfiður
digestion • *n* melting *(f)*
digit • *n* tala, tölustafur
dignity • *n* virðuleiki *(m)*, reisn *(f)*
dilute • *v* þynna, veikja • *adj* þynntur *(m)*, þynnt *(n)*, veikur
dimensional • *adj* -vídd *(f)*, -víður, -víddar-
diminutive • *n* smækkunarending *(f)*
dimple • *n* spékoppur *(n)*
dinghy • *n* julla
dinner • *n* kvöldmatur *(m)*
dinosaur • *n* risaeðla *(f)*
diocese • *n* biskupsdæmi *(n)*
diode • *n* díóða *(f)*, tvistur *(m)*, tvískauta rör *(n)*, tvískauti *(m)*
diphthong • *n* tvíhljóð *(n)*, tvíhljóði *(m)*
diploid • *adj* tvílitna
direction • *n* átt *(f)*, stefna *(f)*
director • *n* leikstjóri *(m)*
dirty • *adj* óhreinn
disaccharide • *n* tvísykra *(f)*
disappear • *v* hverfa
disappointment • *n* vonbrigði
disarm • *v* afvopna
discalced • *adj* berfættur *(m)*
disco • *n* diskó *(n)*, diskótek *(n)*
discontent • *n* einhver sem er óánægður *(m)*, einhver sem er óánægð *(f)*, eitthvað sem er óánægt, eitthvert sem er óánægt *(n)*, uppreisnarseggur *(m)*
discount • *n* afsláttur *(m)*
discourteous • *adj* ókurteis *(f)*, ókurteist *(n)*
discrepancy • *n* misræmi *(n)*, ósamræmi *(n)*
discretionary • *adj* getþótti, vild *(m)*, ákvörðun
disease • *n* sjúkdómur, sýki, mein
disgrace • *n* óvirðing *(f)*
disgusting • *adj* viðbjóðslegur, ógeðslegur
dish • *n* diskur *(m)*, réttur *(m)*, matarréttur *(m)*
dishwasher • *n* uppþvottavél *(f)*, uppvaskari *(m)*
disjoint • *adj* sundurlægur *(m)*, óskaraður *(m)*
disjunction • *n* eðun *(f)*
disk • *n* diskur *(m)*
disobedient • *adj* óhlýðinn
disorder • *n* ringulreið *(f)*, glundroði *(m)*,

röskun *(f)*, kvilli *(m)*
displacement • *n* tilfærsla *(f)*
dissatisfaction • *n* óánægja *(f)*
dissect • *v* kryfja
distaff • *adj* kven-
distance • *n* fjarlægð
distant • *adj* fjarlægur *(m)*
distress • *n* óþægindi *(n)*, vá *(f)*, stórhætta *(f)*
distribute • *v* deila út, útdeila, úthluta, dreifa, útbýta, skipta, flokka
distributive • *adj* dreifinn *(m)*
ditch • *n* skurður *(m)*, síki *(n)*, díki *(n)*, gröftur *(m)*, gröf *(f)*
diurnal • *adj* dagdýr
diver • *n* kafari *(m)*
diverse • *adj* fjölbreyttur, margvíslegur
diversity • *n* fjölbreytni
divide • *v* hluta
dividend • *n* deilistofn *(m)*
divisible • *adj* deilanlegur *(m)*
division • *n* deiling *(f)*, skipting *(f)*
divisor • *n* deilir *(m)*
divorce • *n* skilnaður *(m)*
divorcee • *n* fráskilinn karlmaður *(m)*
do • *v* gera, gjöra
doctor • *n* læknir *(m)*, doktor *(m)*
document • *n* skjal *(n)*
documentary • *n* heimildamynd *(f)* • *adj* heimilda-
documentation • *n* hjálparskjöl
dodo • *n* dúdúfugl *(m)*
dog • *n* hundur *(m)*
doggerel • *n* leirburður *(m)*, hnoð *(n)*, leirrensli *(n)*, kveðskapur *(m)*, skáldskapur *(m)* • *adj* kveðinn *(m)*, stirðkveðinn *(m)*, kímlegur
doldrums • *n* kyrrabelti *(n)*
dole • *n* atvinnuleysisbætur
doll • *n* dúkka *(f)*, brúða *(f)*
dolphin • *n* höfrungur
domain • *n* formengi *(n)*, frámengi *(n)*, skilgreiningarmengi *(n)*, óðal *(n)*
donkey • *n* asni
door • *n* dyr, hurð *(f)*
doorknob • *n* húnn *(m)*
dormitory • *n* svefnsalur *(m)*, heimavist *(f)*
dormouse • *n* heslimús
doubt • *n* efasemd *(f)*
dough • *n* deig *(n)*
doughnut • *n* kleinuhringur *(m)*
dove • *n* dúfa *(f)*
down-to-earth • *adj* jarðbundinn *(m)*
downcast • *adj* gneypur
downtown • *n* miðborg *(f)*, miðbær *(m)*
dragon • *n* dreki *(m)*, lindormur *(m)*

draught • *n* djúprista *(f)*
draughts • *n* dammur *(m)*, dammtafl *(n)*
draw • *v* teikna
drawbridge • *n* vindubrú *(f)*
dream • *v* dreyma • *n* draumur *(m)*
dreamy • *adj* draumkenndur, draumi líkur, dreymandi
dreary • *adj* drungalegur
dregs • *n* dreggjar, botnfall *(n)*, sori *(m)*, úrhrak *(n)*
drenched • *adj* holdvotur
dress • *v* klæða, sig • *n* kjóll *(m)*, klæðnaður *(m)*, fatnaður, föt
drill • *n* bor *(m)*
drink • *v* drekka • *n* drykkur *(m)*
drive • *v* aka
driver • *n* ökumaður *(m)*, bílstjóri *(m)*, rekill *(m)*
drizzle • *n* úði *(m)*
dromedary • *n* drómedari *(m)*
drop • *v* detta • *n* dropi *(m)*
droplet • *n* dropi *(m)*, smádropi *(m)*
drought • *n* þurrkar *(m)*
drug • *n* eiturlyf *(n)*
drum • *v* tromma, berja • *n* tromma *(f)*, tromla *(f)*
drummer • *n* trommuleikari *(m)*, trommari *(m)*
drumstick • *n* trommukjuði *(m)*
drunk • *adj* fullur *(m)*, drukkinn *(m)*
drunkenness • *n* ölvun *(f)*, drykkjuskapur *(m)*, óregla *(f)*, ölæði *(n)*
dry • *adj* þurr
dryer • *n* þurrkari *(m)*
duchy • *n* hertogadæmi *(n)*
duck • *n* önd *(f)*, aliönd *(f)*
duckling • *n* andarungi *(m)*
dude • *n* gaur *(m)*
duke • *n* hertogi *(m)*
dulse • *n* söl *(n)*
dun • *n* grámórautt *(n)*
dunce • *n* tossi *(m)*
dung • *n* mykja *(f)*
dungeon • *n* dýflissa *(f)*
duo • *n* dúó *(n)*, par *(n)*
duologue • *n* tvítal *(n)*
durian • *n* dáraaldin *(m)*
dusk • *v* rökkva, húma, dimma • *n* ljósaskipti *(f)*, húm *(m)*, rökkur *(n)*
dust • *n* ryk *(n)*, duft *(n)*
duty • *n* kvöð *(f)*, skylda *(f)*
dwarf • *n* dvergur *(m)*
dwindle • *v* dvína
dyadic • *adj* tvíunda-
dye • *v* lita • *n* litur *(m)*, litarefni *(n)*
dynamic • *adj* kviklegur *(m)*, kvik-
dyslexia • *n* lesblinda *(f)*

dyslexic • *n* lesblindur • *adj* lesblinda, lesblindur

dysprosium • *n* dysprósín

E

eagle • *n* örn *(m)*
ear • *n* eyra *(n)* • *v* plægja
eardrum • *n* hljóðhimna *(f)*
earl • *n* jarl *(m)*
earless • *adj* eyrnalaus
early • *adj* snemma • *adv* snemma
earring • *n* eyrnalokk
earth • *n* jörð *(f)*
earthquake • *n* jarðskjálfti *(m)*
earthworm • *n* ánamaðkur
east • *n* austur
easy • *adj* einfaldur, léttur, auðvelt
eat • *v* borða, éta, eta
ecclesiology • *n* kirkjufræði *(f)*
echidna • *n* mjónefur *(m)*
echinoderm • *n* skrápdýr
echo • *n* bergmál *(n)*, endurómur *(m)*
eclectic • *adj* velja
eclipse • *n* myrkvi
ecliptic • *n* sólbaugur *(m)*
ecology • *n* vistifræði *(n)*
economics • *n* hagfræði
economy • *n* hagur *(m)*, hagsýni *(f)*, nýtni *(f)*, ráðdeild *(f)*, sparnaður *(m)*, atvinnulif *(n)*, efnahagslíf *(n)*
ecosystem • *n* vistkerfi *(n)*
edge • *n* kantur *(m)*, hlið *(f)*, egg *(f)*, leggur *(m)*
edifice • *n* bygging *(f)*, hús *(n)*
editor • *n* ritill *(m)*, textaritill *(m)*
education • *n* menntun *(f)*
eel • *n* áll *(m)*
efficient • *adj* skilvirkur *(m)*, nýtinn *(m)*
effrontery • *n* ósvífni *(f)*, óskammfeilni *(f)*
egalitarian • *n* jafnréttissinni *(m)* • *adj* jafnrétti
egalitarianism • *n* jafnréttisstefna *(f)*
egg • *n* egg *(n)*, eggfruma *(f)*
eggplant • *n* eggaldin *(n)*
eggshell • *n* eggjaskurn *(f)*, beingulur litur *(m)*, beingulur *(m)* • *adj* beingulur *(m)*
egregious • *adj* svívirðilegur *(m)*, smánarlegur *(m)*, erki-
eider • *n* æður, æðarfugl
eiderdown • *n* æðardúnn *(m)*
eighth • *adj* áttundi
einsteinium • *n* einsteinín
ejaculation • *n* sáðlát *(n)*

elaborate • *adj* ítarlegur
elbow • *n* olnbogi *(m)*
elder • *n* öldungur *(m)*, svartyllir *(m)*, yllir *(m)*
elderberry • *n* ylliber *(n)*
election • *n* kosning
electricity • *n* rafmagn *(n)*
electrode • *n* rafskaut *(n)*, skaut *(n)*, rafpóll *(m)*, rafnemi *(m)*
electrolysis • *n* rafgreining *(f)*
electrolyte • *n* rafklofi *(m)*, rafvaki *(m)*, raflausn *(f)*
electromagnetism • *n* rafsegulfræði
electron • *n* rafeind *(f)*
electronics • *n* rafeindatækni
element • *n* stak *(n)*, íbúi *(m)*
elephant • *n* fíll *(m)*
elephantiasis • *n* fílildi *(n)*
elevator • *n* lyfta
elision • *n* brottfall *(n)*
elitism • *n* úrvalsstefna *(f)*
ellipse • *n* sporbaugur *(m)*
ellipsis • *n* úrfellingarmerki *(n)*
elm • *n* álmur *(m)*
eluvium • *n* útskolun *(f)*
embassy • *n* sendiráð *(n)*
ember • *n* ljóma
embezzlement • *n* fjárdráttur *(m)*
embolism • *n* blóðrek *(n)*
embolus • *n* blóðreki *(m)*
embroider • *v* sauma út, bródera, baldýra
emerald • *n* smaragður *(m)*
emotion • *n* geðshræring *(f)*
empathy • *n* hluttekning *(f)*
emperor • *n* keisari *(m)*
empty • *v* tæma • *adj* tómur
emulsion • *n* þeyta *(f)*
enamel • *v* lakka • *n* lakk *(n)*, glerungur *(m)*
encephalitis • *n* heilabólga *(f)*
enclosure • *n* girðing *(f)*
encompass • *v* felast
encyclopedia • *n* alfræðiorðabók *(f)*
endocrinology • *n* innkirtlafræði
endogamy • *n* innvensl
endoscope • *n* holsjá *(f)*, holspegill *(m)*
endoscopy • *n* holsjárskoðun *(f)*, holspeglun *(f)*
endosperm • *n* fræhvíta *(f)*
enemy • *n* óvinur *(m)*

energy • *n* orka *(f)*
engine • *n* mótor
engineer • *n* verkfræðingur *(m)*
enigma • *n* ráðgáta
ennui • *n* lífsleiði *(m)*, óyndi *(n)*
enter • *v* ganga inn, koma inn
entertainment • *n* skemmtun
enthusiasm • *n* ákafi *(m)*, eldmóður *(m)*
entomology • *n* skordýrafræði *(f)*
entrance • *n* inngangur *(m)*
entropy • *n* Óreiða
ephemeral • *adj* skammvinnur *(m)*, skammær *(m)*, skammlífur *(m)*, hverfull *(m)*, dægurlangur *(m)*
epicene • *n* kynlaus *(n)* • *adj* kynlaus *(m)*
epicycle • *n* aukahringur *(m)*, hjáhringur *(m)*
epidemic • *n* faraldur *(m)*, farsótt *(f)*
epidemiology • *n* faraldsfræði *(f)*, faraldursfræði *(f)*, farsóttafræði *(f)*
epididymis • *n* eistalyppa *(f)*, eistnalyppa *(f)*
epiglottis • *n* speldi *(n)*, barkakýlislok *(n)*, barkalok *(n)*
epilepsy • *n* flogaveiki *(f)*, flog *(n)*, niðurfallssýki *(f)*
epilogue • *n* lokaorð, niðurlagsorð, eftirmáli *(m)*
epiphenomenon • *n* fylgifyrirbæri *(n)*
epistemic • *adj* þekking
epistemology • *n* þekkingarfræði *(f)*
epitaph • *n* grafskrift *(f)*, eftirmæli *(n)*, minningargrein *(f)*
epitome • *n* ímynd
epoxy • *n* epoxíð *(n)* • *adj* epoxý-
equation • *n* jafna *(f)*
equator • *n* miðbaugur
equinox • *n* jafndægur *(n)*
eraser • *n* strokleður *(n)*
erbium • *n* erbín
erection • *n* standpína *(f)*
ermine • *n* hreysiköttur
erotic • *adj* erótískur
error • *n* mistök *(f)*, villa *(f)*, skyssa *(f)*, skekkja *(f)*, Villa *(f)*
escalator • *n* rúllustigi *(m)*
escapee • *n* flóttamaður *(m)*
eschatology • *n* heimsslitafræði *(f)*
escritoire • *n* skatthol *(n)*, skrifborð *(n)*
esophageal • *adj* vélinda
esoteric • *adj* heimullegur *(m)*
espresso • *n* espressó
estuary • *n* ármynni *(n)*, árós *(f)*
eta • *n* eta *(n)*
eternal • *adj* eilífur
eternity • *n* eilífð *(f)*
ether • *n* ljósvaki *(m)*

ethnic • *adj* þjóðernis-
ethnocentric • *adj* þjóðhverfur *(m)*
ethnocentrism • *n* þjóðhverfa *(f)*, þjóðhverfur hugsunarháttur *(m)*, þjóðhverf sjónarmið
ethology • *n* atferlisfræði *(f)*, hátternisfræði *(f)*
ethos • *n* andi *(m)*
etude • *n* etýða *(f)*, æfing *(f)*
etymologist • *n* orðsifjafræðingur *(m)*
etymology • *n* orðsifjafræði *(f)*, orðsifjar
eucalyptus • *n* tröllatré *(n)*, ilmviður *(m)*
eugenics • *n* mannkynbætur *(f)*
eukaryote • *n* heilkjörnungur *(m)*
eunuch • *n* geldingur *(m)*
euphemism • *n* veigrunarorð *(n)*, fegrunarheiti *(n)*, skrautyrði *(n)*, skrauthvörf *(n)*
eureka • *interj* það tókst!, þar kom það!, ég hef fundið það!
europium • *n* evrópín
evangelist • *n* guðspjallamaður *(m)*
even • *adj* jafn, jafn *(m)*, sléttur *(m)*
evening • *n* kvöld *(n)*, kveld *(n)*, aftann *(m)*
event • *n* atburður *(m)*, atvik *(n)*
evergreen • *adj* sígrænn *(m)*, vetrargrænn *(m)*
eversion • *n* úthverfing *(f)*, umsnúningur *(m)*
evert • *v* úthverfa, snúa innhverfunni út
everything • *pron* allt
everywhere • *adv* alls staðar, allstaðar, út um allt, hvarvetna, á hverju strái
evil • *adj* illur *(m)*, ill *(f)*, illt *(n)*, vondur, slæmur
evolution • *n* þróunarkenningin
ewe • *n* ær *(f)*
ex • *n* ex *(n)*, fyrrverandi
exaggerate • *v* ýkja, yfirdrífa
examination • *n* próf *(n)*
example • *n* dæmi
excavator • *n* grafa *(f)*
exceptionally • *adv* undantekningartilvikum
excerpt • *n* brot *(n)*, hluti *(n)*
excessive • *adj* óhóflegur
excite • *v* æsa
exciting • *adj* spennandi
excommunication • *n* bannfæring *(f)*
executioner • *n* böðull *(m)*
exhume • *v* grafa upp
existentialism • *n* tilvistarstefna
existentialist • *n* tilvistarsinni *(m)*
exit • *n* útgangur *(m)*
exosphere • *n* úthvolf *(n)*
expectorate • *v* hósta, hósta upp

expectoration • *n* hræking (*f*), uppgangur (*m*), hráki (*m*)
expensive • *adj* dýr
experience • *v* reyna, verða fyrir, upplifa
expiation • *n* yfirbót (*f*), friðþæging (*f*)
explanation • *n* útskýring (*f*)
explode • *v* sprengja, springa
exponent • *n* veldisvísir (*m*)
expression • *n* svipur (*m*), svipbrigði, segð (*f*)
extra • *adj* auka-, extra

extricate • *v* losa, leysa
eye • *n* auga (*n*)
eyeball • *n* augnknöttur (*m*), auga (*n*)
eyebrow • *n* augabrún (*f*)
eyelash • *n* augnhár (*n*)
eyeless • *adj* augnalaus (*m*), sjónlaus (*m*)
eyelid • *n* augnlok (*n*), brá (*f*), hvarmur (*m*)
eyespot • *n* augndíll (*m*), augnblettur (*m*), sjónblettur (*m*)

F

fable • *n* dæmisaga (*f*)
face • *n* andlit (*n*)
facet • *n* flötur (*m*), fægiflötur (*m*), smáauga (*n*)
facetious • *adj* spaugsamur (*m*), gamansamur (*m*)
fact • *n* raun (*f*), raunveruleiki (*m*), staðreynd (*f*)
factor • *v* þátta, þætta, leysa upp í þætti • *n* þáttur (*m*)
factory • *n* verksmiðja (*f*), smiðja (*f*), fabrikka (*f*)
fair • *adj* fagur
faith • *n* trú (*f*)
falcon • *n* fálki (*m*)
falconry • *n* fálkaveiðar, veiði
fall • *v* falla, detta
fallacy • *n* rökvilla (*f*)
fallen • *n* valur (*m*) • *adj* fallinn (*m*), fallinn í valinn (*m*)
fame • *n* frægð (*f*)
family • *n* fjölskylda (*f*), afkvæmi (*n*), ættingi (*n*), ættingjar, skyldmenni, ætt (*f*)
famine • *n* hungursneyð (*f*)
fan • *n* blævængur (*m*), vifta (*f*)
far • *adj* fjarri
farce • *n* farsi (*m*), skopleikur (*m*), ærlsaleikur (*m*), farsi, skopleikur, skrípaleikur (*m*), sýndarmennska (*f*)
fare • *v* fara, ferðast, reisa
farm • *n* bær (*m*)
farmer • *n* bóndi (*m*)
farrier • *n* járningamaður (*m*)
fart • *v* prumpa, freta
fast • *adj* fastur, hraður, hraðskreiður, skjótur, snöggur, kvikur, fljótur, ör • *adv* fast, hratt • *v* fasta
fat • *n* fita (*f*) • *adj* feitur, þykkur
fate • *n* örlög
father • *n* faðir (*m*)
father-in-law • *n* tengdapabbi (*m*)

fatherland • *n* föðurland (*n*), ættland (*n*)
faun • *n* fán (*m*)
fauna • *n* fána (*f*), dýraríki (*n*)
fear • *n* hræðsla (*f*), beygur (*m*)
feasible • *adj* mögulegt
feather • *n* fjöður (*f*)
federation • *n* samband (*n*)
feed • *v* fóðra, fæða
feel • *v* finna
feeling • *n* tilfinning (*f*), tilfinningar (*f*)
feldspar • *n* feldspat (*n*)
fell • *n* fell (*n*), fjall (*n*)
fellatio • *n* tott (*n*)
feminism • *n* feminismi (*m*)
fence • *n* girðing (*f*)
fennel • *n* fennikka (*f*)
ferment • *v* gerja
fermium • *n* fermín
fern • *n* burkni (*m*)
ferry • *n* ferja (*f*)
ferryman • *n* ferjumaður (*m*)
fescue • *n* vingull (*m*)
festoon • *n* blómsveigur (*m*)
feticide • *n* fósturdráp (*n*)
fetlock • *n* hófskegg (*n*)
fetus • *n* fóstur (*n*)
feudalism • *n* lénsskipulag (*n*), lénskerfi (*n*), lénsveldi (*n*)
fever • *n* hiti (*m*), hitasótt (*f*)
fey • *adj* feigur (*m*)
fiction • *n* skáldskapur (*m*)
fictional • *adj* skáldskapur, uppspunninn (*m*), skáldaður (*m*), tilbúinn (*m*), upploginn (*m*)
ficus • *n* fíkjutré (*n*)
fiddle • *n* fiðla
fidelity • *n* tryggð (*f*)
field • *n* akur (*m*)
fifth • *adj* fimmti (*m*), fimmta (*n*)
fiftieth • *adj* fimmtugasta
fig • *n* fíkja (*f*)

---

fight • *v* slást, berjast, heyja, við, gegn • *n* slagur *(m)*, bardagi *(m)*
file • *n* skrá *(f)*, tölvuskrá *(f)*
film • *n* skán *(f)*
final • *n* úrslit
finance • *n* efnahagur *(m)*, fjárhagur *(m)*
find • *v* finna • *n* fundur *(m)*
finger • *v* putta • *n* fingur *(m)*, putti *(m)*
fingerprint • *n* fingrafar *(n)*
fire • *v* reka, segja upp, sparka • *n* eldur *(m)*, bál *(n)*, ofn *(m)*
firearm • *n* skotvopn *(n)*
firefly • *n* eldfluga *(f)*, blysbjalla *(f)*, glætu-fluga *(f)*, glóbjalla *(f)*, ljósormur *(m)*
fireplace • *n* arinn *(m)*, eldstæði *(n)*, hlóðir
firewall • *n* eldveggur *(m)*
firewood • *n* eldiviður *(m)*
firework • *n* flugeldar
fireworks • *n* flugeldur
firm • *n* firma *(f)*, fyrirtæki *(n)*
firmament • *n* festing *(f)*, himinhvel *(n)*, himinhvolf *(n)*, andlangur *(m)*, himinn *(m)*
first • *adj* fyrstur *(m)*
fish • *n* fiskur *(m)* • *v* veiða, fiska, veiða upp úr
fission • *n* skipting
fist • *n* hnefi *(m)*, kreppt hönd *(f)*
fjord • *n* fjörður *(m)*
flag • *n* fáni *(m)*, flagg *(n)*
flagpole • *n* stöng *(f)*, flaggstöng *(f)*
flagship • *n* flaggskip *(n)*
flame • *n* logi *(m)*
flamethrower • *n* eldvarpa *(f)*
flamingo • *n* flamingói *(m)*, flæmingi *(m)*
flan • *n* bakaður búðingur *(m)*
flank • *n* huppur *(m)*
flashlight • *n* vasaljós *(n)*
flautist • *n* flautuleikari *(m)*
flea • *n* fló *(f)*
flee • *v* flýja
fleeting • *adj* skammær *(m)*, hverfull *(m)*, augnablik
flexible • *adj* sveigjanlegur
flightless • *adj* ófleygur
flint • *n* tinna *(f)*
flip-flop • *n* vippa *(f)*, vippurás *(f)*, san-dali *(m)*
flippant • *adj* virðingarlaus *(m)*
floater • *n* augngrugg *(n)*, flotögn *(f)*
flock • *v* hópast saman • *n* flokkur *(m)*, hópur *(m)*, hjörð *(f)*
floe • *n* ísjaki *(m)*
flood • *v* hlaupa • *n* flóð *(n)*
floor • *n* gólf *(n)*
floppy • *adj* linur *(m)*
flora • *n* flóra *(f)*, gróðurríki *(n)*

floriculture • *n* blómaframleiðslu
flotilla • *n* lítill floti *(m)*, smáfloti *(m)*, flotasveit *(f)*
flour • *n* mjöl *(n)*
flourish • *v* dafna, blómstra, sveifla
flow • *v* renna, streyma, flæða
flower • *v* blómstra • *n* blóm *(n)*
flu • *n* flensa *(f)*, inflúensa *(f)*
fluency • *n* flæði *(n)*
fluent • *adj* reiprennandi, altalandi
flugelhorn • *n* flygilhorn *(n)*
fluorine • *n* flúor *(n)*, flúr
flush • *n* litur *(m)*
flute • *n* flauta *(f)*
fly • *n* fluga *(f)*, fiskifluga *(f)*, rennilás *(m)*
flyleaf • *n* saurblað *(n)*
foal • *v* kasta • *n* folald *(n)*
foam • *n* froða *(f)*
fog • *n* þoka *(f)*
fold • *v* brjóta saman, pakka
folder • *n* mappa *(f)*
foment • *v* bakstur
font • *n* leturgerð *(f)*
fontanelle • *n* hausamót
food • *n* matur *(m)*, fæði *(n)*, matvara *(f)*, matvæli *(n)*
fool • *n* bjáni
foolish • *adj* heimskur
foot • *n* fótur *(m)*, bragliður *(m)*, kveða *(f)*
football • *n* fótbolti
footpath • *n* tá *(n)*
footstool • *n* fótskemill *(m)*, fótaskemill *(m)*, skemill *(m)*
footwear • *n* skófatnaður
forbid • *v* banna
ford • *n* vað *(n)*
forefinger • *n* vísifingur *(m)*, sleikifingur *(m)*, bendifingur *(m)*, vísiputti *(m)*
forehead • *n* enni *(n)*
foreigner • *n* útlendingur *(m)*
forenoon • *n* árdegi, fyrirmiðdagur
forensic • *adj* réttar-
foreplay • *n* forleikur *(m)*
foresee • *v* sjá fyrir
foreseeable • *adj* fyrirsjáanlegur *(m)*
forest • *n* skógur
forget • *v* gleyma
forget-me-not • *n* gleym-mér-ei *(f)*
forgettable • *adj* gleymanleg
forgive • *v* fyrirgefa
forint • *n* fórinta *(f)*, forinta *(f)*
fork • *n* gaffall *(m)*
format • *v* forsníða, strauja, formatta • *n* lögun *(f)*, form *(n)*, snið *(n)*, forsnið *(n)*
fort • *n* virki *(n)*, vígi *(n)*
fortieth • *adj* fertugasta
fortnight • *adv* tvær vikur, hálfur

mánuður (m), fjórtán dagar
fortress • n virki (n)
fortune • n örlög, auðna (f), gæfa (f), lán (n), auður (m)
fossil • n steingervingur (m)
foundation • n grunnur (m), stofnun (f), meik (n)
fountain • n gosbrunnur
fourth • adj fjórði
fowl • n fiðurfé (n)
fox • n refur (m), tófa (f)
fractional • adj brotinn (m), brot
fragrance • n ilmur (m)
franc • n franki (m)
francium • n fransín
frankincense • n reykelsi (n)
freckle • n frekna (f)
free • adj frjáls
freedman • n leysingi (m), frelsingi (m)
freedom • n frelsi (n)
freeze • v frjósa, frysta
frequency • n tíðni (f)
frequent • adj tíður (m), tíð (f), títt (n) • v stunda, sækja, venja komur sínar á, venja komur sínar í
fresh • adj ferskur
fricative • n önghljóð (n)
friend • n vinur (m), vinkona (f), vinstúlka (f), félagi (m), kunningi (m), vina (m), góði (m), góða (f)
friendless • adj vinalaus
friendliness • n vingjarnleiki (m)
friendly • n vináttuleikur (m) • adj vingjarnlegur, vinalegur
friendship • n vinátta (f)

frightened • adj hræddur
frisk • v leita á • adj frískur (m)
frog • n froskur (m)
from • prep frá, á móti
frost • v hríma • n frost (n), frostavetur (m)
froth • n froða (f)
frown • v hnykla brýnnar, hleypa brúnum, yggla sig • n gretta, ygglibrún, vanþóknunarsvipur
fructose • n frúktósi (m)
fruit • n ávöxtur (m), aldin (n), faggi (m)
frustum • n stúfur (m)
fuck • v ríða, hafa kynmök, sofa hjá, hafa mök við • n dráttur (m), uppáferð (f), kynmök, mök, samfarir, samræði (n) • interj helvítis, fjandans, djöfulsins, andskotinn, djöfullinn, djöfulsins helvíti
fuel • n eldsneyti (n)
fugue • n fúga (f)
full • adj fullur (m)
fulmar • n fýll (m), múkki (m)
function • n fall
funeral • n útför
fungible • adj jafngengur, útskiptanlegur
fungicide • n sveppadeyðir (m)
fungus • n sveppur
funnel • n trekt
funny • n brandari (m) • adj fyndinn (m), skemmtilegur (m), hnyttinn (m), smellinn (m)
furniture • n húsgagn (n)
future • n framtíð (f)

G

gadolinium • n gadólín
gait • n göngulag (n), gangtegund (f)
galaxy • n stjörnuþoka (f), vetrarbraut (f)
galleon • n galíon
galley • n galeiða (f)
gallium • n gallín
gallows • n gálgi (m)
game • n leikur (m), spil (n), tafl (n) • adj með
gamete • n kynfruma (f)
gamut • n skali (m), svið (n), röð (f), tónaróf (n), tónaskali (m)
gangling • adj renglulegur (m)
gangrene • n ýldudrep (n), átudrep (n), brandur (m), kolbrandur (m), drep í holdi (n)
gannet • n súla (f)

garage • n bílskúr (m)
garbage • n rusl (n)
garden • n garður (m)
gardening • n garðyrkja (f)
garlic • n hvítlaukur
garment • n flík (f), spjör (f)
garnish • v skreyta
garret • n háaloft (n), ris (n)
gas • n gas (n)
gasoline • n bensín (n)
gate • n hlið (n)
gather • v safna
gauge • n kvarði (m)
gear • n tannhjól (n), gír (m)
gee • n gé ((gyeh (w:Hard and soft G))
geezer • n karlfauskur (m)
geisha • n geisja (f)

gem • *n* gimsteinn *(m)*
gender • *n* kyn *(n)*
genealogy • *n* ættfræði *(f)*
generator • *n* spönnuður *(m)*
genetics • *n* erfðafræði *(f)*
genitive • *n* eignarfall *(n)* • *adj* eignarfall
genocide • *n* þjóðarmorð *(n)*
genome • *n* erfðamengi *(m)*
genotype • *n* arfgerð *(f)*, erfðafar *(n)*, erfðagervi *(n)*
gentleman • *n* herra *(m)*, herramaður *(m)*, aðalsmaður *(m)*, heiðursmaður *(m)*, ljúfmenni *(m)*, prúðmenni *(m)*, valmenni, herramenn *(m)*, karlaklósett *(n)*
gentlemanliness • *n* prúðmennska *(f)*
gentleness • *n* blíða *(f)*
genuflection • *n* knébeyging *(f)*, knéfall *(f)*
geodesic • *n* gagnvegur *(m)* • *adj* gagnvegur
geodesy • *n* landmæling *(f)*, landmælingafræði *(f)*
geography • *n* landafræði *(f)*, landfræði *(f)*
geology • *n* jarðfræði *(f)*
geometry • *n* rúmfræði *(f)*
germanium • *n* german
germinate • *v* spíra, skjóta frjóöngum
geyser • *n* goshver *(m)*
gherkin • *n* smágúrka *(f)*
ghoul • *n* náæta *(f)*
gibberish • *n* djöflaþýska *(f)*, golfranska *(f)*
gift • *n* gjöf *(f)*
gigabyte • *n* gígabæti
gill • *n* tálkn *(n)*
ginger • *n* engifer *(n)*
giraffe • *n* gíraffi *(f)*
girl • *n* stúlka *(f)*, stelpa *(f)*, telpa *(f)*, þerna *(f)*, þjónustustúlka *(f)*
girlfriend • *n* kærasta *(f)*, vinkona *(f)*
girth • *n* gjörð *(f)*, söðulgjörð *(f)*
gist • *n* aðalatriði *(n)*, kjarni *(m)*
give • *v* gefa
gizzard • *n* fóarn *(n)*
glacier • *n* jökull *(m)*, ísbreiða *(f)*
gladly • *adv* gjarnan, gjarna
glass • *n* gler *(n)*, glas *(n)*
glaucoma • *n* gláka *(f)*
glitter • *v* glitra • *n* glitur *(n)*
glockenspiel • *n* klukkuspil
glossary • *n* orðasafn *(n)*
glove • *n* hanski *(m)*
glucose • *n* glúkósi *(m)*
glutton • *n* átvagl *(n)*, mathákur *(m)*, svelgur *(m)*
glycogen • *n* glýkógen *(n)*, dýrasterkja *(f)*

gnaw • *v* naga
go • *v* fara
goalkeeper • *n* markvörður *(m)*
goat • *n* geit *(f)*
goatee • *n* hökutoppur *(m)*
goblet • *n* bikar *(m)*
goblin • *n* svartálfur
god • *n* guð *(m)*
goddess • *n* gyðja *(f)*
gold • *n* gull
goldfish • *n* gullfiskur *(m)*
goldsmith • *n* gullsmiður *(m)*
golf • *n* golf *(n)*
good • *adj* góður *(m)*, góð *(f)*, gott *(n)*
goodbye • *interj* bless, bæ, vertu sæll, vertu sæl
goose • *n* gæs, aligæs
gooseberry • *n* stikilsber *(n)*
gore • *n* dreyri *(m)*
gorgeous • *adj* gullfallegur
gorilla • *n* górilla *(f)*
goshawk • *n* gáshaukur
gospel • *n* guðspjall *(n)*
government • *n* stjórn *(f)*, ríkisstjórn *(f)*
governor • *n* ríkisstjóri *(m)*, landstjóri *(m)*, guvernör *(m)*
graffiti • *n* veggjakrot *(n)*
grammar • *n* málfræði *(f)*, málfræði *(f)*, málfræðibók *(f)*
granddaughter • *n* sonardóttir *(m)*, dótturdóttir *(f)*
grandfather • *n* afi *(m)*
grandmother • *n* amma
grape • *n* vínber *(n)*, þrúga *(f)*
grapefruit • *n* greipaldin *(n)*, greipaldintré *(n)*, greip *(f)*, tröllaldin *(n)*
grapevine • *n* vínviður *(m)*
graphite • *n* grafít *(n)*, ritblý
grass • *n* gras *(n)*
grasshopper • *n* engispretta
grassy • *adj* grösugur
grateful • *adj* þakklátur
grater • *n* rifjárn *(n)*
grave • *n* gröf *(f)*
gray • *n* grár • *adj* grár
graze • *v* bíta gras
great • *adj* stór *(m)*, mikill *(m)*
greed • *n* græðgi *(f)*
green • *n* grænn • *adj* grænn
greenhouse • *n* gróðurhús *(n)*, vetrargarður *(m)*, gróðurskáli *(m)*
greeting • *n* kveðja *(f)*
grenade • *n* handsprengja *(f)*
grin • *n* glott *(n)*
group • *n* grúpa *(f)*
grove • *n* lundur *(m)*
grub • *v* róta, róta í • *n* maðkur *(m)*, lirfa

(f), matur (m), æti (n)
guanine • n gúanín (n)
guano • n drit (n)
guard • n vörður (m)
guardian • n verndari (m), fjárhaldsmaður (m)
guerrilla • n skæruliði (m)
guess • v geta, giska
guest • n gestur (m)
guile • v véla, tæla • n vélabrögð, kænska
(f), slægð (f)
guitar • n gítar (m)
gulf • n flói (m)
gull • n máfur (m)
gullible • adj trúgjarn, auðtrúa
gum • n gómur (m)
gun • n byssa (f), fallbyssa (f), skotvopn

(n)
gunpowder • n byssupúður (n)
gust • n gustur (m), vindhviða (f)
gustation • n bragðskyn (n)
gustatory • adj bragðskyn
gutta-percha • n gúttaperka (n)
gymnasium • n íþróttahús (n),
leikfimisalur (m), menntaskóli (m),
framhaldsskóli (m)
gymnastics • n fimleikar
gynecological • adj kvensjúkdómur
gynecology • n kvensjúkdómafræði (f)
gypsum • n gifs (n)
gypsy • n sígauni (m)
gyrfalcon • n fálki (m), valur (m)

H

haddock • n ýsa (f)
hafnium • n hafnín
haggle • v prútta
haha • interj haha
haiku • n hæka (f)
hail • n haglél (n) • v heilsa
hailstone • n hagl (n)
hair • n hár (n)
hairbrush • n hárbursti
hajj • n hadsjí (n)
halberd • n atgeir (m), bryntröll (n)
halberdier • n hermaður vopnaður bryn-
trölli (m), hermaður vopnaður atgeir (m)
half • n helmingur (m) • adj hálf-
half-hour • n hálftími (m)
halibut • n lúða (f), heilagfiski (m), flyðra
(f)
halitosis • n andremma (f), andfýla (f)
hallelujah • n hallelúja (n) • interj hallelúja
halo • n geislabaugur (m)
halyard • n falur (m)
ham • n skinka (f)
hamburger • n hamborgari (m)
hammer • n hamar (m)
hamster • n hamstur (m)
hand • n hönd (f), mund (f)
handball • n handbolti (m)
handbook • n handbók (f)
handicap • n forgjöf (f), fötlun (f)
handkerchief • n vasaklútur
handshake • n handaband (n)
hang • v hanga
hanging • n henging (f)
hangman • n hengimann (m)

hangnail • n annögl
hangover • n timburmenn, þynnka (f)
haphazard • adj tilviljunarkenndur,
óskipulegur
haploid • adj einlitna
happen • v bera við, henda, verða, vilja
til
happiness • n gleði (f), hamingja (f),
lukka (f)
happy • adj hamingjusamur, heppilegur
harbinger • n boðberi (m), fyrirboði (m),
undanfari (m)
hard • adj hart (n), hörð (f), harður (m),
erfiður (m)
hard-boiled • adj harðsoðinn
hardly • adv af hörku, hakalega, með nau-
mindum, naumlega, ekki meira en svo,
varla, tæplega, með erfiði, með fyrirhöfn
hardship • n þrengingar
hardy • adj herkinn
hare • n héri (m)
harelip • n héravör (f)
harem • n kvennabúr (n)
harmful • adj skaðlegur
harmonium • n harmóníum (n)
harmony • n jafnvægi (n), samlyndi (n),
samræmi (n), samhljómur (m), hljómfræði (f)
harp • n harpa
harpoon • n skutull (m)
harpsichord • n semball (m)
harpsichordist • n semballeikari (m)
harrow • v herfa • n herfi (n)
hat • n hattur (m), höfuðfat
hate • v hata

hatred • *n* hatur *(n)*
hatter • *n* hattari
haunting • *n* reimleiki *(m)*
have • *v* hafa
hawk • *n* haukur *(m)*
hay • *n* hey *(n)*
haystack • *n* heystakkur *(m)*, hey *(n)*
hazelnut • *n* heslihneta *(f)*
he • *pron* hann
head • *n* höfuð *(n)*, haus *(m)*
headache • *n* höfuðverkur *(m)*, hausverkur *(m)*
headdress • *n* höfuðbúnaður *(m)*
header • *n* skalli *(m)*
headgear • *n* höfuðbúnaður *(m)*
headlight • *n* ökuljós
health • *n* heilsa *(f)*
hear • *v* heyra
heart • *n* hjarta *(n)*
heartburn • *n* brjóstsviði *(m)*
heath • *n* lyng *(n)*, heiði
heathen • *n* heiðingi *(m)* • *adj* heiðinn *(m)*
heavy • *adj* þungur
heddle • *v* draga í höföld • *n* hafald *(n)*
hedge • *n* limgerði *(n)*, hekk *(n)*
hedgehog • *n* broddgöltur *(m)*
heel • *n* hæll *(m)*
heifer • *n* kvíga *(f)*
heinous • *adj* viðbjóðslegur
helicopter • *n* þyrla *(f)*, þyrilvængja *(f)*, kofti *(m)*
heliport • *n* þyrluvöllur *(m)*
helium • *n* helín, helíum
hello • *interj* halló, hæ, góðan dag, góðan daginn
helmet • *n* hjálmur *(m)*
help • *n* hjálp *(f)*, aðstoð *(f)*, fulltingi *(n)*, hjálparhella *(f)*, heimilishjálp *(f)* • *v* hjálpa • *interj* hjálp
helpful • *adj* hjálpsamur, gagnlegt
hem • *v* humma, falda • *n* faldur *(m)*, brydding *(f)*
hemiplegia • *n* helftarlömun *(f)*, lömun öðrum megin í líkamanum *(f)*
hemoglobin • *n* blóðrauða *(n)*
hemorrhoid • *n* gyllinæð *(f)*, raufaræðahnútur *(m)*
hence • *adv* héðan, þess vegna
henceforth • *adv* héðan í frá, upp frá þessu
heptagon • *n* sjöhyrningur *(m)*
heraldry • *n* skjaldarmerkjafræði *(f)*
herd • *n* hjörð *(f)*, stóð *(n)*, hirðir *(m)*
here • *adv* hér, hingað
hereby • *adv* hérmeð
hermaphrodite • *n* tvíkynjungur *(m)* • *adj* tvítóla, tvítólaður, tvítóli *(m)*

hermit • *n* einsetumaður *(m)*, einsetumunkur *(m)*
hero • *n* hetja
heroin • *n* heróín *(n)*
heron • *n* hegri *(m)*
herring • *n* síld *(f)*
hers • *pron* hennar
hesitant • *adj* hikandi *(m)*, efablandinn *(m)*, tvístígandi *(m)*, óákveðinn *(m)*, óráðinn *(m)*, á báðum áttum
hexagon • *n* sexhyrningur *(m)*
hi • *interj* halló, hæ
high • *adj* skakkur *(m)*, skökk *(f)*, skakkt *(n)*
hight • *v* heita
highway • *n* hraðbraut *(f)*, þjóðvegur *(m)*
highwayman • *n* vegaræningi *(m)*, stigamaður *(m)*
hill • *n* hæð *(f)*, hlíð *(f)*, brekka *(f)*, hóll *(m)*
hilly • *adj* hæðóttur
hilt • *n* hjalt *(n)*
hin • *n* hín *(f)*
hind • *n* hind *(f)*
hinder • *v* varna, tálma
hindrance • *n* hindrun *(f)*
hip • *n* mjöðm *(f)*
hippie • *n* hippi *(m)*
hippopotamus • *n* flóðhestur *(m)*
hiss • *v* hvæsa, hvissa
histamine • *n* lostefni *(n)*, histamín *(n)*
histogram • *n* súlurit *(n)*, stuðlarit *(n)*
history • *n* saga *(f)*, sagnfræði *(f)*
histrionic • *adj* leiklist, uppgerðarlegur, leikaralegur, tilgerðarlegur
hit • *v* slá, hitta
hither • *adj* sem er nær • *adv* hingað
ho • *n* hóra *(f)*
hoarse • *adj* hás, rámur
hoarseness • *n* hæsi *(f)*
hockey • *n* hokkí
hold • *v* halda, rúma
hole • *v* gera gat á • *n* hola *(f)*, gat *(n)*
holiday • *n* helgidagur *(m)*
holmium • *n* holmín
home • *n* heimili *(n)*, heiman, að heiman, heim, heima • *adv* heima, heim
homesick • *adj* með heimþrá, haldinn heimþrá
homesickness • *n* heimþrá *(f)*
homework • *n* heimavinna *(f)*
homicide • *n* manndráp *(n)*
homogeneous • *adj* einsleitur *(m)*, einleitur *(m)*, eingerður *(m)*, samkynja *(m)*, samleitur *(m)*
homonymous • *adj* samnefndur
homophobia • *n* hommafælni *(f)*, ótti við samkynhneigð *(m)*, hommahatur *(n)*

homophone • *n* samhljóma orð
homosexual • *n* samkynhneigður *(m)*, hommi
homosexuality • *n* samkynhneigð *(f)*
honest • *adj* heiðarlegur *(m)*, ráðvandur *(m)*, sómakær *(m)*, réttsýnn *(m)*, heiðarlega fenginn *(m)*
honey • *n* hunang *(n)*, elskan *(f)*
honeycomb • *n* vaxkaka *(f)*
honeymoon • *n* hveitibrauðsdagar, brúðkaupsferð *(f)*
hood • *n* hetta *(f)*, vélarhlíf *(f)*, húdd *(n)*
hoof • *n* hófur *(m)*, klauf *(f)*
hook • *n* krókur *(m)*, haki *(m)*
hop • *n* humall *(m)*
hope • *n* von *(f)*, vona • *v* vona, gera sér vonir um
hopefully • *adv* vonandi
horizon • *n* sjóndeildarhringur *(m)*, sjónbaugur *(m)*
horizontal • *adj* lárétt
hormone • *n* hormón *(n)*
horn • *n* horn *(n)*
hornblende • *n* hornblendi *(n)*
horniness • *n* gredda *(f)*
horny • *adj* graður *(m)*, gröð *(f)*
horrible • *adj* hræðilegur
horse • *v* tuskast, láta illa, sjá einhverjum fyrir hesti • *n* hestur *(m)*, hross *(n)*, riddari *(m)*
horseback • *n* hestbak
horsefly • *n* kleggi *(m)*
horsemeat • *n* hrossakjöt *(n)*
horseradish • *n* piparrót
horseshoe • *v* járna • *n* skeifa *(f)*
horsetail • *n* elfting
horticultural • *adj* garðyrkju
horticulture • *n* garðyrkjufræði *(f)*, garðrækt *(f)*, garðyrkja *(f)*
horticulturist • *n* garðyrkjufræðingur *(m)*, garðyrkjumaður *(m)*
hosanna • *interj* hósanna
hospitable • *adj* gestrisinn
hospital • *n* sjúkrahús *(n)*, spítali *(m)*
host • *v* hýsa • *n* gestgjafi *(m)*, hýsill *(m)*, kynnir
hot • *adj* heitur
hotel • *n* hótel *(n)*, gistihús *(n)*
hound • *n* hundur
hour • *n* klukkustund, klukkutími
house • *n* hús *(n)*, híbýli *(n)*
housewife • *n* húsfrú *(f)*, húsmóðir *(f)*, húsmóðir
hovel • *n* hreysi *(n)*, kofi *(m)*
how • *adv* hve, hversu, hvernig, en
hubris • *n* hroki *(m)*, ofdramb *(n)*
hue • *n* litblær *(m)*, litur *(m)*, farfi *(m)*

hug • *v* faðma, knúsa • *n* knús *(n)*, faðmlag *(n)*
huge • *adj* risastór, gríðarstór
huh • *interj* ha
hullabaloo • *n* hamagangur *(n)*
hum • *v* raula
humane • *adj* mannúðlegur
humanely • *adv* mannúðlega
humility • *n* hógværð *(f)*, auðmýkt *(f)*
hummingbird • *n* kólibrífugl *(m)*
hundred • *n* hérað *(n)*
hunger • *n* hungur *(n)*, sultur *(m)*
hungry • *adj* svangur *(m)*, hungraður *(m)*, soltinn *(m)*
hunt • *v* veiða, leita • *n* veiði *(f)*, veiðiferð *(f)*
hunter • *n* veiðimaður *(m)*
hurricane • *n* fellibylur, fárviðri *(n)*
hurt • *v* vera vont, meiða, særa
husband • *n* eiginmaður
husk • *v* afhýða
husky • *adj* rámur
hyaline • *adj* glær *(m)*
hydrate • *n* hýdrat *(n)*
hydride • *n* hýdríð *(n)*
hydrocarbon • *n* vetniskol *(n)*, kolvatnsefni *(n)*, kolvetni *(n)*
hydrocephalus • *n* vatnshöfuð *(n)*
hydrogen • *n* vetni *(n)*
hydrology • *n* vatnafræði *(f)*, vatnsfræði *(f)*
hydrolysis • *n* vatnsrof
hydrophilic • *adj* vatnssækinn *(m)*, vatnsfíkinn *(m)*
hydroxide • *n* hýdroxíð *(n)*
hyena • *n* híena *(f)*
hygiene • *n* hreinlæti *(n)*
hygroscopic • *adj* ídrægur *(m)*
hymen • *n* meyjarhaft *(n)*, meydómsmerki *(n)*
hymn • *n* sálmur *(m)*, lofsöngur *(m)*
hymnal • *n* sálmabók *(f)*
hyperbolic • *adj* breiðger *(m)*
hyperglycemia • *n* blóðsykurshækkun *(f)*
hypernym • *n* yfirheiti *(n)*
hypertext • *n* stiklutexti *(m)*
hyperventilation • *n* oföndun *(f)*
hyphen • *n* bandstrik *(n)*
hypochondria • *n* ímyndunarveiki *(f)*, sóttsýki *(f)*, sótthræðsla *(f)*
hypochondriac • *adj* ímyndunarveikur *(m)*, ímyndunarveiki, geislungasvæði
hypocrisy • *n* hræsni *(f)*, yfirdrepsskapur *(m)*, uppgerð *(f)*
hypodermic • *n* stungulyf *(n)*, sprauta *(f)* • *adj* undir húðinni, húðbeðs-
hypodermis • *n* frumulag rétt undir

yfirhúð í plöntum, undirhúð *(f)*
hypoglycemia • *n* blóðsykurskortur *(m)*,
blóðsykurslækkun *(f)*, blóðsykursekla *(f)*
hyponym • *n* undirheiti *(n)*
hypoplasia • *n* vanþroski líffæra *(m)*,
vanþroski vefja *(m)*
hypotension • *n* lágþrýstingur *(m)*,
óeðlilega lágur blóðþrýstingur *(m)*
hypotensive • *adj* sem varðar lágþrýsting,
með óeðlilega lágan blóðþrýsting, sjúkur
af of lágum blóðþrýstingi
hypotenuse • *n* langhlið *(f)*
hypothalamus • *n* undirstúka *(f)*, heiladyngjubotn *(m)*
hypothecate • *v* veðsetja

hypothecation • *n* veðsetning *(f)*
hypothetical • *adj* reistur á tilgátu *(m)*,
reist á tilgátu *(n)*, skilyrtur *(m)*, skilyrt *(n)*
hypoxia • *n* súrefnisskortur *(m)*
hyrax • *n* hnubbi *(m)*, klettagrefingi *(m)*,
stökkhéri *(m)*
hysterectomy • *n* legnám *(n)*
hysterical • *adj* sefasjúkur, móðursjúkur,
æstur, í uppnámi, í geðshræringu, mjög
fyndinn
hysterics • *n* móðursýkiskast *(n)*, stjórnlaust grátkast *(n)*, stjórnlaust hláturkast
(n)

I

ibex • *n* fjallageit *(f)*
ice • *n* ís *(m)*, rjómaís *(m)*, meth *(n)*
iceberg • *n* borgarísjaki *(m)*, ísjaki *(m)*
ichthyologist • *n* fiskifræðingur *(m)*
ichthyology • *n* fiskifræði *(f)*
icicle • *n* grýlukerti *(n)*
ideology • *n* hugmyndafræði *(f)*
idiolect • *n* einkamállýska *(f)*
idiot • *n* hálviti *(m)*, asni *(m)*, grasasni *(m)*,
skynskiptingur *(m)*
idolatry • *n* skurðgoðadýrkun *(f)*
if • *conj* ef, hvort
igloo • *n* snjóhús *(n)*
ignoramus • *n* fávís *(m)*, fáfróður *(m)*
ignorance • *n* fáfræði *(f)*, fáviska *(f)*,
vanþekking *(f)*, þekkingarleysi *(n)*, fákunnátta *(f)*, vankunnátta *(f)*
ignore • *v* hunsa
ill • *adj* veikur
illegible • *adj* ólæsilegur
image • *n* mynd *(f)*
imagination • *n* ímyndunarafl *(n)*, ímyndun *(f)*
imbricate • *v* skara
imitative • *adj* hermi-
immigrant • *n* innflytjandi
immigration • *n* aðflutningur
immortal • *adj* ódauðlegur
immortality • *n* ódauðleiki *(m)*
impale • *v* stjaksetja, stinga á tein, setja á
nál, reka í gegn
impatient • *adj* óþolinmóður
imperative • *n* nauðsyn *(f)* • *adj* mikilvægur
imperialism • *n* heimsvaldastefna *(f)*, imperíalismi *(m)*
implore • *v* grátbiðja

imply • *v* gefa í skyn, benda til
importance • *n* mikilvægi *(n)*
important • *adj* mikilvægur *(m)*
impossible • *adj* ómögulegur
imprison • *v* fangelsa
in • *prep* eftir
inadvertent • *adj* óviljandi
incense • *n* reykelsi *(n)*
inception • *n* upphaf *(n)*, byrjun *(f)*
incessant • *adj* sífelldur, þrálaus, þrálátur,
viðstöðulaus, stöðugur
incest • *n* sifjaspell
inch • *n* tomma *(f)*, þumlungur *(m)*
incognito • *adj* fara huldu höfði • *adv*
huldu höfði, undir dulnefni, undir fölsku
nafni
inconsolable • *adj* óhuggandi
incontinent • *adj* óskírlífur *(m)*, óskrírlíf
(n), óskírlíft *(n)*
increase • *v* ágerast, waxa, fjölga, auka
incus • *n* steðji *(m)*
indeclinable • *adj* óbeygjanlegur
independence • *n* sjálfstæði *(n)*, óhæði
(n)
index • *n* atriðaskrá *(m)*, röðunarskrá *(m)*,
veldisvísir *(m)*, vísitala *(m)*
indicative • *n* framsöguháttur *(m)*
indium • *n* indín
indivisible • *adj* ódeilanlegur *(m)*
indoctrination • *n* innræting *(f)*
indubitable • *adj* efalaus, ótvíræður,
óhrekjandi, vafalaus
indubitably • *adv* ótvíræðlega, óhrekjanlega
induction • *n* aðleiðsla *(f)*, þrepun *(f)*,
stærðfræðileg þrepun *(f)*
industry • *n* iðnaður *(m)*

inequality • *n* ójafna *(f)*
inexpensive • *adj* ódýrt
infanticide • *n* barnsmorð *(n)*, barnsmorðingi *(n)*
infection • *n* sýking *(f)*
infectious • *adj* smitandi
infinitive • *n* nafnháttur *(m)*
infinity • *n* óendanleiki
inflammation • *n* bólga *(f)*, þroti *(m)*
inflation • *n* verðbólga *(f)*
inflection • *n* beyging *(f)*, raddblær *(m)*
inflexible • *adj* ósveigjanlegur
influence • *n* áhrif
influenza • *n* inflúensa *(f)*, flensa *(f)*
informal • *adj* óformlegur
information • *n* upplýsingar
injection • *n* innspýting *(f)*
injure • *v* slasa
injury • *n* sár *(n)*
ink • *n* blek *(n)*
inkwell • *n* blekbytta *(f)*
inlet • *n* vík *(f)*, vogur *(m)*
inn • *n* gistihús *(n)*, krá *(f)*
innate • *adj* meðfæddur
innocence • *n* sakleysi *(n)*, barnaskapur *(m)*, grandaleysi *(n)*, meinlaus *(f)*, meinlaust *(n)*, saklaus *(f)*, saklaust *(n)*, skaðlaus *(f)*, skaðlaust *(n)*
insect • *n* skordýr *(n)*
inshore • *adj* nærri, við, grunnsævi, álands- • *adv* nærri landi, við land, uppi í landsteinum, að landi
insomnia • *n* svefnleysi *(n)*, andvaka *(f)*
insomniac • *n* svefnleysi *(m)* • *adj* svefnleysi
inspire • *v* hvetja
instep • *n* rist *(f)*
institution • *n* stofnun *(f)*
instrumentalist • *n* hljóðfæraleikari *(m)*
insufflation • *n* innblástur *(m)*
insulator • *n* einangrari *(m)*, einangri *(m)*, einangur *(m)*
insulin • *n* insúlín, eyjavaki *(m)*
insult • *n* móðgun *(f)*
insurance • *n* trygging *(f)*, trygging
insurrection • *n* uppreisn *(f)*
integral • *n* heildun *(f)*, tegrun *(f)*
integrate • *v* tegra, heilda
intelligence • *n* greind *(f)*
intelligent • *adj* gáfaður
intentional • *adj* viljandi
inter • *v* jarða, greftra, jarðsetja
intercession • *n* meðalganga *(f)*, fyrirbæn *(f)*, bænarstaður *(m)*
interdisciplinary • *adj* þverfaglegur *(m)*,

þverfræðilegur *(m)*
interested • *adj* áhugasamur
interesting • *adj* athyglisverður
interjection • *n* upphrópun *(f)*
interleave • *v* flétta
interloper • *n* boðflenna *(f)*, aðskotadýr *(n)*
intermission • *n* hlé *(n)*, hvíld *(f)*, aflát *(n)*
international • *adj* alþjóðlegur
internationalization • *n* alþjóðavæðing *(f)*
interpreter • *n* túlkur *(m)*
intersection • *n* vegamót, gatnamót, sniðmengi *(n)*, skurðpunktur *(m)*, snið *(n)*, skurðmengi *(n)*, skarmengi *(n)*
interview • *n* viðtal *(n)*
interviewee • *n* viðmælandi *(m)*
interviewer • *n* spyrill *(m)*, spyrjandi *(m)*
intestine • *n* görn *(f)*
into • *prep* inn í
intuitionism • *n* innsæiskenning *(f)*
invariant • *n* óbreyta *(f)* • *adj* óbreyttur
invent • *v* finna upp
invention • *n* uppfinning *(f)*
investment • *n* fjárfesting *(f)*
invincible • *n* ósigrandi
invisibility • *n* ósýnileiki *(m)*
invisible • *adj* ósýnilegur
invite • *v* bjóða • *n* boð *(n)*
involution • *n* sjálfhverfa *(f)*, sjálfhverf vörpun *(f)*
iodine • *n* joð
ion • *n* jón *(f)*, fareind *(f)*
ionization • *n* jónun *(f)*
iridium • *n* iridín *(n)*
iron • *v* strauja, straua • *n* járn *(n)*, straujárn *(n)*
irrational • *n* óræð tala *(f)* • *adj* óræður *(m)*
irregular • *adj* óreglulegur *(m)*
is • *v* er
island • *n* ey *(f)*, eyja, eyja *(f)*, eyland *(n)*
isomorphism • *n* einsmótun *(f)*
isoperimetric • *adj* jafn að ummáli *(m)*, ummálsjafn *(m)*
isotope • *n* samsæta *(f)*, ísótópur *(m)*
isotropic • *adj* stefnusnauður *(m)*, einsátta *(m)*, jafnátta *(m)*
isthmus • *n* eiði
it • *pron* það
itemize • *v* sundurliða
iterative • *adj* ítrekun
ivory • *n* fílabein *(n)*

J

jack • *n* tjakkur *(m)*, gosi *(m)*
jackdaw • *n* dvergkráka *(f)*
jacket • *n* jakki *(m)*, frakki *(m)*
jaeger • *n* kjói *(m)*
jam • *n* sulta *(f)*
jammed • *adj* sneisafullur
jar • *n* krukka *(f)*
jaundice • *n* gula *(f)*
jaw • *n* kjálki *(m)*
jay • *n* skrækskaði, joð *((yoth))*
jazz • *n* djass *(m)*
jeep • *n* jeppi *(m)*
jellyfish • *n* marglytta *(f)*
jib • *n* fokka *(f)*, framsegl *(n)*, lyftiarmur *(m)*, bóma *(f)*
jibe • *n* hnjóðsyrði *(n)*
job • *n* verkefni *(n)*, verk *(n)*, vinna *(f)*, starf *(n)*
jogging • *n* skokk *(n)*
join • *v* sameina
joint • *n* jóna *(f)*, marijúanavindlingur *(m)*
joke • *v* grínast, spauga • *n* brandari *(m)*, grín *(n)*, spaug *(n)*
jot • *v* skrifa hjá sér, punkta, punkta niður, hripa, hripa niður, hripa hjá sér • *n* punktur *(m)*, depill *(m)*, angarögn *(f)*
jotun • *n* jötunn
journalism • *n* blaðamennska *(f)*, fréttamennska *(f)*
journalist • *n* blaðamaður *(m)*
journey • *v* ferðast • *n* leiðangur, ferð
joy • *n* gleði *(f)*
joystick • *n* stýripinni *(m)*, stýristautur *(m)*, leikvölur *(m)*
judge • *n* dómari *(m)*, dómbær *(m)*, sér-fróður *(m)*, hafa gott vit á, hafa vit á
judo • *n* júdó *(n)*
jug • *v* sjóða í leirpotti, sjóða í leirpotti með loki, fangelsa, setja í fangelsi, stinga í steininn, stinga inn, henda í fangelsi • *n* kanna *(f)*, krús *(f)*, fangelsi *(m)*, steininn *(m)*, tútta *(f)*, túttur, bobblingur *(m)*, bob-blingar
juggling • *n* djögl, gegl, gripl
juice • *n* safi *(m)*, djús *(m)*
juicy • *adj* safaríkur, safamikill
jump • *v* hoppa
jungle • *n* frumskógur *(m)*
juniper • *n* einer *(m)*
junk • *n* rusl *(n)*, drasl *(n)*, djúnka *(f)*, júnka *(f)*
jurisprudence • *n* lögfræði *(f)*
juror • *n* kviðdómari *(m)*, kviðdómandi *(m)*
jury • *n* kviðdómur *(m)*, dómnefnd *(f)*
just • *adv* áðan

K

kale • *n* grænkál
kangaroo • *n* kengúra *(f)*
karate • *n* karate *(n)*
karyotype • *n* kjarngerð *(f)*, kjarnagerð *(f)*
kayak • *n* kajak *(m)*
keelhaul • *v* kjöldraga
keg • *n* legill *(m)*
kelp • *n* þari *(m)*
kenning • *n* kenning *(f)*
keratin • *n* hyrni *(n)*, hornefni *(n)*, keratín *(n)*
kernel • *n* kjarni *(m)*, stýrikjarni *(m)*
kestrel • *n* fálki *(m)*, haukur, valur, turn-fálki
kettle • *n* ketill *(m)*
key • *n* lykill *(m)*, takki *(m)*, hnappur *(m)*, tóntegund *(f)*
keyboard • *n* lyklaborð *(n)*, hnappaborð *(n)*, leturborð *(n)*, hljómborð *(n)*
kick • *v* sparka, sparka í, sparka út,
sparka út af • *n* spark *(n)*
kid • *n* kið *(n)*, barn *(n)*, krakki *(m)*
kidney • *n* nýra *(n)*
kill • *n* dráp, morð
killer • *n* morðingi *(m)*
kilogram • *n* kílógramm
kilt • *n* skotapils *(n)*
kin • *n* ættmenni, skyldmenni • *adj* skyl-dur
kind • *n* gerð *(f)*, tegund *(f)* • *adj* góður *(m)*, vinalegur *(m)*
kindergarten • *n* leikskóli *(m)*
king • *n* konungur *(m)*, kóngur *(m)*
kingdom • *n* konungsríki *(n)*, konungs-dæmi *(n)*, konungsveldi *(n)*
kiosk • *n* skáli *(m)*, söluskáli *(m)*, söluturn *(m)*, sjoppa *(f)*, kiosk
kismet • *n* örlög *(n)*, sköp *(n)*
kiss • *v* kyssa • *n* koss
kitchen • *n* eldhús *(n)*

kite • *n* flugdreki *(m)*
kitten • *n* kettlingur *(m)*
kittiwake • *n* rita *(f)*
kleptomania • *n* stelsýki *(f)*
klutz • *n* klossi *(m)*
knee • *n* hné *(n)*, kné *(n)*
knife • *n* hnífur *(m)*
knight • *n* riddari *(m)*
knot • *v* hnýta • *n* hnútur *(m)*, flækja *(f)*,

klípa *(f)*
know • *v* vita, þekkja
knowledge • *n* þekking *(f)*, vitneskja *(f)*, kunnátta *(f)*
knuckle • *n* kjúka *(f)*
koala • *n* pokabjörn *(n)*
krill • *n* ljósáta
krypton • *n* krypton

L

laboratory • *n* rannsóknarstofa, tilraunastofa, rannsóknarstofu
lack • *v* skorta • *n* skortur *(m)*
lacrimation • *n* táraflæði *(n)*, táraflóð *(n)*, táramyndun *(f)*
lactose • *n* laktósi
ladder • *n* stigi *(m)*
ladle • *v* ausa • *n* ausa *(f)*
lag • *n* lagg, hökt *(n)*, töf *(f)*, seinkun *(f)*
lake • *n* vatn *(n)*, tjörn *(f)*
lamb • *n* lamb *(n)*, lambakjöt *(n)*
lament • *v* harma, syrgja
lamp • *n* lampi *(m)*
lampshade • *n* lampaskermur *(m)*, skermur *(m)*
land • *v* lenda • *n* land, jörð *(f)*
landlocked • *adj* landlukt
language • *n* mál *(n)*, tungumál *(n)*, tunga *(n)*
lanolin • *n* ullarfeiti *(f)*
lantern • *n* lampi *(m)*
lanthanum • *n* lanþan *(n)*
lap • *n* skaut *(n)*
laptop • *n* fartölva *(f)*, ferðatölva *(f)*
lapwing • *n* vepja *(f)*
larboard • *n* bakborði *(m)*
larceny • *n* stuldur *(m)*, þjófnaður *(m)*
larch • *n* lerki, lerkitré *(n)*
large • *adj* mikill, stór
lark • *n* lævirki *(m)*
larva • *n* lirfa *(f)*
larvicide • *n* lirfueyðir *(m)*
laryngitis • *n* barkakýlisbólga *(f)*, barkakýliskvef *(n)*, raddbandakvef *(n)*, barkabólga *(f)*
larynx • *n* barkakýli *(n)*
lasagna • *n* lasanja *(n)*, lasagna *(n)*
laser • *n* leysir *(m)*, leysigeisli *(m)*
lasso • *v* snara • *n* snara *(f)*, slöngvivaður *(m)*
last • *adj* síðast
late • *adj* seint *(n)*, heitinn • *adv* seinn
latency • *n* biðtími *(m)*

lateness • *n* seinleiki *(m)*
later • *interj* heyrumst, sjáumst
lathe • *n* rennibekkur *(m)*
lattice • *n* grind *(f)*
laugh • *v* hlæja • *n* hlátur
laughable • *adj* hlægilegur
laughter • *n* hlátur *(m)*
lava • *n* hraun
law • *n* lögmál *(n)*
lawrencium • *n* lárensín
lawyer • *n* lögfræðingur *(m)*
layman • *n* leikmaður *(m)*
lead • *n* blý *(n)*
leader • *n* leiðsögumaður *(m)*
leaf • *n* lauf *(n)*, laufblað *(n)*
leak • *n* leki *(m)*
leapfrog • *n* höfrungahlaup
learn • *v* læra, nema
leather • *n* leður *(n)*
lecithin • *n* lesitín *(n)*
leech • *n* blóðsuga *(f)*, iglur
leek • *n* blaðlaukur *(m)*
lees • *n* dreggjar, botnfall *(n)*
left • *adj* vinstri
leg • *n* fótur *(m)*, fótleggur *(m)*, leggur *(m)*, buxnaskálm *(f)*, skálm *(f)*, áfangi *(m)*
legible • *adj* læsilegur
legless • *adj* án fóta, fótalaus *(m)*
legume • *n* belgaldin *(n)*
leisure • *n* frístund *(f)*, tómstund *(f)*
lemming • *n* læmingi *(m)*
lemon • *n* sítróna *(f)*
lemonade • *n* límonaði *(n)*, sítrónudrykkur *(m)*
lemur • *n* lemúr *(m)*
lend • *v* lána
length • *n* lengd *(f)*
lentil • *n* lentil
leopard • *n* hlébarði *(m)*
leprosy • *n* holdsveiki *(f)*, líkþrá *(f)*, holdsveiki
lesbian • *n* lesbía *(f)*
letter • *n* bókstafur *(m)*, stafur *(m)*, bréf

(n), sendibréf (n)
lettuce • n salat
leukemia • n hvítblæði (n), blóðlýsa (f)
level • v jafna, jafna við jörðu • n hallamál (n), stig (n), borð (n), hæð (f)
lexeme • n les (n), flettiorð (n)
lexicography • n orðabókafræði (f), orðabókargerð (f), samning orðabókar (f)
lexicon • n orðabók (f), orðasafn (n), lesforði (m), lessafn (n)
liar • n lygari (m)
liberate • v frelsa
liberty • n frelsi (n)
library • n bókasafn (n), bókhlaða (f), bókahús (n)
libration • n tunglvik (n)
lichen • n flétta (f)
lick • v sleikja
licorice • n lakkrís (m)
lie • v liggja, ljúga • n lygi
life • n líf (n)
lifeboat • n björgunarbátur (m)
lift • n lyfta (f)
ligament • n liðband (n), band (n)
light • n ljós (n) • v kveikja, lýsa • adj bjart (n), bjartur (m), björt (f), fölur, ljós, léttur (m), létt (n), fitulítill (m), fituskertur (m), fitusnauður (m)
lighthouse • n viti (m), vitaturn (m)
lightning • n elding (f)
like • v líka
likewise • adv sömuleiðis
lily • n lilja (f)
lime • n gulgrænn
limerick • n limra (f)
limestone • n kalksteinn
limnology • n vatnalíffræði
limousine • n limmósína (f), glæsivagn (m), eðalvagn (m)
linden • n lind (f)
line • n lína (f)
ling • n langa (f)
linguist • n málvísindamaður (m)
linguistics • n málvísindi
linseed • n hörfræ (n)
lintel • n dyratré (n), ofdyri (n)
lion • n ljón (n)
lip • n vör (f)
lipid • n lípíð (n)
lipophilic • adj fitusækinn (m)
lipstick • n varalitur (m)
liquid • n vökvi (m)
lisp • v vera smámæltur (m), vera smámælt (n) • n smámæli (n)
list • n listi (m), skrá (f)
listen • v hlusta, á, eftir
literal • adj bókstaflegur

literature • n bókmenntir
lithium • n litín (n), liþín (n), litíum (n)
litter • n samburi, got (n), ungi, rusl (n), drasl (n)
little • adj lítill • adv lítið
liturgical • adj litúrgískur
live • v lifa, búa • adj lifandi • adv beint
livelihood • n lifibrauð (n), viðurværi (n)
liver • n lifur (f)
livestock • n búfé (n)
lizard • n eðla (f)
llama • n lamadýr (n)
loaf • n hleifur (m), brauð (n) • v slóra
loanword • n tökuorð (n)
lobe • n blað (n)
lobster • n humar (m)
local • adj staðbundinn, staðbundinn (m), staður
lock • n lás (m), lokkur (m)
lodger • n leigjandi (m)
logarithm • n logri (m)
logarithmic • adj logri
logorrhea • n munnræpa (f), orðaflaumur (m), óhamið málæði (n)
loiter • v slóra
lollipop • n sleikipinni (m), sleikjó (m), sleikibrjóstsykur (m), sleikjubrjóstsykur (m)
lonely • adj einmana
long • adj langur • adv langt, lengi • v þrá
look • v kíkja, horfa, sjá, líta, líta út, virðast, sýnast, leita
loom • n vefstóll (m)
loop • n snara (f)
loose • v missa, sleppa, fyrirgjöra
lord • n herra (m), húsbóndi (m), lávarður (m)
lore • n fróðleikur (m), þjóðlegur fróðleikur (m)
lose • v týna
lost • adj týndur
lottery • n happdrætti (n), lottó (n)
lotus • n lótus (n), lótusblóm (n)
loudspeaker • n hátalari (m)
louse • n lús (f)
love • n elska, ást, kærleikur (m)
low • n lágþrýstisvæði (n)
luck • n heppni (f), lukka (f)
lucky • adj lánsamur, heppinn, gæfusamur
lucrative • adj arðbær (m), ábatasamur (m), arðsamur (m), gróða-
lugubrious • adj raunamæddur (m), hryggð, sorg, sorgbitinn
lullaby • n vögguvísa (f)
lumbago • n þursabit (n)
lumbar • adj lend

lumpsucker • *n* hrognkelsi
lunatic • *n* brjálæðingur *(m)*, geðsjúklingur *(m)*
lung • *n* lunga, lungu
lute • *n* lúta *(f)*
lutetium • *n* lútesín
lye • *n* lútur

lymph • *n* vessi *(m)*, sogæðavökvi *(m)*
lymphocyte • *n* eitilfruma *(f)*
lymphoma • *n* eitlaæxli *(n)*, eitilfrumukrabbamein *(n)*
lynx • *n* gaupa *(f)*
lyre • *n* lýra *(f)*

M

machination • *n* ráðabrugg *(n)*, leynimakk *(n)*
machine • *n* vél *(f)*
macro • *n* fjölvaskipun *(f)*, fjölvi *(m)*
macromolecule • *n* stórsameind *(f)*
macron • *n* lengdarmerki *(n)*
macrophage • *n* gleypifruma *(f)*, stóræta *(f)*, stórátfruma *(f)*
mad • *adj* ær
madrigal • *n* madrígal *(m)*, madrígali *(m)*
magazine • *n* tímarit *(n)*, skothylkjahólf *(n)*
mage • *n* galdramaður *(m)*
magical • *adj* galdra-, göldróttur *(m)*, töfrandi, töfrum líkt
magma • *n* bergkvika
magnesium • *n* magnesín *(n)*, magnín *(n)*, magníum *(n)*, magnesíum *(n)*
magnet • *n* segull *(m)*
magpie • *n* skjór *(m)*
maim • *v* limlesta
mainland • *n* meginland *(n)*, fastland *(n)*
mainmast • *n* stórsigla *(f)*
makeup • *n* farði *(m)*, meik *(n)*
malice • *n* illgirni *(f)*, meinfýsni *(f)*
mallard • *n* stokkönd
mammal • *n* spendýr
mammoth • *n* loðfíll *(m)*, fornfíll *(m)*, mammút *(m)*
man • *v* manna • *n* manneskja *(f)*, maður *(m)*, karlmaður *(m)*, karl *(m)*
man-made • *adj* manngerður, tilbúinn
manacle • *n* handjárn
mane • *n* makki *(m)*, fax *(n)*
manganese • *n* mangan *(n)*
manger • *n* jata *(f)*
mango • *n* mangó
mangrove • *n* leiruviðarskógur
manhole • *n* mannop *(n)*, mannsmuga *(f)*
mankind • *n* mannkyn *(n)*
manna • *n* manna *(n)*
mannequin • *n* gína *(f)*
manservant • *n* heimilisþjónn *(m)*, þjónn *(m)*, einkaþjónn *(m)*
mantle • *n* möntull *(m)*

manure • *n* mykja *(f)*
map • *n* kort *(n)*, vörpun *(f)*, færsla *(f)*, myndun *(f)*, ummyndun *(f)*
maple • *n* hlynur
mapping • *n* vörpun *(f)*, færsla *(f)*, myndun *(f)*, ummyndun *(f)*
marble • *n* marmari *(m)*
march • *v* marsera *(f)* • *n* marsering *(f)*, ganga *(f)*, kröfuganga *(f)*, mars *(m)*, gangur *(m)*
mare • *n* hryssa *(f)*, meri *(f)*
margarine • *n* smjörlíki *(n)*
marigold • *n* morgunfrú *(f)*, gullfífill *(m)*
marine • *adj* sjór
mark • *v* dekka, valda
market • *n* markaður *(m)*
marmot • *n* múrmeldýr
maroon • *n* rauðbrúnn *(m)*, dumbrauður *(m)* • *adj* rauðbrúnn *(m)*, dumbrauður *(m)*
marquess • *n* markgreifi *(m)*
marriage • *n* hjónaband *(n)*
marrow • *n* mergur *(m)*
marry • *v* gifta, kvæna, gefa saman, vígja
marsh • *n* mýri
marshmallow • *n* sykurpúði *(m)*
marsupial • *n* pokadýr *(n)*
marten • *n* mörður
marvelous • *adj* undursamlegur, stórkostlegur, undraverður
mascara • *n* maskari *(m)*
mask • *n* gríma *(f)*
masochist • *n* masókisti *(m)*
mass • *n* massi *(m)*, messa • *v* messa
massage • *n* nudd
masseur • *n* nuddari *(m)*
mast • *n* mastur *(n)*, siglutré *(n)*
mastectomy • *n* brjóstnám *(n)*, brottnám *(n)*
masterpiece • *n* meistaraverk *(n)*
masticate • *v* kremja, hnoða
masturbation • *n* sjálfsfróun *(f)*, rúnk *(n)*
mat • *n* motta *(f)*
mathematical • *adj* stærðfræðilegur
mathematician • *n* stærðfræðingur *(m)*
mathematics • *n* stærðfræði *(f)*

matriculate • *v* innrita, innritast
matriculation • *n* innritun *(f)*
matrix • *n* mergur, grind, uppistöðuefni, fylki, innrúm, mót, afsteypumót
mattress • *n* dýna *(f)*
may • *v* mega, geta
maybe • *adv* kannski, kannske, máske, máski, ef til vill
mayonnaise • *n* majónes *(n)*
mayor • *n* borgarstjóri *(m)*, bæjarstjóri *(m)*
me • *pron* mig, mér, ég, minn *(m)*, mín *(f)*, mitt *(n)*
mead • *n* mjöður *(m)*
meadow • *n* engi *(n)*, grund *(f)*, grasflöt *(f)*
meal • *n* máltíð *(f)*
mean • *v* ætla, meina, þýða • *n* meðaltal *(n)*, hreint meðaltal *(n)*, venjulegt meðaltal *(n)*, milliliður *(m)*, innliður *(m)*
meaning • *n* meining *(f)*, merking
meat • *n* kjöt *(n)*
meatball • *n* kjötbolla *(f)*
media • *n* miðill *(m)*
median • *n* miðgildi *(n)*, miðtala *(f)*
medicine • *n* lyf *(n)*, læknisfræði *(f)*
medium • *n* miðilsgáfa
megabyte • *n* megabæti
megalomania • *n* mikilmennskubrjálæði *(n)*
megalopolis • *n* risaborg
melancholy • *n* þunglyndi *(n)*
melanoma • *n* sortuæxli *(n)*
member • *n* félagi *(m)*
membrane • *n* himna
memento • *n* minjagripur *(m)*, minningargripur *(m)*
memorable • *adj* eftirminnilegur, minnistæður
memory • *n* minni *(n)*
menarche • *n* fyrstu tíðir *(f)*
mendelevium • *n* mendelevín
meningitis • *n* heilahimnubólga *(f)*, mengisbólga *(f)*
menstruation • *n* blæðingar, tíðir
mention • *v* minnast á, nefna, orða, geta, koma á framfæri, hafa orð á, vekja máls á, koma inn á, víkja að, drepa á, impra á • *n* umtal *(n)*
menu • *n* matseðill *(m)*
meow • *v* mjálma • *interj* mjá
mercenary • *n* málaliði *(m)*
mercury • *n* kvikasilfur
mercy • *n* náð *(n)*
meritocracy • *n* gáfumannaveldi *(n)*, veldi hæfileikamanna *(n)*
mermaid • *n* hafmey *(f)*
mesh • *n* lykkja *(f)*, möskvi *(m)*

mesosphere • *n* miðhvolf *(n)*
message • *n* skilaboð, boðskapur *(m)*
messenger • *n* sendiboði *(m)*, boðberi *(m)*
metabolism • *n* efnaskipti *(n)*
metabolite • *n* myndefni *(n)*
metacarpal • *n* miðhandarbein *(n)*, hnúaleggur *(m)*, handarbaksleggur *(m)* • *adj* miðhandar-, handarbaks-
metacarpus • *n* miðhönd *(f)*, miðhandarbein *(n)*
metal • *n* málmur *(m)*
metalanguage • *n* hjálparmál *(n)*, lýsimál *(n)*
metalloid • *n* málmleysingi *(m)*, hálfmálmur *(m)*, málmbróðir *(m)*
metamathematics • *n* yfirstærðfræði *(f)*
metarule • *n* yfirregla *(f)*
metathesis • *n* hljóðavíxl, stafavíxl
meteor • *n* stjörnuhrap *(n)*
meteorite • *n* loftsteinn *(m)*
meteoroid • *n* reikisteinn *(m)*, geimsteinn *(m)*, geimgrýti *(n)*
meteorologist • *n* veðurfræðingur *(m)*
meteorology • *n* veðurfræði *(f)*
methane • *n* metan
methanol • *n* metanól *(n)*
method • *n* aðferð *(f)*, háttur *(m)*, skipulag *(n)*
methylphenidate • *n* metýlfenídat *(n)*
metonymy • *n* nafnhvörf, merkingarskipti
metrology • *n* mælifræði *(f)*
microbe • *n* örvera *(f)*
microcosm • *n* smáheimur *(m)*, örheimur *(m)*
microorganism • *n* örvera *(f)*
microphone • *n* hljóðnemi *(m)*
microwave • *n* örbylgja *(f)*
midnight • *n* miðnætti *(m)*, miðnótt *(f)*
midsummer • *n* miðsumar *(n)*, miðsumarsdagur *(m)*
mile • *n* míla
millennium • *n* árþúsund *(n)*, þúsöld *(f)*
millet • *n* hirsi
millionaire • *n* milljónamæringur *(m)*, milli *(m)*
millisecond • *n* millísekúnda
millstone • *n* kvarnarsteinn *(m)*, myllusteinn *(m)*
milt • *n* svil
mine • *pron* minn *(m)* • *n* náma *(f)*, jarðsprengja *(f)*
miner • *n* námumaður *(m)*
mineralogy • *n* steindafræði
minesweeper • *n* sprengjuleit
minim • *n* hálfnóta *(f)*
minimum • *n* lágmark *(n)*
ministry • *n* klerkdómur *(n)*

mink • *n* minkur *(m)*
minuet • *n* menúett *(m)*
minus • *n* neikvæð tala *(f)*, tala sem er minni en núll *(f)*, mínus *(m)*, ókostur *(m)* • *adj* mínus, sem lýtur að frádrætti, frádráttar, neikvæður, minni en núll • *conj* mínus
minute • *n* mínúta *(f)*, augablik *(n)*
miracle • *n* kraftaverk *(n)*
mirage • *n* hilling *(f)*
mirror • *v* spegla • *n* spegill *(m)*
miscegenation • *n* kynþáttablöndun *(f)*
miser • *n* nirfill *(m)*
misnomer • *n* rangnefni *(n)*
misogynist • *n* kvenhatari *(m)*
misogyny • *n* kvenhatur *(n)*
miss • *n* ungfrú
missive • *n* bréf *(n)*, langur og virðulegur pistill *(m)*
mist • *n* mistur *(m)*
mister • *n* herra *(m)*
mistletoe • *n* mistilteinn *(m)*
misunderstand • *v* misskilja
mitochondrion • *n* hvatberi *(m)*
mitten • *n* vettlingur *(m)*, lúffa *(f)*
moat • *n* kastalasíki *(n)*, síki *(n)*, virkisgröf *(f)*, kastaladíki *(n)*, díki *(n)*
mockingbird • *n* hermikráka *(f)*
mode • *n* tíðasta gildi *(n)*, algengasta gildi *(n)*, líklegasta gildi *(n)*
modestly • *adv* með kurt og pí
modulation • *n* mótun *(f)*
modulus • *n* leifastofn *(m)*, lengd *(f)*, algildi *(n)*, tölugildi *(n)*
moist • *adj* rakur, tárvotur
mold • *n* mygla
mole • *n* moldvarpa *(f)*
molecule • *n* sameind *(f)*, mólekúl *(n)*
molybdenum • *n* mólýbden
moment • *n* augnablik *(n)*
monadic • *adj* einstæður *(m)*
monarch • *n* einvaldsherra *(m)*, konungur *(m)*, drottning *(f)*, fursti *(m)*, keisari *(m)*, einvaldur *(m)*, einvaldur þjóðhöfðingi konungsríkis *(m)*, einvaldur þjóðhöfðingi keisaradæmis *(m)*, einvaldur þjóðhöfðingi furstadæmis *(m)*, höfðingi *(m)*, jöfur *(m)*
monarchy • *n* konungsríki, konungdæmi
monastery • *n* klaustur *(n)*
money • *n* peningur *(m)*, fé *(n)*, gjaldmiðill *(m)*, ríkidæmi *(n)*
monitor • *n* mænir *(m)*, tölvuskjár *(m)*
monk • *n* munkur *(m)*
monkey • *n* api *(m)*
monocle • *n* einglyrni *(n)*
monogamous • *adj* einkvænis-, einkvæni

monolingual • *adj* eintyngdur *(m)*, einmálga
monomer • *n* einliða *(f)*
mononucleosis • *n* einkirningasótt *(f)*, eitlasótt *(f)*, kossasótt *(f)*
monosyllabic • *adj* einkvæður *(m)*
monotheism • *n* eingyðistrú
monotonic • *adj* einhalla *(m)*
monotony • *n* einhalli *(m)*
monotreme • *n* nefdýr *(n)*
monster • *n* ófreskja
month • *n* mánuður
monument • *n* minnismerki *(n)*
moo • *v* baula • *n* baul *(n)* • *interj* mu, mö
mood • *n* skap *(n)*
moon • *n* tungl, máni *(m)*, tungl *(n)*, fylgihnöttur *(m)*
moor • *n* mýri *(f)*, heiði *(f)*
moose • *n* elgur *(m)*
moratorium • *n* greiðslustöðvun *(f)*, frestur *(m)*, stöðvun *(f)*
moreover • *adv* einnig, þar á ofan, þar að auki
morgue • *n* líkhús *(n)*
moribund • *adj* dauðvona *(m)*, liggja fyrir dauðanum, að dauða kominn *(m)*
morning • *n* morgunn *(m)*
morpheme • *n* myndan *(f)*, morfem *(f)*, minnsta, merkingarbær, eining, mál *(f)*
morphine • *n* morfín *(n)*
morphology • *n* orðhlutafræði *(f)*
mortal • *adj* dauðlegur
mosque • *n* moska *(f)*
mosquito • *n* moskítófluga *(f)*
mote • *n* ögn *(f)*, rykögn *(f)*, korn *(n)*
motet • *n* mótetta *(f)*
moth • *n* mölur *(m)*
mother • *n* mamma *(f)*, móðir *(f)*
mother-in-law • *n* tengdamamma *(f)*
mother-of-pearl • *n* perlumóðir *(f)*
motherless • *adj* móðurlaus *(f)*, móðurlaust *(n)*
motionless • *adj* grafkyrr, hreyfingarlaus
motor • *n* mótor
motorcade • *n* bílalest *(f)*
motorcycle • *n* mótorhjól *(n)*
mountain • *n* fjall *(n)*, haugur *(m)*
mourn • *v* syrgja
mouse • *n* mús *(f)*, mús, tölvumús
moustache • *n* yfirvaraskegg *(n)*, yfirskegg *(n)*, motta *(f)*
mouth • *n* munnur *(m)*, kjaftur, op *(n)*, mynni *(n)*
move • *v* flytja, flytjast, búferlum, færa, keyra, snerta, leggja, til
movie • *n* bíómynd *(f)*, mynd *(f)*, kvikmynd *(f)*

mow • *v* slá, slá gras
mucus • *n* slím *(n)*
muff • *n* múffa *(f)*
muffin • *n* múffa *(f)*
mule • *n* múldýr *(n)*, múlasni *(m)*
multilateral • *adj* marghliða *(m)*
multilingual • *adj* fjöltyngdur
multiparous • *adj* fjölbyrja *(f)*
mummy • *n* múmía *(f)*, mamma *(f)*
municipal • *adj* borgar-, bæjar-, sveitar-
municipality • *n* sveitarfélag
mural • *n* veggskreyting *(f)*
murder • *v* myrða, rústa • *n* morð *(n)*
murderer • *n* morðingi *(m)*
muscle • *n* vöðvi *(m)*, styrkur *(m)*
muscular • *adj* vöðvi, vöðvastæltur, vöðvamikill, massaður
museum • *n* safn *(n)*
mushroom • *n* sveppur *(m)*
music • *n* tónlist, músík
musket • *n* framhlaðningur *(m)*
muskrat • *n* moskusrotta, bísamrotta
mustard • *n* sinnep *(n)*

mutation • *n* stökkbreyting *(f)*
mutter • *v* muldra, tauta, hvísla, tuða • *n*
muldur *(n)*, taut *(n)*
mutton • *n* kindakjöt *(n)*
mutual • *adj* gagnkvæmur, sameiginlegur
muzzle • *v* mýla, múlbinda, setja
munnkörfu á, dýr, þagga niður í • *n* trýni
(n), múli *(m)*, snoppa *(f)*, grön, byssukjaftur *(m)*, múll *(m)*, bitmúli *(m)*, mýli *(n)*,
munnkarfa *(f)*
muzzleloader • *n* framhlaðningur *(m)*
mycology • *n* sveppafræði *(f)*
myoglobin • *n* vöðvarauði *(m)*,
mýóglóbín *(n)*, vöðvaglóbín *(n)*
myriad • *n* mýgrútur *(m)*, urmull *(f)*, ótal
(n), ógrynni *(n)*, aragrúi *(m)*
myrrh • *n* myrra *(f)*
mystery • *n* ráðgáta *(f)*
myth • *n* saga *(f)*, uppspuni *(m)*, skröksaga *(f)*

N

nag • *n* bikkja *(f)*, trunta *(f)*
nail • *n* nögl *(f)*, nagli *(m)*, saumur *(m)*
naked • *adj* nakinn *(m)*, ber *(m)*, naktur
(m), ber, óvarinn
nakedness • *n* nekt *(f)*
name • *v* nefna, útnefna • *n* nafn *(n)*
nameless • *adj* nafnlaus *(m)*, óþekktur *(m)*
namely • *adv* nefnilega
nape • *n* hnakki *(m)*
napkin • *n* servíetta *(f)*
narcissus • *n* páskalilja *(f)*
narcolepsy • *n* drómasýki
narrow • *adj* þröngur, þéttur
narwhal • *n* náhvalur *(m)*
nascent • *adj* myndun *(f)*, mótun *(f)*,
fæðast
nation • *n* þjóð *(f)*, ríki *(n)*
nature • *n* náttúra *(f)*, eðli *(n)*, umhverfi
(n)
navel • *n* nafli *(m)*
navy • *n* sjóher *(m)*
near • *v* nálgast • *adj* skammt
necessary • *adj* nauðsynlegur *(m)*
necklace • *n* hálsfesti *(f)*
neckline • *n* hálsmál *(n)*
necktie • *n* bindi *(n)*, slifsi *(n)*
necrology • *n* dánarskrá *(f)*, dánartilkynning *(f)*, dánarfregn *(f)*
necromancer • *n* andasæringamaður *(m)*,

uppvakningamaður *(m)*
necromancy • *n* andasæring *(f)*
necrosis • *n* drep *(n)*
needle • *n* nál *(f)*, saumnál *(f)*
needlework • *n* saumaskapur *(m)*
negation • *n* neitun *(f)*
neglected • *adj* vanræktur *(m)*
neigh • *v* hneggja • *n* hnegg *(n)*
neighborhood • *n* nágrenni *(n)*
neighboring • *adj* nágranni
neither • *conj* hvorki X né Y
neodymium • *n* neodým
neon • *n* neon
nephew • *n* bróðursonur *(m)*, systursonur *(m)*
nephology • *n* skýjafræði *(f)*
nepotism • *n* frændhygli *(f)*
neptunium • *n* neptún
nerve • *n* taug *(f)*
ness • *n* nes
nest • *n* hreiður *(n)*
net • *n* net *(n)* • *adj* nettó
network • *n* net *(n)*
neurology • *n* taugafræði *(f)*
neutrality • *n* hlutleysi *(n)*
neutrino • *n* fiseind *(f)*
neutron • *n* nifteind *(f)*
never • *adv* aldrei
nevertheless • *adv* engu að síður, samt

sem áður, eigi að síður
new • *adj* nýr *(m)*, ný *(f)*, nýtt *(n)*, nýr
newborn • *adj* nýfæddur
news • *n* frétt
newspaper • *n* dagblað *(n)*, fréttablað *(n)*, dagblaðapappír *(m)*
next • *adj* næstur
nickel • *n* nikkel *(n)*
nickname • *v* uppnefna
niece • *n* bróðurdóttir *(f)*, systurdóttir *(f)*
nigger • *n* negri
night • *n* nótt *(f)*, nátt *(f)*, njóla *(f)*
nightfall • *n* rökkurbil, ljósaskipti, næturkoma, nótt *(f)*
nightingale • *n* næturgali *(m)*
nightmare • *n* martröð *(f)*, hryllingur *(m)*
nihilism • *n* tómhyggja, níhílismi
nincompoop • *n* beinasni *(m)*, fábjáni *(m)*, einfeldningur *(m)*, fáviti *(m)*, fífl *(n)*
ninetieth • *adj* nítugasta
ninth • *adj* níggjundi
niobium • *n* nióbín
nipple • *n* brjóstvarta *(f)*, geirvarta *(f)*
nit • *n* nit *(f)*
nitrate • *n* nítrat *(n)*
nitrite • *n* nítrít *(n)*
nitrogen • *n* köfnunarefni *(n)*, nitur *(n)*
no • *n* neitun *(f)*, nei *(n)*
nobelium • *n* nóbelín
nod • *v* að kinka kolli, að sofna
nomad • *n* hirðingi *(m)*
nomadism • *n* hjarðmennska *(f)*
nominate • *v* tilnefna
nomogram • *n* samanbuðartafla *(f)*, venslarit *(n)*
none • *pron* enginn
nonnegative • *adj* ekki neikvæður *(m)*, frekar jákvæður *(m)*, ófrádrægur *(m)*, stærri eða jafn núlli *(m)*
nonsense • *n* rugl *(n)*, bull *(n)*
noodle • *n* núðla *(f)*
noose • *n* lykkja *(f)*, rennilykkja *(f)*

nor • *conj* né
north • *n* norður *(n)*
nose • *n* nef *(n)*
nosebleed • *n* blóðnasir
nosegay • *n* blómvöndur *(m)*
nostalgia • *n* nostalgía *(f)*, fortíðarþrá *(f)*
nostril • *n* nös *(f)*
not • *adv* ekki, ei, eigi • *interj* ekki • *conj* ekki, ei, eigi
nothing • *pron* ekkert *(n)*, neitt
notice • *v* taka eftir
notify • *v* láta vita, tilkynna
notorious • *adj* alræmdur
notwithstanding • *adv* samt sem áður, engu að síður • *conj* enda þótt, þó að • *prep* þrátt fyrir
noun • *n* nafnorð *(n)*
novel • *n* skáldsaga *(f)*
now • *adv* nú
nowhere • *adv* hvergi, ekki neins staðar, ekki nokkursstaðar
nuclear • *adj* frumeinda-, kjarna-, atóm-, kjarnorku-, atómsprengju-
nucleolus • *n* kjarnakorn *(n)*
nucleoplasm • *n* kjarnasafi, kjarnafrymi
nucleotide • *n* kirni *(n)*, núkleótíð *(n)*
nucleus • *n* atómkjarni *(m)*, frumeindarkjarni *(m)*, kjarni *(m)*, frumukjarni *(m)*
nudity • *n* nekt *(f)*
number • *v* númera, tölusetja • *n* tala *(f)*, tölustafur *(m)*, númer *(f)*, fjöldi *(m)*
numerator • *n* teljari *(m)*
numismatics • *n* myntfræði *(f)*
numismatist • *n* myntfræðingur *(m)*
nurse • *n* barnfóstra *(f)*, fóstra *(f)*, hjúkrunarfræðingur *(m)*, hjúkrunarkona *(f)*, hjúkka *(f)*
nut • *n* hneta *(f)*, hnota *(f)*
nutcracker • *n* hnetubrjótur *(m)*
nutmeg • *v* klobba • *n* múskat *(n)*
nylon • *n* nælon *(n)*, nælonsokkur *(m)*

O

o'clock • *adv* klukkan
oak • *n* eik *(f)*, eikitré *(n)*
oaken • *adj* eikinn *(m)*
oar • *n* ár *(f)*
oasis • *n* vin *(f)*
oat • *n* hafri *(m)*
oath • *n* eiður *(m)*
oatmeal • *n* haframjöl *(n)*
obedient • *adj* hlýðinn
obesity • *n* offita

obituary • *n* minning
object • *v* mótmæla, malda í mórinn, mæla á móti • *n* hlutur *(m)*, andlag *(n)*, andl. *(n)*
objection • *n* andmæli, mótbára *(f)*
oblong • *adj* ílangur
oboe • *n* óbó *(n)*
observe • *v* skoða
obsidian • *n* hrafntinna *(f)*
obsolete • *adj* úreltur *(m)*

ocarina • *n* okkarína *(f)*
ocean • *n* haf *(n)*, sjór *(m)*, ægir *(m)*, úthaf *(n)*
octagon • *n* átthyrningur *(m)*
octane • *n* oktan *(n)*
octave • *n* áttund *(f)*
octet • *n* áttund *(f)*, átta bita bæti *(n)*
octopus • *n* kolkrabbi *(m)*
odalisque • *n* ódalíska
odd • *adj* odda-, ójafn, hvass
office • *n* skrifstofa *(f)*
offside • *n* rangstaða *(f)* • *adj* rangstæður
often • *adv* oft, ósjaldan, iðulega, oftlega, títt, þrá-
oh • *interj* ó
ohm • *n* óm
oil • *n* olía *(f)*
old • *adj* gamall
old-fashioned • *adj* gamaldags
olive • *n* ólífa *(f)*
olivine • *n* ólivín *(n)*
omnibus • *n* strætó *(m)*
omnifarious • *adj* af öllu tagi, alls kyns
omnipotence • *n* almætti *(n)*
omnipotent • *adj* almáttugur
omnipresence • *n* alnánd *(f)*
omnipresent • *adj* alls staðar nálægur
omniscience • *n* alviska *(f)*
omniscient • *adj* alvitur
omnivore • *n* alæta *(f)*
omophagia • *n* hrákjötsát *(n)*
once • *adv* einu sinni
oncology • *n* æxlafræði *(f)*
one-eyed • *adj* eineygður, eineygur
one-sided • *adj* einhliða *(m)*
onion • *n* laukur *(m)*
onomatopoeia • *n* hljóðgerving *(f)*, hljóðlíkingarorð *(n)*, hljóðgervingur *(m)*
ontology • *n* verufræði *(f)*
onus • *n* sönnunarbyrði *(f)*
oocyte • *n* eggfruma *(f)*
opal • *n* ópall *(m)*
opaque • *adj* ógagnsær
opera • *n* ópera *(f)*
operand • *n* þolandi *(m)*
operation • *n* starf *(n)*, vinnsla *(f)*, starfsemi *(f)*, starfræksla *(f)*, rekstur *(m)*, framkvæmd *(f)*, aðgerð *(f)*, uppskurður *(m)*, skurðaðgerð *(f)*, hernaðaraðgerð *(f)*
operator • *n* virki *(m)*
ophthalmologist • *n* augnlæknir *(m)*
ophthalmology • *n* augnlækningar
opinion • *n* álit
opium • *n* ópíum *(n)*
opossum • *n* pokarotta *(f)*
opponent • *n* andstæðingur *(m)*, mótherji *(m)*

optative • *n* óskháttur *(m)*
optics • *n* ljósfræði *(f)*, sjónfræði *(f)*
optimum • *n* kjörgildi *(n)*, besta gildi *(n)*, kjörstaða *(f)*
or • *conj* eða
orally • *adv* munnlega
orange • *n* appelsína *(f)*, appelsínugulur • *adj* appelsínugulur *(m)*
orc • *n* orki *(m)*
order • *v* panta • *n* röð *(f)*, pöntun *(f)*, ættbálkur *(m)*
orderly • *adj* skipulegur *(m)*, reglulegur *(m)*
ore • *n* málmgrýti
oregano • *n* óriganó *(m)*
organ • *n* líffæri *(n)*, orgel *(n)*, málgagn *(n)*
organelle • *n* frumulíffæri *(n)*
organism • *n* lífvera *(f)*
organist • *n* orgelleikari *(m)*, organisti *(m)*
orgy • *n* orgía *(f)*
orifice • *n* op *(n)*, munnur *(m)*
original • *n* frumeintak *(n)*, orginall *(m)*, frumrit *(n)*
ornithology • *n* fuglafræði *(f)*
orphan • *n* munaðarleysingi *(m)*
orphanage • *n* munaðarleysingjahæli *(n)*
orthodoxy • *n* rétttrúnaður *(m)*
orthography • *n* réttritun *(f)*
osmium • *n* osmín
osmosis • *n* himnuflæði
osprey • *n* gjóður
ossuary • *n* beinabúr, beinaklefi, beinahús
osteoporosis • *n* beinþynning
ostracism • *n* útskúfun *(f)*
ostrich • *n* strútur
otter • *n* otur *(m)*
outdoor • *adj* útivistar-
outdoors • *adv* úti, utandyra, utanhúss, undir berum himni
outlaw • *v* útlægja • *n* útlagi *(m)*
outskirt • *n* útjaðar *(m)*
outstandingly • *adv* ágætlega
ovary • *n* eggjastokkur
ovation • *n* lófatak *(n)*, fagnaðarlæti, hylling *(f)*
oven • *n* ofn *(m)*
over • *adj* búinn • *prep* yfir
over-the-counter • *adj* ólyfseðilsskyldur
overcoat • *n* yfirhöfn *(f)*
overdraft • *n* yfirdráttur *(m)*
overdraw • *v* yfirdraga
overlord • *n* lénsdrottinn *(m)*, lénsherra *(m)*
overrate • *v* ofmeta
oversleep • *v* sofa yfir sig

overtone • *n* yfirtónn *(m)*
ovulation • *n* egglos *(n)*
ovum • *n* eggfruma *(f)*, egg *(n)*
owl • *n* ugla *(f)*
own • *v* eiga
oxide • *n* oxíð *(n)*

oxidoreductase • *n* oxídóredúktasi *(m)*
oxygen • *n* súrefni
oxymoron • *n* refhvörf
oystercatcher • *n* tjaldur *(m)*
ozone • *n* óson *(n)*

P

pachyderm • *n* þykkskinnungur *(m)*
pacific • *adj* friðsæll *(m)*, kyrrlátur *(m)*, kyrr *(m)*
package • *v* pakka • *n* pakki *(m)*, böggull *(m)*
paddle • *v* paddla, róa
paddy • *n* hrísgrjónaakur *(m)*
paganism • *n* heiðni *(f)*
pain • *n* sársauki *(m)*, verkur *(m)*
paint • *v* mála • *n* málning *(f)*, litir
paintbrush • *n* pensill *(m)*
painting • *n* málverk *(n)*
pair • *n* tvenna *(f)*, par *(n)*
pajamas • *n* náttföt
palace • *n* palata *(f)*, höll *(f)*
palatal • *adj* framgómmæltur
pale • *adj* fölur
paleness • *n* fölvi *(m)*
paleontologist • *n* steingervingafræðingur *(m)*
paleontology • *n* steingervingafræði *(f)*
palimpsest • *n* uppskafningur *(m)*, skafið handrit *(n)*, skafgígur *(m)*
palladium • *n* palladín
pallor • *n* fölvi *(m)*
palm • *n* lófi *(m)*
palsy • *n* lömun *(f)*
panacea • *n* undralyf *(n)*, kynjalyf, allra meina bót *(f)*, töfraformúla
pancake • *n* pönnukaka *(f)*
pancreas • *n* bris *(n)*, briskirtill *(m)*
pandemic • *adj* heimsfaraldur *(m)*
pandemonium • *n* ringlulreið *(f)*
pandiculation • *n* syfjuteygjur, morgunteygjur
panegyric • *n* lofgerð *(f)*, lof *(n)*, lofkvæði *(n)*
panic • *n* læti
pantheist • *n* algyðistrúarmaður *(m)*
panther • *n* pardusdýr *(n)*
pantomime • *n* látbragðsleikur *(m)*
pants • *n* buxur
paper • *n* pappír *(m)* • *adj* pappírs-, pappa-
paperback • *n* pappírskilja *(f)*
paperboy • *n* blaðburðardrengur *(m)*,

blaðadrengur *(m)*, blaðberi *(m)*
papist • *n* pápisti *(m)*
parabola • *n* fleygbogi
parachute • *n* fallhlíf
parade • *n* skrúðganga *(f)*
paradigm • *n* fyrirmynd *(f)*, viðmið *(n)*, beygingardæmi *(n)*, hugarfar *(n)*
paradise • *n* himinn *(m)*
parallel • *adj* samhliða *(m)*
paralysis • *n* lömun *(f)*
paraplegia • *n* þverlömun *(f)*, lömun fyrir neðan mitti *(f)*
paraplegic • *n* maður lamaður fyrir neðan mitti *(m)* • *adj* þverlamaður *(m)*, lamaður fyrir neðan mitti *(m)*
parasite • *n* sníkjudýr *(n)*, afæta *(f)*, sníkill *(m)*
parent • *n* foreldri
parenthesis • *n* svigi *(m)*
parhelion • *n* hjásól *(f)*, aukasól *(f)*, gíll *(m)*, úlfur *(m)*, úlfakreppa *(f)*
park • *v* leggja, parkera • *n* park
parlance • *n* talsmáti *(m)*, málvenja *(f)*, málfar *(n)*, mál *(n)*
parliament • *n* þing *(n)*
parole • *n* reynslulausn *(f)*
parrot • *n* páfagaukur *(m)*, hermikráka *(f)*, eftirherma *(f)*
parse • *v* þátta
parsley • *n* steinselja
parsnip • *n* pastínakka *(f)*
part • *v* fara • *n* hluti *(m)*, partur *(m)*
participant • *n* þátttakandi *(m)*
participle • *n* lýsingarháttur *(m)*
particle • *n* smáorð *(n)*
partitive • *n* deildarfall *(n)*
partridge • *n* akurhæna *(f)*
party • *n* partí *(n)*, veisla *(f)*, teiti *(n)*
parvenu • *n* stéttskiptingur *(m)*, uppskafningur *(m)*
passenger • *n* farþegi *(m)*
passion • *n* ákafi *(m)*, passía *(f)*
passport • *n* vegabréf
password • *n* lykilorð *(n)*, leyniorð *(n)*, aðgangsorð *(n)*
pastern • *n* hófhvarf *(n)*

pastry • *n* bakkelsi *(n)*
pasture • *n* vin *(n)*
path • *n* leið *(f)*
pathology • *n* meinafræði *(f)*, sjúkdómafræði *(f)*, sjúklegt ástand *(n)*
patient • *n* sjúklingur *(m)* • *adj* þolinmóður *(m)*
patriot • *n* föðurlandsvinur *(m)*, ættjarðarvinur *(m)*
pattern • *n* mynstur *(n)*
pavement • *n* gangstétt *(f)*, fortóv *(n)*
paw • *n* loppa *(f)*
pay • *v* borga, greiða, gjalda
pea • *n* baun *(f)*, erta *(f)*
peace • *n* friður *(m)*, friðartími *(m)*
peach • *n* ferskja *(f)*
peacock • *n* páfugl *(m)*
peafowl • *n* páfugl *(m)*
peahen • *n* páhæna *(f)*
peanut • *n* jarðhneta *(f)*
pear • *n* pera *(f)*
pearl • *n* perla *(f)*
peasant • *n* bóndi *(m)*
peat • *n* torf *(n)*, mór *(m)*
pebble • *n* steinn
peckish • *adj* svangur *(m)*
pedagogue • *n* kennari *(m)*, barnakennari
(m), smásmigill *(m)*
pedant • *n* uppfullur af lærdómshroka
(m), uppfull af lærdómshroka *(f)*, smámu-
nasamur maður *(m)*, smámunasöm kona
(f)
pedantry • *n* smámunasemi *(f)*, smásmygli *(f)*
pediment • *n* bjór *(m)*, gaflbrík *(f)*, gaflhlað *(n)*
pedometer • *n* skrefamælir *(m)*,
skrefmælir *(m)*, skrefateljari *(m)*
pee • *n* pé *((pyeh))*
peel • *n* hýði
peg • *n* snagi *(m)*
pelican • *n* pelíkani *(m)*
pelt • *n* feldur *(m)*, loðskinn *(n)* • *v* láta
rigna á, láta dynja á, ausa yfir, hellirigna,
steypast, steypast niður
pelvis • *n* mjaðmargrind *(f)*
pen • *n* kví *(f)*, tröð *(f)*, stía *(f)*, rétt *(f)*,
penni *(m)*
pencil • *n* blýantur *(m)*
pendant • *n* nisti *(n)*, men *(n)*, hálsmen
(n)
pendulum • *n* pendúll *(m)*, dingull *(m)*,
hengill *(m)*, kólfur *(m)*
penguin • *n* mörgæs *(f)*
penicillin • *n* penisillín
peninsula • *n* skagi *(m)*
penis • *n* typpi *(n)*, limur *(m)*, getnaðar-

limur *(m)*
pennant • *n* fáni *(m)*, veifa *(f)*
pentagon • *n* fimmhyrningur *(m)*
penthouse • *n* þakhýsi *(n)*, þakíbúð *(f)*
penultimate • *adj* næstsíðastur
people • *n* þjóð *(f)*, fólk *(n)*
pepper • *v* pipra • *n* pipar *(m)*
peppermint • *n* piparminta *(f)*
pepsin • *n* pepsín *(n)*
percussion • *n* samsláttur *(m)*, sláttur *(m)*,
barningur *(m)*, slagverk *(n)*
perdition • *n* glötun *(f)*
perennial • *adj* fjölær *(m)*
perfume • *n* ilmur *(m)*, ilmvatn *(n)*
perimeter • *n* ummál *(m)*, jaðar
periodontics • *n* tannslíðurssjúkdómafræði *(f)*
peritoneum • *n* lífhimna *(f)*
perjury • *n* meinsæri *(n)*
permanent • *n* permanent *(n)* • *adj* varanlegur
perpetrate • *v* fremja
perseverance • *n* þrautseigja *(f)*, þolgæði
(n), harðfylgi *(n)*
persevere • *v* halda ótrauður áfram, sei-
glast við, láta ekki deigan síga, láta engan
bilbug á sér finna
persimmon • *n* döðluplóma, persimónía
person • *n* manneskja *(f)*, persóna *(f)*
perusal • *n* lestur *(m)*
peruse • *v* lesa gaumgæfilega, lesa
pervert • *n* pervert *(m)*, perri *(m)*, öfuggi
(m)
pessimistic • *adj* svartsýnn, bölsýnn
pest • *n* meindýr *(n)*
pesticide • *n* skordýraeitur *(n)*,
plágueyðir *(m)*, eyðingarlyf *(n)*
phalanx • *n* kjúka *(f)*
phallus • *n* reður *(m)*
pharmacist • *n* apótekari *(m)*, lyfsali *(m)*
pharmacology • *n* lyfjafræði
pharmacy • *n* apótek *(n)*, lyfjabúð *(f)*
pheasant • *n* fashani
phenotype • *n* svipgerð *(f)*, svipfar *(n)*
philatelist • *n* frímerkjasafnari *(m)*
philately • *n* frímerkjasöfnun *(f)*
philology • *n* textafræði *(f)*
phlegm • *n* öndunarfæraslím *(n)*, kvefslím *(n)*, rólyndi *(n)*, deyfð *(f)*
phoenix • *n* fönix *(m)*
phone • *v* hringja • *n* sími *(m)*
phoneme • *n* hljóðan
phonology • *n* hljóðkerfisfræði *(f)*
phosphorus • *n* fosfór *(n)*
photo • *n* mynd *(f)*
photograph • *n* ljósmynd *(f)*
photon • *n* ljóseind *(f)*, fótóna *(f)*, ljósögn

(f)
photosynthesis • *n* ljóstillífun *(f)*
phrase • *n* frasi, málsháttur
phylum • *n* fylking *(f)*
physicist • *n* eðlisfræðingur *(m)*
physiology • *n* lífeðlisfræði *(f)*
pi • *n* pí *(n)*
pianist • *n* píanóleikari *(m)*, píanisti *(m)*
piano • *n* píanó *(n)*, slagharpa *(f)*, fortepíanó *(n)* • *adv* veikur
pianoforte • *n* píanó *(n)*
picaroon • *v* sjóræningjast
pick • *v* lesa
picket • *n* staur *(m)*, rimill *(m)*, pílári *(m)*, hervörður *(m)*, verkfallsvörður *(m)*
picture • *n* mynd *(f)*, ljósmynd *(f)*
pie • *n* baka *(f)*
piece • *n* hluti *(m)*, stykki *(n)*, verk *(n)*
pier • *n* bryggja *(f)*
pig • *n* svín *(n)*, löggusvín *(n)*
pigeon • *n* dúfa *(f)*
piglet • *n* grís *(m)*, gríslingur *(m)*
pigsty • *n* svínastía *(f)*
pike • *n* gedda *(f)*
pillow • *n* koddi *(m)*
pilot • *n* flugmaður *(m)*
pimiento • *n* allrahanda *(n)*
pimp • *n* melludólgur *(m)*, hórumangari *(m)*
pimple • *n* nabbi *(m)*, bóla *(f)*, graftarbóla *(f)*
pin • *v* næla • *n* títuprjónn *(m)*, keila *(f)*
pine • *n* fura *(f)*, fýri *(n)*
pineapple • *n* ananas *(m)*, granaldin *(n)*
pink • *adj* bleikur
pinstriped • *adj* teinóttur *(m)*
pipette • *n* pípetta *(f)*
pirate • *n* sjóræningi *(m)* • *adj* sjóræningi
piss • *v* pissa, míga • *n* hland *(n)*, sull *(n)*
pistachio • *n* pistasíutré *(n)*, pistasíuhneta *(f)*, pistasía *(f)*
piston • *n* stimpill *(m)*, bulla *(f)*
pit • *n* hola *(f)*, gryfja *(f)*, steinn *(m)*
pitch • *n* tónhæð *(f)*
pitcher • *n* kanna *(f)*
pitchfork • *n* heygaffall *(m)*
pituitary • *n* dingull *(m)*, heiladingull *(m)* • *adj* dingull
pity • *n* samúð *(m)*
pixel • *n* díll *(m)*, myndeining *(f)*, punktur *(m)*
pizza • *n* flatbaka *(f)*, pítsa *(f)*, pitsa *(f)*, pizza
placate • *v* róa, sefa, fróa
place • *n* staður *(m)*
placebo • *n* lyfleysa *(f)*, þóknunarhrifslyf *(n)*

placenta • *n* fylgja *(f)*, legkaka *(f)*
plagioclase • *n* plagíóklas *(n)*
plague • *n* plága *(f)*
plaice • *n* koli *(m)*
plain • *n* flatlendi *(n)*
plaintiff • *n* stefnandi *(m)*
plan • *v* ætla
plane • *v* hefla • *n* hefill *(m)*
planet • *n* reikistjarna *(f)*, pláneta *(f)*
plant • *n* jurt *(f)*, planta *(f)*
plasma • *n* rafgas *(n)*, blóðvökvi *(m)*
plastic • *n* plast *(n)*
plate • *n* diskur *(m)*
platinum • *n* platína
platitude • *n* gömul tugga *(f)*, margþvæld tugga *(f)*, innantómur frasi *(m)*
platonic • *adj* lostalaus *(m)*, platónskur *(m)*, andlegur *(m)*, háleitur *(m)*, laus við holdlega fýsn *(m)*
platypus • *n* breiðnefur *(m)*
platyrrhine • *adj* flatnefja *(m)*
play • *v* leika, leika sér, spila, spila á
playwright • *n* leikritaskáld *(n)*
plaza • *n* torg *(n)*
pleat • *n* felling *(f)*
plebiscite • *n* þjóðaratkvæðagreiðsla *(f)*, þjóðaratkvæði *(n)*
plenipotentiary • *n* fulltrúi *(m)*
plod • *v* arka
plosive • *n* lokhljóð *(n)*
plot • *v* brugga launráð, kortleggja • *n* ráðabrugg *(n)*, reitur *(m)*, skiki *(m)*, blettur *(m)*, lóð *(f)*, teikning *(f)*, graf *(n)*
plough • *v* plægja • *n* plógur *(m)*
pluck • *n* táp *(n)*
plum • *n* plóma *(f)*, plómutré *(f)*, plómublár *(f)*
plummet • *v* steypast, stingast
plural • *n* fleirtala *(f)* • *adj* fleir-, marg-, fleirtölu-, í fleirtölu
plus • *n* plús *(n)*, viðbót *(f)*, viðauki *(m)*, kostur • *adj* jákvæður, pósitífur, stærri en núll *(f)*, stærra en núll *(n)*, með jákvæða hleðslu • *conj* auk, og
plutonium • *n* plúton
pluvial • *adj* regn, rigning, úrkoma
pneumatic • *adj* gas-, loft-, loftaflfræði-, loftknúinn *(m)*, þrýstilofts-, loftfylltur *(m)*, fullur af þrýstilofti *(m)*, hol-
pochard • *n* skutulönd *(f)*
pocket • *n* vasi *(m)*
poem • *n* ljóð *(n)*, kvæði *(n)*, dikt *(n)*, skáldskapur *(m)*
poet • *n* skáld *(n)*, ljóðskáld *(n)*
poetess • *n* skáldkona *(f)*
poetry • *n* ljóðlist
poinsettia • *n* jólastjarna *(f)*

pointer • *n* bendir *(m)*
poison • *n* eitur *(n)*
poker • *n* skörungur *(m)*, potari *(m)*, póker *(m)*
pole • *n* póll *(m)*
polemic • *n* deilurit *(n)*
police • *n* lögregla *(f)*
policeman • *n* lögreglumaður *(m)*, lögga *(f)*
polite • *adj* kurteis
political • *adj* pólitísk *(m)*, pólitíska *(f)*
politician • *n* stjórnmálamaður *(m)*
politics • *n* stjórnmál
pollen • *n* frjókorn *(n)*
polonium • *n* pólon
polyester • *n* pólýester
polygamous • *adj* fjölkvænis-, fjölkvæni
polymer • *n* fjölliða *(f)*
polymorphic • *adj* fjölbreytinn *(m)*, fjölmóta *(m)*
polymorphism • *n* fjölbrigðni *(f)*, fjölbreytni *(f)*, fjölmótun *(f)*
polynomial • *n* margliða *(f)*
polyp • *n* sepi *(m)*, holsepi *(m)*
polyphony • *n* fjölröddun *(f)*, pólýfónía *(f)*
polysemous • *adj* margræður *(n)*
polystyrene • *n* pólýstýren *(n)*
polytheism • *n* fjölgyðistrú *(f)*
polyurethane • *n* pólýúretan *(n)*
pomegranate • *n* granatepli *(n)*, kjarnepli *(n)*
pond • *n* tjörn *(f)*
ponder • *v* íhuga
ponytail • *n* tagl *(n)*, stertur *(m)*
poodle • *n* púðluhundur *(m)*, púðli *(m)*
pool • *n* pollur *(m)*
popcorn • *n* poppkorn *(n)*
pope • *n* páfi *(m)*
poppy • *n* draumsóley *(f)*, valmúi *(m)*
popular • *adj* vinsæll
popularity • *n* vinsældir
population • *n* fólksfjöldi *(m)*, íbúar, mannfjöldi *(m)*, þýði *(n)*, hópur *(m)*, stofn *(m)*, lýður *(m)*
porbeagle • *n* hámeri *(f)*, hamar *(m)*
porcelain • *n* postulín *(n)*, postulín
pornographic • *adj* klámfenginn
pornography • *n* klám *(n)*
porpoise • *n* hnísa *(f)*, marsvín *(n)*
port • *n* höfn *(f)*, tengi *(n)*, púrtvín *(n)*, portvín *(n)*
positron • *n* jáeind *(f)*
posology • *n* lyfjunarfræði *(f)*, stærð skammta *(f)*
possibility • *n* möguleiki *(m)*
possible • *adj* hægur, mögulegur

postcard • *n* póstkort *(n)*, kort *(n)*, bréfspjald *(n)*
postmodernism • *n* póstmódernismi *(m)*
postpone • *v* fresta
postposition • *n* eftirsetning *(f)*
posy • *n* blómvöndur *(m)*
potassium • *n* kalín, kalíum *(n)*
potato • *n* kartafla *(f)*, jarðepli *(n)*
potentate • *n* valdamaður *(m)*, burgeis *(m)*, höfðingi *(m)*, þjóðhöfðingi *(m)*
potential • *adj* mögulegur
pound • *v* banga
pour • *v* hella
pout • *v* setja á sig stút, setja upp fýlusvip, setja stút á munninn • *n* stútur *(m)*, fýlustútur *(m)*, fýlusvipur *(m)*
poverty • *n* fátækt *(f)*
powder • *n* duft *(n)*
powerful • *adj* öflugur *(m)*, voldugur *(m)*, máttugur *(m)*, kröftugur *(m)*, kraftmikill *(m)*, valdamikill *(m)*
praise • *v* hrósa • *n* lof
praseodymium • *n* praseódým
prawn • *n* rækja *(f)*
pray • *v* biðja, bæna
preach • *v* predika
preamble • *n* formáli *(m)*, inngangur *(m)*, inngangsorð, formálsorð
precious • *adj* dýrmætur
precipitation • *n* það að steypast áfram *(n)*, það að æða áfram *(n)*, það að flæða áfram *(n)*, úrkoma *(f)*, flýtir *(m)*, óðagot *(n)*, bráðræði *(n)*
predicate • *n* umsögn *(f)*, umsagnarliður *(m)*, umsagnarökfræði *(f)* • *v* byggja á, grundvalla á
pregnancy • *n* meðganga
pregnant • *adj* óléttur, ófrískur, þungaður, barnshafandi, vanfær
prehensile • *adj* grip-
prejudiced • *adj* fordómafullur
premeditated • *adj* yfirlagður, að yfirlögðu ráði
premise • *n* forsenda *(f)*
premolar • *n* forjaxl *(m)*, framjaxl *(m)*
premonition • *n* fyrirboði *(m)*, viðvörun
preposition • *n* forsetning *(f)*
preposterous • *adj* fáránlegur
prepuce • *n* forhúð *(f)*
presentation • *n* afhending
president • *n* forseti *(m)*, forstjóri *(m)*
presuppose • *v* ganga út frá
presupposition • *n* forsenda *(f)*
pretext • *n* yfirskin *(n)*
preview • *n* stikla *(f)*
previously • *adv* áður
prey • *n* bráð *(f)*

price • *n* verð *(n)*
pride • *n* stolt *(n)*
priest • *n* prestur *(m)*
primarily • *adv* aðallega, fyrst og fremst
primate • *n* prímati *(m)*, fremdardýr *(n)*
primordial • *adj* frum-, upprunalegur *(m)*, upphaf
prince • *n* prins *(m)*, fursti *(m)*, mikilmenni *(n)*
princess • *n* prinsessa *(f)*
principality • *n* furstadæmi *(n)*
principle • *n* prinsipp *(n)*
print • *v* prenta
printer • *n* prentari *(m)*
prison • *n* fangelsi *(n)*
prisoner • *n* fangi *(m)*, bandingi *(m)*
pristine • *adj* óspilltur *(m)*, ósnortinn *(m)*, óskemmdur *(m)*, upprunalegur *(m)*, upphaflegur *(m)*
probably • *adv* líklega, sennilega
prodigal • *n* eyðslukló *(f)* • *adj* hóflaus *(f)*, hóflaust *(n)*
produce • *v* framleiða, pródúsa, pródúsera, útvega
product • *n* vara *(f)*
profession • *n* atvinna *(f)*
professor • *n* prófessor *(m)*, háskólakennari *(m)*
proficient • *adj* fær, snjall
progeny • *n* afkvæmi *(n)*, afsprengi *(n)*, afkomandi *(m)*
prognosis • *n* horfur, spá *(f)*
program • *v* forrita • *n* program, forrit *(n)*, tölvuforrit *(n)*
programmer • *n* forritari *(m)*
programming • *n* forritun *(f)*
progressive • *n* framfarasinni *(m)*
projection • *n* frávarp *(n)*, ofanvarp *(n)*
prokaryote • *n* dreifkjörnungur *(m)*
prolapse • *v* síga, falla fram • *n* framfall *(n)*, sig *(n)*
promethium • *n* prómetín
promise • *v* lofa, heita, strengja heit • *n* loforð *(n)*
pronoun • *n* fornafn *(n)*
pronunciation • *n* framburður *(m)*
proof • *n* sönnun *(f)*
proofreader • *n* prófarkalesari *(m)*
propaganda • *n* áróður *(m)*
propane • *n* própan *(n)*
propeller • *n* hreyfill *(m)*
propensity • *n* tilhneigingu
property • *n* eign *(f)*, landeign *(f)*, fasteign *(f)*, eiginleiki *(m)*
prophet • *n* spámaður *(m)*
proposition • *n* fullyrðing *(f)*, yrðing *(f)*
prose • *n* prósa *(f)*

prosody • *n* bragfræði *(f)*
prosperity • *n* velmegun *(f)*
prostate • *n* hvekkur, blöðruhálskirtill
prostitute • *n* vændiskona *(f)*, skækja *(f)*, gleðikona *(f)*, hóra *(f)*
protactinium • *n* protaktín
protect • *v* hlífa
protist • *n* frumvera *(f)*
protium • *n* einvetni *(n)*, prótín *(n)*
proton • *n* róteind *(f)*
protoplasm • *n* frymi *(n)*
prototype • *n* frumgerð
protractor • *n* gráðubogi *(m)*, mælibogi *(m)*, hornmál *(n)*
protrude • *v* skaga fram, standa út
provident • *adj* fyrirhyggjusamur *(m)*, forsjáll *(m)*, framsýnn *(m)*, aðgætinn *(m)*
prow • *n* trjóna *(f)*, skegg *(n)*
prune • *n* sveskja *(f)*
psalm • *n* sálmur
pshaw • *interj* svei, iss, uss, fussum svei
psychiatrist • *n* geðlæknir *(m)*
psychology • *n* sálfræði *(f)*
psychosomatic • *adj* geðvefrænn *(m)*
ptarmigan • *n* rjúpa *(f)*
pterygium • *n* glæruvængur *(m)*
pub • *n* krá *(f)*
public • *adj* opinber
publish • *v* gefa út
pudding • *n* blóðmör *(m)*, slátur *(n)*, búðingur *(m)*
puddle • *n* pollur *(m)*
puffin • *n* lundi *(m)*
pulchritudinous • *adj* fagur *(m)*, fallegur *(m)*
pulley • *n* trissa *(f)*
pulmonary • *adj* lunga-, lungna-
pulse • *n* æðasláttur *(m)*, púls *(m)*, sláttur *(m)*, taktslag *(n)*
pumice • *n* vikur
pump • *n* dæla *(f)*
pumpkin • *n* grasker *(n)*
punctuation • *n* greinarmerki
punishment • *n* refsing *(f)*
punk • *n* pönk *(n)*, pönkari *(m)*
pupil • *n* nemandi *(m)*
puppet • *n* brúða *(f)*, leikbrúða *(f)*, strengjabrúða *(f)*
puppy • *n* hvolpur *(m)*
pure • *adj* hreinn
purebred • *adj* hreinræktaður *(m)*
purgatory • *n* hreinsunareldur *(m)*
purloin • *v* stela, taka, ræna
purple • *adj* fjólublár, purpuralitur
purpose • *v* ætla
purr • *v* mala
pus • *n* gröftur *(m)*

push • *v* hrinda, ýta
pussy • *n* kisa *(f)*, kisi *(m)*, píka *(f)*, kunta
(f), pjalla *(f)*, pussa, vagína *(f)*
putative • *adj* meintur *(m)*
puzzle • *n* púsl *(n)*
pyramid • *n* pýramídi

pyromania • *n* íkveikjuæði *(n)*
pyromaniac • *n* brennuvargur *(m)*
pyrophobia • *n* eldfælni *(f)*
pyroxene • *n* pýroxen *(n)*

Q

quack • *v* gagga, gussa • *n* andagagg *(n)*,
guss *(n)*, skottulæknir *(m)*, fúskari *(m)*,
loddari *(m)*, falsari *(m)*, svikari *(m)* • *adj*
svika-, fals-, skottu-
quackery • *n* skottulækningar
quadrilateral • *n* ferhliðungur *(m)*,
fjórhliðungur *(m)*
quadriplegia • *n* lömun allra útlima *(f)*,
allömun útlima *(f)*, lömun á höndum og
fótum *(f)*
quadruped • *n* ferfætlingur *(m)*
quail • *n* kornhæna
qualitative • *adj* eigindlegur
quantitative • *adj* megindlegur
quantity • *n* magn *(n)*
quantization • *n* skömmtun *(f)*
quark • *n* kvarki *(m)*
quarter • *n* fjórðungur, fjórðungur *(m)*,
hverfi *(m)*
quartz • *n* kvars *(m)*
quaver • *n* áttundapartsnóta *(f)*, áttundipartur *(m)*
queen • *n* drottning *(f)*, drolla *(f)*, læða *(f)*
queer • *adj* hinsegin
question • *n* spurning *(f)*
queue • *n* biðröð *(f)*
quick • *adj* fljótur, kvikur
quiet • *adj* hljóður
quill • *n* fjaðurstafur *(m)*, fjaðurpenni *(m)*,
broddur *(m)*
quinine • *n* kínín *(n)*
quiver • *n* örvamælir *(m)*
quotation • *n* tilvitnun *(f)*
quote • *v* vitna í

R

rabbit • *n* kanína
raccoon • *n* þvottabjörn *(m)*
racism • *n* kynþáttafordómar, rasismi *(m)*,
kynþáttahyggja *(f)*, kynþáttastefna *(f)*,
kynþáttarembingur *(m)*, kynþáttahatur
(n), kynþáttahroki *(m)*
racist • *n* rasisti *(m)*, kynþáttahatari *(m)*,
kynþáttahroki *(m)* • *adj* kynþáttafordómar, kynþáttahyggja, kynþáttahatur,
rasista-, kynþáttahroki
radar • *n* ratsjá
radio • *n* útvarp *(n)*, útvarpstæki *(n)*
radioactive • *adj* geislavirkur
radiograph • *n* röntgenmynd *(f)*
radiography • *n* röntgenljósmyndun *(f)*
radiologist • *n* geislalæknir *(m)*
radiology • *n* geislalækningar, geislunarfræði *(f)*
radish • *n* hreðka *(f)*, radísa *(f)*
radius • *n* radíus *(m)*, geisli *(m)*
radon • *n* radon *(n)*
raft • *n* fleki *(m)*
railway • *n* járnbraut *(f)*, lestarspor *(n)*,
járnbani *(m)*, járngata
raiment • *n* voð *(f)*
rain • *n* rigning, regn *(n)*
rainbow • *n* regnbogi *(m)*, friðarbogi *(m)*,
njólubaugur *(m)*
raincoat • *n* regnkápa *(f)*
raindrop • *n* regndropi
raisin • *n* rúsína *(f)*
ram • *n* hrútur *(m)*
ramification • *n* kvíslun *(f)*, greining *(f)*
ramify • *v* kvíslast, greinast
randy • *adj* graður *(m)*, lostafullur *(m)*,
lostafenginn *(m)*, grófur *(m)*, ruddalegur
(m), dónalegur *(m)*, illa siðaður *(m)*
range • *n* myndmengi *(n)*, mynd *(f)*
ransom • *n* lausnargjald *(n)*, lausnarfé *(n)*
rape • *v* nauðga, valda spjöllum á, spilla
• *n* nauðgun *(f)*
rapeseed • *n* repjufræ *(n)*
rapid • *adj* fljótur
rapport • *n* samband *(n)*, tengsl
raspberry • *n* hindberjum *(m)*, hindber
(n)

ratify • *v* staðfesta
ratio • *n* hlutfallstala *(f)*, hlutfall *(n)*, hlutfall milli tveggja stærða *(n)*
rational • *adj* ræður *(m)*
raven • *n* hrafn *(m)*
raw • *adj* hrár, óunninn
ray • *n* skata *(f)*
raze • *v* rífa niður, leggja í rúst, jafna við jörðu
razor • *n* rakvél *(f)*
reaction • *n* hvörf, hvarf *(n)*
reactionary • *n* afturhaldsseggur *(m)* • *adj* afturhaldssamur *(m)*
read • *v* lesa • *n* lesning *(f)*
reader • *n* lesandi *(m)*
ready • *adj* tilbúinn *(m)*, undirbúinn *(m)*
real • *adj* satt *(n)*
really • *adv* sannarlega, virkilega, raunar, raunverulega • *interj* virkilega?
realm • *n* ríki *(n)*, veldi *(n)*
recalcitrant • *adj* þverúðarfullur, þrjóskur
recant • *v* taka aftur, draga til baka
recently • *adv* nýlega
receptacle • *n* geymsla *(f)*, hirsla *(f)*
reciprocal • *n* umhverfa *(f)*, margföldunarumhverfa *(f)*, margföldunarandhverfa *(f)*
recompense • *v* launa, borga bætur • *n* bætur, þóknun *(f)*
record • *n* skrá *(f)*, skýrsla *(f)*, heimild *(f)*, menjar *(f)*, plata *(f)*, hljómplata *(f)*, færsla *(f)*, met *(n)*
recorder • *n* flauta *(f)*, blokkflauta *(f)*
recrimination • *n* gagnásökun *(f)*, gagnsök *(f)*
rectangle • *n* rétthyrningur *(m)*
red • *n* rauður • *adj* rauður
red-hot • *adj* rauðglóandi *(m)*, eldheitur *(m)*, blossandi *(m)*
reddish • *adj* rauðleitur
redneck • *n* jói
reed • *n* hræll *(m)*
reef • *n* rif *(n)*
referendum • *n* þjóðaratkvæðagreiðsla *(f)*, þjóðaratkvæði *(n)*
reflexive • *adj* afturbeygður *(m)*, sjálfhverfur *(m)*, spegilvirkur *(m)*
reflexivity • *n* afturbeyging *(f)*
reflux • *n* bakflæði *(n)*
refraction • *n* ljósbrot *(n)*
refrigerator • *n* kæliskápur *(m)*, ísskápur *(m)*
reggae • *n* reggí *(n)*
region • *n* hérað *(n)*
register • *n* gisti *(n)*
regression • *n* aðhvarf *(n)*
regulation • *n* reglugerð *(f)*

reindeer • *n* hreindýr *(n)*
reiterate • *v* margítreka, margendurtaka
reject • *v* hafna
related • *adj* skyldur, tengdur, skyldur *(m)*
relative • *n* ættingi *(m)*
relay • *n* liði *(m)*, rafliði *(m)*, boðhlaup *(n)*
religion • *n* trúarbrögð
reliquary • *n* helgiskrín *(n)*
relish • *v* njóta
remember • *v* muna
repeat • *v* endurtaka
repercussion • *n* eftirmál, eftirköst
replica • *n* eftirmynd *(f)*, eftirlíking *(f)*
reprehensible • *adj* ámælisverður
reprimand • *v* ávíta
reproof • *n* ávítur
reptile • *n* skriðdýr *(n)*
republic • *n* lýðveldi *(n)*
repudiation • *n* neitun *(f)*, höfnun *(f)*
requiem • *n* sálumessa *(f)*
rescind • *v* rifta, ógilda, nema úr gildi, fella úr gildi
residence • *n* bústaður *(m)*
resignation • *n* uppsögn *(f)*
resistance • *n* viðnám *(n)*, mótstaða *(f)*
resistor • *n* viðnám *(n)*, viðnámstæki *(n)*, mótstaða *(f)*
respect • *v* virða, bera virðingu fyrir • *n* virðing *(f)*, leyti *(n)*
rest • *n* hvíld *(f)*, þögn *(f)*, afgangur *(m)*, rest *(f)* • *v* hvíla
restaurant • *n* veitingastaður *(m)*, veitingahús *(n)*, matsölustaður *(m)*, veitingasalur *(m)*
restlessness • *n* órói *(m)*, óró *(f)*
resurrection • *n* upprisa *(f)*
retaliate • *v* svara í sömu mynt, hefna sín, gjalda líku líkt
reticle • *n* þráðkross *(m)*, sjónkvarði *(m)*, hárkross *(m)*
retire • *v* draga sig í hlé, setjast í helgan stein
retreat • *v* hörfa
retrovirus • *n* víxlveira *(f)*, retróveira *(f)*
return • *v* skila
revelation • *n* opinberun *(f)*
revenge • *n* hefnd *(f)*
revolution • *n* bylting *(f)*
revolver • *n* marghleypt skammbyssa *(f)*
rhenium • *n* renín *(n)*, reníum *(n)*
rheology • *n* flotfræði
rhinoceros • *n* nashyrningur *(m)*
rhodium • *n* ródín
rhombus • *n* tígull *(m)*, tigull *(m)*
rhubarb • *n* rabarbari *(m)*
rhyme • *n* rím

rhyolite • *n* líparít *(n)*
rhythm • *n* taktur *(m)*
ribosome • *n* netkorn
rice • *n* hrís *(n)*, hrísgrjón
rich • *adj* ríkur *(m)*
ricochet • *v* endurkastast, kastast frá, skoppa, fleyta kerlingar • *n* endurkast *(n)*, skopp *(n)*
rider • *n* viðauki *(m)*
riffraff • *n* pakk *(n)*, skríll *(m)*, illþýði *(n)*
rifle • *n* riffill *(m)*
right • *adj* beint *(n)*, beinn *(m)*, bein *(f)*, rétt, horn, rétt *(n)*, réttur *(m)*, hægri
ring • *n* baugur *(m)*, hringur *(m)*
rising • *adj* rísandi *(n)*
rite • *n* helgiathöfn *(f)*, helgisiður *(m)*
river • *n* fljót *(n)*, á *(f)*, elfur *(f)*
road • *n* vegur *(m)*, gata *(f)*, leið *(f)*
robin • *n* farþröstur *(m)*
robotics • *n* þjarkafræði *(f)*
rocket • *n* klettasalat, rukola
rod • *n* stöng *(f)*
rodent • *n* nagdýr *(n)*
roe • *n* hrogn *(n)*
roller • *n* rúlla *(f)*
roof • *n* þak *(n)*
rook • *n* bláhrafn *(m)*, hrókur
room • *n* rúm
root • *n* rót *(f)*, rætur
rope • *n* reipi *(n)*, tog *(n)*
rose • *n* rós *(f)*
roundabout • *n* hringtorg *(n)*, umferðarhringur *(m)*, hringekja *(f)*, krókaleið *(f)*, krókvegur *(m)* • *adj* óbeinn *(m)*, ví-

filengjur, krókóttur *(m)*, króka-, beinn *(m)*
rove • *v* vappa
row • *v* róa, paddla
rowan • *n* ilmreynir *(m)*, reynir *(m)*, reynitré *(n)*, reyniberjatré *(n)*
rowing • *n* róður *(m)*
royal • *adj* konunglegur
rubber • *n* gúmmí
rubidium • *n* rúbidín
ruble • *n* rúbla *(f)*
ruby • *n* rúbín *(m)* • *adj* rúbínrauður
ruddy • *adj* rjóður *(m)*, rauðleitur *(m)*, roði, rauður *(m)*, bölvaður *(m)*, fjárans, skrambans, fjári, skrambi, ansi
rue • *n* rúturunni
ruin • *n* rúst
rule • *v* stjórna, drottna, ráða , ríkja • *n* regla *(f)*
ruler • *n* reglustika *(f)*
rum • *n* romm *(n)*
ruminate • *v* jórtra
run • *v* hlaupa
run-of-the-mill • *adj* venjulegur *(m)*, hversdagslegur *(m)*, fábrotinn *(m)*, miðlungs-
rune • *n* rún *(f)*
rung • *n* trappa *(f)*, þrep *(n)*
runway • *n* flugbraut *(f)*
rust • *v* ryðga
rustle • *v* skrjáfa • *n* skrjáf *(n)*, þrusk *(n)*
rusty • *adj* ryðgaður
ruthenium • *n* rúten
rye • *n* rúgur *(m)*

S

sabotage • *n* skemmdarverk *(n)*
sack • *n* sekkur *(m)*, poki *(m)*, posi *(m)*
sacral • *adj* spjald-, spjaldbein, spjaldhryggur, krosslliður
sacrifice • *v* fórna, gefa til • *n* fórn *(f)*
sacrum • *n* spjaldbein *(n)*, spjaldliðir, spjaldhryggur *(m)*
sad • *adj* dapur
saddle • *n* hnakkur, söðull *(m)*, hnakkur *(m)*
sadness • *n* sorg *(f)*
safe • *n* peningaskápur *(m)*
safety • *n* öryggi *(n)*
saga • *n* saga *(f)*
sail • *n* segl *(n)*, sigling *(f)* • *v* sigla
sailboat • *n* kútter
sailor • *n* sjómaður *(m)*, sjóari *(m)*
saint • *n* dýrlingur *(m)*

sake • *n* hrísgrjónavín *(n)*, sake *(n)*
salad • *n* salat *(n)*
salary • *n* laun, föst laun, kaup *(n)*
sale • *n* sala *(f)*, útsala *(f)*
salesman • *n* sölumaður *(m)*
salesperson • *n* sölumaður
saliva • *n* slef *(n)*, munnvatn *(m)*
salmon • *n* lax *(m)* • *adj* laxbleikur
salt • *v* salta • *n* salt *(n)*, sjóari *(m)* • *adj* saltur
salubrious • *adj* heilsusamlegt
samarium • *n* samarín
same • *adj* samur
samurai • *n* samúræji *(m)*
sand • *n* sandur *(m)*
sandal • *n* sandali *(m)*
sandbox • *n* sandkassi *(m)*
sandstone • *n* sandsteinn *(m)*

sandwich • *n* samloka *(f)*
sap • *n* skotgröf *(f)*
sapodilla • *n* sapódillatré *(n)*, tyggigúmmítré *(n)*, sapódilla *(f)*, sapódillaplóma *(f)*
sapphire • *n* safír *(m)* • *adj* safírblár
sarcoidosis • *n* sarklíki *(n)*
sarcomere • *n* vöðvaliður *(m)*, vöðvadeild *(f)*
sari • *n* sarí *(m)*
satellite • *n* gervitungl *(n)*, gervihnöttur *(m)*
sauce • *n* sósa *(f)*
sauerkraut • *n* súrkál *(n)*
sauna • *n* sána *(f)*, baðstofa *(f)*, eimbað *(n)*, gufubað *(n)*
sausage • *n* pylsa *(f)*
save • *v* bjarga, vista
saw • *v* saga • *n* sög *(f)*
sawdust • *n* sag *(n)*
say • *v* segja
scab • *n* hrúður *(n)*
scabbard • *n* skálpur *(m)*
scalar • *n* einvíð stærð *(f)*, tölustærð *(f)*, stigastærð *(f)*
scallop • *n* hörpuskel *(f)*, hörpudiskur *(m)*
scandium • *n* skandín
scanner • *n* skanni *(m)*
scapegoat • *n* blóraböggull *(m)*
scar • *n* ör *(n)*
scarecrow • *n* fuglahræða
scarf • *n* trefill *(m)*
scheme • *n* ráð *(n)*, ráðagerð *(f)*, brugg *(n)*
schizophrenia • *n* geðklofi *(m)*
school • *n* skóli *(m)*
schooner • *n* skonnorta
science • *n* vísindi *(n)*, fræði *(n)*
scientist • *n* vísindamaður *(m)*
scissors • *n* skæri
sclerosis • *n* hersli *(n)*, sigg *(n)*
scoff • *v* hæða, draga dár, gera gys
scold • *v* skamma, hundskamma, ávíta, láta skömmunum rigna yfir, sneypa, fá skömm í hattinn
scorpion • *n* sporðdreki *(m)*
scrapie • *n* riða
scrawl • *v* krota, krassa, hripa, pára, skrifa flausturslega • *n* krot *(n)*, klór *(n)*, pírumpár *(n)*
screamer • *n* öskrari *(m)*
screen • *n* skjár *(m)*
screw • *n* skrúfa *(f)*
scribe • *v* skrifa, rita, skrá
scroll • *n* bókrolla *(f)*
scrotum • *n* pungur *(m)*, böllur *(m)*
scurvy • *n* skyrbjúgur *(m)*
scythe • *v* slá, slá með orfi og ljá • *n* orf

og ljár
sea • *n* haf *(n)*, sjór *(m)*, ægir *(m)*, úthaf *(n)*
seal • *n* selur *(m)*, innsigli • *v* innsigla
search • *v* leita • *n* leit
seasickness • *n* sjóveiki *(f)*
season • *n* árstíð *(f)*, vertíð *(f)*, þáttaröð *(f)*
seaworthy • *adj* haffær
sebum • *n* húðfeiti *(f)*
second • *n* tvíund *(f)*, sekúnda *(f)* • *adj* annar *(m)*
secondhand • *adj* notaður
secret • *n* leyndarmál *(n)* • *adj* leynilegur
secrete • *v* seyta
sect • *n* sértrúarsöfnuður *(m)*
security • *n* öryggi *(n)*
sedentary • *adj* kyrrsetu-, hreyfingarleysis-

sediment • *n* botnfall *(n)*, syrja *(f)*, botnlag *(n)*, dreggjar *(n)*, set *(n)*, vatnborin jarðvegsefni, vindborin jarðvegsefni
seduce • *v* tæla, lokka
see • *v* sjá, skynja, skil, fatta
seed • *n* fræ *(n)*
seek • *v* leita
seesaw • *v* vega salt • *n* vegasalt *(n)*
seismic • *adj* jarðskjálfta-
seismograph • *n* jarðskjálftamælir *(m)*
seismologist • *n* jarðskjálftafræðingur *(m)*, skjálftafræðingur *(m)*
seismology • *n* jarðskjálftafræði *(f)*, skjálftafræði *(f)*
seldom • *adv* sjaldan
selenium • *n* selen *(n)*
self-deception • *n* sjálfsblekking *(f)*
self-pity • *n* sjálfsvorkunn *(f)*, sjálfsmeðaumkun *(f)*
sell • *v* selja
semantic • *adj* merkingarlegur, merkingarfræðilegur
semaphore • *n* veif *(f)*
semen • *n* sæði *(n)*, sáð *(n)*, sáðvökvi *(m)*, brundur *(m)*
semibreve • *n* heilnóta *(f)*
semiconductor • *n* hálfleiðari *(m)*
seminoma • *n* sæðiskrabbi *(m)*
semiquaver • *n* sextándapartsnóta *(f)*, sextándipartur *(m)*
senate • *n* öldungadeild *(f)*
senator • *n* öldungaráðsmaður
send • *v* senda
sentence • *n* setning *(f)*
sepal • *n* bikarblað *(n)*
separate • *adj* aðkilinn
sepsis • *n* graftarsótt *(f)*, blóðsýking *(f)*, blóðeitrun *(f)*
series • *n* röð *(f)*, þáttaröð *(f)*
serious • *adj* alvarlegur

sermon • *n* predikun *(f)*
serotonin • *n* serótónín *(n)*
serpent • *n* höggormur *(m)*, naðra *(f)*
sesquipedalian • *adj* margkvæður *(m)*, atkvæði, gefinn fyrir long orð *(m)*
set • *n* mengi *(n)*
seventh • *adj* sjöundi
sew • *v* sauma
sex • *n* kyn *(n)*
sexism • *n* kynjamismunun
sexy • *adj* sexí, kynþokkafullur, kynæsandi
shack • *n* kofi, skúr, hreysi
shadow • *n* skuggi *(m)*
shag • *n* toppskarfur *(m)*
shake • *v* takast í hendur, dansa • *n* hristingur *(m)*, sjeik *(m)*, mjólkurhristingur *(m)*
shale • *n* leirsteinn *(m)*, leirflögur
shallot • *n* skalottlaukur *(m)*, sjalottulaukur *(m)*, skalotlaukur *(m)*, sandlaukur *(m)*
shame • *n* háðung *(f)*, skömm *(f)*
shampoo • *n* sjampó *(n)*
shamrock • *n* músasmári *(m)*
shanty • *n* kofi *(m)*, hreysi *(n)*
shantytown • *n* kofaþorp *(n)*
shark • *n* hákarl *(m)*
she • *pron* hún
shears • *n* klippur
sheathe • *v* slíðra, setja í slíður
shed • *n* skúr *(m)*, skemma *(f)*
shell • *n* skel *(f)*
shelter • *n* skjól *(n)*, athvarf *(n)*
sheriff • *n* fógeti, skerfari *(m)*
shield • *n* skjöldur *(m)*, skjöldur • *v* skýla, hlífa, vernda
shine • *v* ljóma
ship • *n* skip *(n)*
shire • *n* skíri *(n)*
shirk • *v* koma sér undan
shirt • *n* skyrta *(f)*
shit • *n* skítur *(m)* • *v* kúka, skíta, að, á, sig • *interj* helvítis, fjandinn, fjandans, djöfullsins, andskotans
shiver • *v* skjálfa
shoal • *n* vaða *(f)*, torfa *(f)*
shoe • *v* járna • *n* skór *(m)*
shoehorn • *n* skóhorn *(n)*
shoot • *v* skjóta
shop • *n* verslun *(f)*, búð *(f)*
shoplifter • *n* búðarþjófur *(m)*
shore • *n* strönd, bakki *(m)*
shorebird • *n* vaðfugl *(m)*
short • *adj* lágur *(m)*, lágvaxinn *(m)*, stuttur *(m)*, stuttvaxinn *(m)*
shorthand • *n* stytting *(f)*

shorts • *n* stuttbuxur
shotgun • *n* haglabyssa *(f)*, framhlaðningur *(m)*, framsæti *(n)*
should • *v* eiga að
shoulder • *v* axla • *n* öxl *(f)*, vegöxl *(f)*
shout • *v* hrópa, æpa, skrækja, öskra
shower • *v* fara í sturtu, fara í steypibað • *n* skúr *(f)*, demba *(f)*, skvetta *(f)*, sturta *(f)*, steypibað *(n)*
shrew • *n* snjáldurmús *(f)*, snjáldra *(f)*
shrimp • *n* rækja *(f)*
shudder • *v* skjálfa, hrylla við • *n* hrollur *(m)*, skjálfti *(m)*
shuffle • *v* stokka • *n* stokkun *(f)*
shut • *v* loka
shutter • *n* gluggahleri *(m)*, hleri *(m)*, lokari *(m)*
shuttle • *v* skutla • *n* skytta *(f)*, skutla *(f)*
shy • *adj* feiminn
sibling • *n* systkin
sic • *v* siga, etja
sickle • *n* sigð *(f)*
side • *n* blaðsíða
sidewalk • *n* gangstétt *(f)*, fortóv *(n)*
sieve • *n* sáldur *(n)*
sign • *v* undirrita, skrifa undir
signature • *n* undirskrift *(f)*
silence • *n* þögn *(f)*, ró *(f)* • *interj* þögn
silent • *adj* hljóður *(m)*
silicon • *n* kísill
silk • *n* silki
silkworm • *n* silkiormur
silver • *n* silfur *(n)*, silfur, mynnt, silfurlitaður
similar • *adj* einslaga *(m)*, einslagaður *(m)*, einshyrndur *(m)*
simile • *n* líking *(f)*, samlíking *(f)*
simple • *adj* einfaldur *(m)*
simplex • *n* hyrna *(f)*
simply • *adv* einfaldlega
sin • *v* syndga • *n* synd *(f)*, misgjörð, misgerð, yfirsjón
since • *prep* síðan
sine • *n* sínus *(m)*
sinful • *adj* syndugur
sing • *v* syngja
singe • *v* svíða, brenna, sviðna, brenna lítillega
singer • *n* söngvari *(m)*, söngkona *(f)*
singleton • *n* einstökungur *(m)*, einsstaksmengi *(n)*
singular • *n* eintala *(f)* • *adj* eintala *(f)*, et. *(f)*
sink • *v* sökkva • *n* vaskur *(m)*
sinless • *adj* syndlaus
sinusoid • *n* sínusferill *(m)*
sinusoidal • *adj* sínus-, sínuslaga *(f)*

sip • *v* bergja • *n* sopi *(m)*
sir • *n* herra *(m)*
sister • *n* systir *(m)*
sister-in-law • *n* mágkona, mágkona *(f)*,
svilkona *(f)*
sit • *v* sitja
sixth • *adj* sjötti
sixtieth • *adj* sextugasta
size • *n* stærð
skald • *n* skáld
skate • *n* skata *(f)*
skateboard • *v* skeita • *n* hjólabretti *(n)*
skeleton • *n* beinakerfið
skeptical • *adj* vantrúaður *(m)*
skepticism • *n* efahyggja
skewer • *n* spýta *(f)*
ski • *v* skíða • *n* skíði *(n)*, andri *(m)*, öndur *(m)*
skier • *n* skíðamaður *(m)*
skin • *n* húð *(f)*, skinn *(n)*, hörund *(n)*
skirt • *n* pils *(n)*
skull • *n* höfuðkúpa, hauskúpa *(f)*
skunk • *n* skunkur *(m)*
sky • *n* himinn *(m)*
skyrocket • *n* eldflaug *(f)*, raketta *(f)*
skyscraper • *n* skýjakljúfur *(m)*
slave • *v* þræla, púla • *n* þræll *(m)*
slay • *v* bana
sledge • *n* sleði *(m)*
sleep • *v* sofa • *n* svefn *(m)*, stírur
sleepiness • *n* svefnhöfgi *(f)*, syfja *(f)*
sleepyhead • *n* svefnpurka *(f)*
sleet • *v* setja niður slyddu, slydda • *n*
ískorn *(n)*, ísing *(f)*, slydda *(f)*, kraparigning *(f)*, bleytukafald *(n)*
sleeve • *n* ermi *(f)*
slide • *v* renna • *n* renna *(f)*, rennibraut
(f), sleði *(m)*, skyggna *(f)*
slipper • *n* inniskór *(m)*
sliver • *n* flís *(f)*, flaski *(m)*
sloop • *n* slúppa
sloth • *n* leti *(f)*, ómennska *(f)*, dugleysi
(n), letidýr *(n)*
slowly • *adv* hægt, rólega
slush • *n* slabb *(n)*, krap *(n)*
small • *adj* smár, lítill
smart • *adj* snjall
smash • *v* mölva
smegma • *n* reðurfarði *(m)*, limfarði *(m)*,
forhúðarostur *(m)*, ostur *(m)*
smell • *v* lykt, lykta • *n* lykt *(f)*, lyktarskyn
(f)
smile • *v* brosa • *n* bros *(n)*
smog • *n* þreykur *(m)*, reykjarmóða *(f)*,
mengunarmóða *(f)*
smoke • *v* reykja • *n* reykur *(m)*
smoker • *n* reykingamaður *(m)*

smoking • *n* reykingar
snail • *n* snigill *(m)*
snake • *n* snákur *(m)*, slanga *(f)*
sneeze • *v* hnerra
snide • *adj* illkvittinn *(m)*, meinhæðinn
(m), fyrirlítanlegur *(m)*
snip • *n* snifsi *(n)*
sniper • *n* leyniskytta *(f)*
snob • *n* snobb *(n)*
snooker • *n* snóker
snore • *v* hrjóta
snot • *n* hor *(n)*
snout • *n* trýni *(n)*
snow • *v* snjóa, fenna • *n* snjór *(m)*, snær
(m), fönn *(f)*, snjókoma *(f)*
snow-blind • *adj* snjóblindur
snowflake • *n* snjókorn *(n)*
snowman • *n* snjókarl *(m)*
so • *adv* svona
soap • *n* sápa
sob • *v* snökta, stynja, andvarpa, gráta,
stynja upp, segja frá með ekka • *n* snökkt
(n), ekki *(m)*, ekkasog *(n)*, andvarp *(n)*
soccer • *n* fótbolti *(m)*, knattspyrna *(f)*
socialism • *n* jafnaðarstefna, sósíalismi
socialization • *n* félagsmótun *(f)*
society • *n* samfélag *(n)*, þjóðfélag *(n)*,
félag *(n)*
sock • *n* sokkur *(m)*
socket • *n* innstunga *(f)*
sodium • *n* natrín *(n)*, natríum *(n)*
sofa • *n* sófi *(m)*
soft • *adj* mjúkur
soft-boiled • *adj* linsoðinn
software • *n* hugbúnaður *(m)*
sojourn • *v* dveljast um tíma, hafa viðdvöl • *n* dvöl *(f)*, viðdvöl *(f)*
solder • *v* lóða, brasa, sjóða saman,
kveikja, kveikja saman • *n* lóðmálmur *(m)*, lóðtin *(n)*, brasmálmur *(m)*,
loðningarefni *(n)*
soldering • *n* lóðun *(f)*, tinlóðun *(f)*
soldier • *n* hermaður *(m)*, dáti *(m)*
sole • *n* il *(f)*, sóli *(m)*, skósóli *(m)*
solicitor • *n* lögfræðingur *(m)*,
málafærslumaður *(m)*, dyrasölumaður
(m), sölumaður *(m)*
solid • *adj* storkuhamur *(m)*
soliloquy • *n* eintal *(n)*, einræða *(f)*, einræða persónu *(f)*
solitude • *n* einsemd *(f)*
solstice • *n* sólstöður, sólhvörf
solution • *n* útkoma *(f)*
sombrero • *n* mexíkanahattur *(m)*
some • *pron* sum, sumar, sumir
somebody • *pron* einhver *(m)*
somersault • *n* kollhnís *(m)*, heljarstökk

(n)
something • *pron* eitthvað
sometimes • *adv* stundum, af og til
somewhere • *adv* einhvers staðar
son • *n* sonur *(m)*
sonar • *n* ómsjá *(f)*, sónar *(m)*
sonata • *n* sónata *(f)*
song • *n* söngur *(m)*, lag *(n)*
soon • *adv* bráðum, brátt, fljótlega
soothsayer • *n* spámaður, spákona
sorrow • *n* sorg *(f)*
sorry • *interj* fyrirgefðu, afsakið, fyrirgefðu mér
sort • *n* gerð *(f)*, tegund *(f)*, sort *(f)* • *v* flokka
soul • *n* sál *(f)*
sound • *v* hljóma, hljóða • *n* hljóð *(n)*, sund *(n)*
sour • *adj* súr
south • *n* suður *(n)*
sow • *n* sýr *(f)*
space • *n* geimur *(m)*
spacecraft • *n* geimfar
spaceship • *n* geimskip *(n)*
spade • *n* skófla, spaði *(m)*, surtur *(m)*, negri *(m)*, niggari *(m)*, svertingjahundur *(m)*, blámaður *(m)*
spam • *n* ruslpóstur *(m)*
sparingly • *adv* sparlega
spark • *n* neisti *(m)*
spathe • *n* hulsturblað *(n)*
spatula • *n* spaði *(m)*
spawn • *v* gjóta
speaker • *n* hátalari *(m)*
spear • *n* spjót *(n)*
specialty • *n* sérréttur *(m)*
spectacles • *n* gleraugu
speculum • *n* spegill *(m)*, slanga *(f)*
speech • *n* mál *(n)*, tal *(n)*, málhæfileiki *(m)*, málfar *(n)*, mæli *(n)*, framburður *(m)*, ræða *(f)*, ávarp *(n)*, tala *(f)*
speechless • *adj* orðlaus
spell • *n* galdraþula *(f)*, álög • *v* stafa
spelt • *n* spelt *(n)*, speldi *(n)*
spendthrift • *n* eyðslukló *(f)*
sperm • *n* sæðisfruma *(f)*, sæði *(n)*
spermatozoon • *n* sæðisfruma *(f)*, sáð *(n)*, sáðfruma *(f)*
spermicide • *n* sáðfrumnadeyðir *(m)*
sphere • *n* hnöttur
sphincter • *n* hringvöðvi *(m)*
spice • *n* krydd *(n)*
spider • *n* kónguló *(f)*, könguló *(f)*
spinach • *n* spínat *(n)*
spine • *n* hryggur *(m)*, hryggjarsúla *(f)*, kjölur *(m)*
spiracle • *n* andop *(n)*, loftæðaop *(n)*, blás-

turshola *(f)*, blástursop *(n)*
spire • *n* spíra *(f)*, turnspíra *(f)*
spit • *n* spýta *(f)* • *v* hrækja
spleen • *n* milta *(n)*
split • *v* klofna
spoilsport • *n* gleðispillir *(m)*
spoke • *n* spæll *(m)*
sponge • *n* svampur *(m)*
spool • *v* biðfæra • *n* spóla *(f)*, kefli *(n)*
spoon • *n* skeið *(f)*, spúnn *(m)*
spoonful • *n* skeið *(f)*, skeiðarfylli *(f)*
sport • *n* íþrótt *(f)*
spout • *v* spúa
spring • *n* vor *(n)*
springboard • *n* stökkpallur *(m)*
sprout • *n* spíra *(f)*, frjónál *(f)*
spruce • *n* greni, greni *(n)*, greni-
spud • *n* grefill *(m)*, kartafla *(f)*
spurious • *adj* óekta *(m)*, falskur *(m)*, falsaður *(m)*, tál-, fals-, óskilgetinn *(m)*
spy • *v* njósna, koma auga á • *n* njósnari *(m)*
squall • *n* él *(n)*
square • *n* ferningur *(m)*, réttskeið *(f)*, torg *(n)*, ferningstala *(f)* • *adj* ferningslaga, hornréttur, fer-
squib • *n* háðsgrein *(f)*, níðkvæði *(n)*, atlaga *(f)*
squid • *n* smokkfiskur *(m)*, smokkur *(m)*
squirrel • *n* íkorni *(m)*
stable • *n* gripahús *(n)*, hesthús *(n)*, fjós *(n)*
stack • *n* stafli *(m)*, hlaði *(m)*, troðröð *(f)*
stadium • *n* leikvangur *(m)*
stag • *n* hjörtur *(m)*
stage • *n* svið *(n)*
stainless • *adj* ryðfrír *(m)*
stair • *n* trappa, þrep, stigi, tröppur
stairs • *n* stigi *(m)*
stairwell • *n* stigagangur *(m)*
stallion • *n* stóðhestur *(m)*, graðhestur *(m)*
stamp • *v* stimpla • *n* stimpill *(m)*
stand • *v* standa
staple • *v* hefta • *n* hefti *(n)*, kengur *(m)*, vírhefti *(n)*
star • *n* stjarna
starboard • *n* stjórnborði *(m)*
stare • *v* stara, glápa
starfish • *n* krossfiskur *(f)*, sæstjarna *(f)*
starling • *n* stari *(m)*
start • *n* byrjun *(f)*, upphaf *(n)* • *v* hrökkva við, hrökkva upp
state • *n* ríki *(n)*, fylki *(n)*, ástand *(n)*
static • *adj* kyrrlegur *(m)*, kyrr-
statics • *n* stöðufræði
station • *n* stöð *(f)*

statue • *n* stytta *(f)*
status • *n* staða *(f)*
stay • *v* dvelja, vera, halda
stead • *n* staður *(m)*, bær *(m)*
steal • *v* stela
steam • *n* gufa *(f)*
steamship • *n* Gufuskip *(n)*
steel • *n* stál *(n)*
steeple • *n* kirkjuturn *(m)*
steeplechase • *n* hindrunarhlaup *(n)*
steeplejack • *n* viðgerðarmaður turna *(m)*, viðgerðarmaður reykháfa *(m)*
stem • *n* stefni *(n)*
stepbrother • *n* stjúpbróðir *(m)*
stepchild • *n* stjúpbarn *(n)*
stepdaughter • *n* stjúpdóttir *(f)*
stepfather • *n* stjúpfaðir *(m)*, stjúpi *(m)*
stepmother • *n* stjúpmóðir *(f)*, stjúpa *(f)*, stjúpmamma *(f)*
stepson • *n* stjúpsonur *(m)*
sterilize • *v* gelda, sótthreinsa
stern • *n* skutur *(m)*
sternal • *adj* bringubein
sternpost • *n* afturstefni *(n)*
steroid • *n* steri *(m)*
stethoscope • *n* hlustunarpípa *(f)*
stick • *n* prik *(n)*
stiffen • *v* stífna
stigma • *n* fræni *(n)*
stillborn • *adj* andvanafæddur *(m)*
stilted • *adj* tilgerðarlegur *(m)*, uppskrúfaður *(m)*, klúsaður *(m)*
stinger • *n* broddur *(m)*
stingray • *n* stingskötur *(f)*
stipend • *n* framfærslufé *(n)*, lífeyrir *(m)*, styrkur *(m)*, námsstyrkur *(m)*
stirrup • *n* ístað *(n)*
stochastic • *adj* slembi-, slembinn *(m)*, tilviljanakenndur *(m)*
stockfish • *n* harðfiskur *(m)*
stockpile • *v* koma upp varabirgðum, safna varabirgðum, hamstra • *n* varabirgðir, varaforði *(m)*, vopnabirgðir
stoke • *v* kynda undir, bæta eldsneyti á
stole • *n* stóla *(f)*
stomach • *n* magi *(m)*
stomachache • *n* magapína *(f)*
stone • *n* steinn *(m)*, gimsteinn *(m)*, eðalsteinn *(m)*
stony • *adj* grýttur
stool • *n* kollur *(m)*
stork • *n* storkur
storm • *n* stormur
story • *n* saga
stowaway • *n* laumufarþegi *(m)*, farþjófur *(m)*
straight • *n* röð *(f)* • *adj* beinn

strainer • *n* sigti *(n)*
strait • *n* sund *(n)*
strand • *n* strönd *(f)*
stratosphere • *n* heiðhvolf *(n)*
stratus • *n* þokuský *(n)*, lágský *(n)*
strawberry • *n* jarðarber *(n)*, jarðarberjaplanta *(f)*
street • *n* gata *(f)*, stræti *(n)*
stress • *n* streita *(f)*, stress *(n)*, áhersla *(f)*
strike • *n* verkfall
string • *n* band *(n)*, snæri *(n)*, spotti *(m)*, strengur *(m)*
strip • *n* strimill *(m)*, braut *(f)*, nektardans *(m)*, stripp *(n)* • *v* svipta, fjarlægja, afklæðast, strippa
stripper • *n* fatafella *(f)*, nektardansmær *(f)*
stroll • *n* rölt
strontium • *n* strontín
structure • *n* bygging
stubble • *n* skeggbroddur *(m)*, broddur *(m)*
stud • *n* foli *(m)*
student • *n* nemandi *(m)*
studies • *n* fræði
study • *v* læra, lesa, stúdera • *n* nám *(n)*, bóknám *(n)*, lærdómur *(m)*, fræðiiðkan *(f)*, athugun *(f)*, rannsókn *(f)*, könnun *(f)*, skoðun *(f)*, námsefni *(n)*, rannsóknarefni *(n)*, fræðigrein *(f)*, lesstofa *(f)*, lesherbergi *(n)*, bókaherbergi *(n)*, etýða *(f)*, æfing *(f)*
stupid • *adj* heimskur
stupor • *n* sljóleiki *(m)*, hálfmeðvitundarleysi *(n)*
styrofoam • *n* frauðplast *(n)*
subatomic • *adj* smærri en frumeind *(m)*, innan atóms
subcutaneous • *adj* húðbeðs-
subdirectory • *n* undirmappa *(f)*
subgroup • *n* undirflokkur *(m)*, hlutgrúpa *(f)*
subject • *n* frumlag *(n)*, efni *(n)*, umræðuefni *(n)*, umtalsefni *(n)*, viðfangsefni *(n)*, yrkisefni *(n)*, fag *(n)*, námsgrein *(f)*, grein *(f)*, þegn *(m)*
sublimation • *n* þurrgufun *(f)*, göfgun *(f)*
submarine • *n* kafbátur *(m)*
subphylum • *n* undirfylking *(f)*
subscribe • *v* undirrita
subset • *n* hlutmengi *(n)*
subsidiary • *n* dótturfyrirtæki *(n)*
subtitle • *n* undirtitill *(m)*, undirfyrirsögn *(f)*, aukafyrirsögn *(f)*, texti *(m)*, þýðing *(f)*, þýðingartexti *(m)*, kvikmyndatexti *(m)*
suburb • *n* úthverfi
success • *n* árangur *(m)*
successor • *n* eftirfari *(m)*

suck • *v* sökka, ömurlegur *(m)*
sucrose • *n* súkrósi *(m)*, sakkarósi *(m)*
suction • *n* sog *(n)*, loftsog *(n)*
suddenly • *adv* brátt, skyndilega, snögglega, hastarlega
suet • *n* mör *(m)*
suffering • *n* þjáning *(f)* • *adj* þjáður *(m)*
suffix • *v* skeyta við • *n* viðskeyti *(n)*
suffrage • *n* atkvæðisréttur *(m)*, kosningaréttur *(m)*
sugar • *n* sykur *(m)*
sugary • *adj* sætur
suicide • *n* sjálfsmorð *(n)*, sjálfsvíg *(n)*, sjálfsmorðingi *(m)*, sjálfsbani *(m)*
suit • *n* jakkaföt
sulfur • *n* brennisteinn *(m)*
sultan • *n* soldán *(m)*
sum • *n* summa *(f)*, samtala *(f)*
summation • *n* summumyndun *(f)*
summer • *n* sumar *(n)*
sundial • *n* sólúr *(n)*
sunfish • *n* tunglfiskur
sunflower • *n* sólblóm *(n)*
sunlight • *n* sólarljós *(n)*
sunrise • *n* sólarupprás *(f)*, sólris *(n)*, sólaruppkoma *(f)*, dögun *(f)*
sunset • *n* sólsetur *(n)*, sólarlag *(n)*, sólfall *(n)*
sunshine • *n* sólskin
sunstroke • *n* sólstingur *(m)*
superficial • *adj* yfirborðskenndur
superlative • *n* efsta stig *(n)*
supermarket • *n* kjörbúð *(f)*, stórmarkaður *(f)*
supernova • *n* sprengistjarna *(f)*
superphylum • *n* yfirfylking *(f)*
superstition • *n* hjátrú *(f)*
supersymmetry • *n* ofursamhverfa
supine • *adj* á bakinu, liggja upp í loft, útafliggjandi
suppository • *n* stikkpilla *(f)*, endaþarmsstíll *(m)*
supreme • *adj* æðstur *(m)*
surf • *n* brim *(n)*
surgeon • *n* skurðlæknir *(m)*
surname • *n* eftirnafn, kenninafn
surreptitious • *adj* laumulegur *(m)*, í laumi, leynilegur *(m)*
surround • *v* umkringja
sushi • *n* sushi
sustenance • *n* viðurværi *(n)*, fæði *(n)*, matur *(m)*, næring *(f)*
swallow • *n* svala, landsvala
swamp • *n* mýri *(f)*
swan • *n* álft *(f)*, svanur *(m)*
swastika • *n* hakakross *(m)*
swear • *v* sverja, blóta
sweat • *n* sviti *(m)* • *v* svitna, hafa, áhyggjur
sweater • *n* peysa *(f)*
sweet • *adj* sætur
sweetness • *n* sætleik *(f)*
swim • *v* synda • *n* sund *(n)*
swimsuit • *n* sundföt, sundbolur *(m)*
swindle • *v* svindla á, svindla • *n* svindl *(n)*, svik *(n)*
swing • *v* sveiflast, róla, hanga • *n* sveifla *(f)*, róla *(f)*
sword • *n* sverð *(n)*
swordfish • *n* sverðfiskur *(m)*
sycophant • *n* smjaðrari *(m)*, höfðingjasleikja *(f)*, undirlægja *(f)*
syllable • *n* atkvæði *(n)*, samstafa *(f)*
syllabus • *n* námsáætlun *(f)*
syllogism • *n* rökhenda *(f)*
symbol • *n* tákn *(n)*
symbolically • *adv* táknrænt
symmetrical • *adj* samhverfur *(m)*
symphony • *n* sinfónía *(f)*
synagogue • *n* samkunduhús *(n)*, sýnagóga *(f)*
synchronous • *adj* samstilltur *(m)*
syncope • *n* brottfall *(n)*
syndactyly • *n* samtáun *(f)*, samfingrun *(f)*
synergy • *n* samvirkni *(f)*
synonym • *n* samheiti *(n)*
syntax • *n* málskipan *(f)*, setningafræði *(f)*, orðskipunarfræði *(f)*
syphilis • *n* sárasótt *(f)*
syrup • *n* síróp *(n)*
system • *n* kerfi *(n)*

T

table • *n* borð *(n)*
tablecloth • *n* borðdúkur *(m)*
tablespoon • *n* matskeið *(f)*
tabloid • *n* æsifréttablað *(n)*
tachometer • *n* snúningshraðamælir *(m)*
tadpole • *n* halakarta *(f)*, froskungi *(m)*
tail • *n* hali *(m)*, skott *(n)*, rófa *(f)*, tagl, dindill *(m)*, stél *(n)*, sporður *(m)*
tailor • *n* klæðskeri *(m)*, skraddari *(m)*
take • *v* taka, nema

takeoff • *n* flugtak *(n)*
tale • *n* saga *(f)*
talent • *n* talenta *(f)*, hæfileiki *(m)*, gáfa *(f)*, hæfileikafólk *(n)*, hæfileikamaður *(m)*
talk • *v* tala, mæla, ávarpa
talkative • *adj* málglaður, skrafhreifinn
talkativeness • *n* málgleði *(f)*, skrafhreifni *(f)*
tall • *adj* hár
tallow • *n* tólg *(f)*
tame • *adj* taminn, gæfur, spakur
tamper • *v* eiga við, fikta, fikta í
tampon • *n* tíðatappi *(m)*
tangent • *n* snertill *(m)*, tangens *(m)*
tank • *n* tankur *(m)*, skriðdreki, tank *(m)*
tantalum • *n* tantal
tapeworm • *n* bandormur *(m)*
tapir • *n* káputapír *(m)*
tar • *v* tjarga • *n* tjara *(f)*, sjóari *(m)*, sjómaður *(m)*, tar-skrá *(f)*
tarantula • *n* tarantúla *(f)*
tarn • *n* tjörn *(f)*
taste • *v* bragða, smakka, bragðast • *n* bragð *(n)*, smekkur *(m)*, forsmekkur *(m)*
tattoo • *v* húðflúra, tattóvera, tattúera • *n* húðflúr *(n)*, tattú *(n)*, tattó *(n)*
tau • *n* tá *(n)*
taunt • *v* smána, brigsla, hæða • *n* smán *(n)*, brigsl *(n)*, hæðni *(f)*
tautology • *n* sísanna *(f)*
tax • *n* skattur *(m)*
taxi • *v* taxa • *n* leigubíll *(m)*, taxi *(m)*, leigubifreið *(f)*
taxonomy • *n* flokkunarfræði *(m)*
tea • *n* te *(m)*
teach • *v* kenna
teacher • *n* kennari *(m)*, kennslukona *(f)*
teakettle • *n* ketill *(m)*
tear • *n* tár *(n)*
teaser • *n* stikla *(f)*
technetium • *n* teknetín
technique • *n* tækni
technobabble • *n* tæknibull *(n)*
technology • *n* tækni *(f)*
tee • *n* té *((tyeh))*, teigur *(m)*, tí *(n)*
teethe • *v* taka tennur
telephone • *v* hringja, hringja í • *n* sími *(m)*
telescope • *n* sjónauka
television • *n* sjónvarp *(n)*, imbakassi *(m)*, sjónvarp, sjónvarpstæki *(n)*
tell • *v* segja
tellurium • *n* tellúr
temperature • *n* hitastig *(n)*
temple • *n* musteri *(n)*, hof *(n)*, gagnauga *(n)*
tenacious • *adj* fastheldinn, haldgóður, minnisgóður
tendon • *n* sin *(f)*
tennis • *n* tennis *(m)*
tense • *n* tíð *(f)* • *adj* upptrekktur, órólegur
tensor • *n* þinur *(m)*
tent • *n* tjald *(n)*
tenth • *adj* tíundi *(m)*
terbium • *n* terbín
termite • *n* maur *(m)*
tern • *n* þerna *(f)*
ternary • *adj* þríunda-, þrístæður *(m)*
terrible • *adj* hræðileg
territory • *n* landsvæði, yfirráðasvæði
terrorist • *n* hryðjuverkamaður
terse • *adj* stuttur og gagnorður, stuttur og laggóður
tertiary • *adj* þriðji *(m)*
testosterone • *n* testósterón *(n)*
text • *n* texti *(m)*
textbook • *n* kennslubók *(f)*, skólabók *(f)*
thallium • *n* þallín
than • *prep* en
thanatophobia • *n* dauðafælni *(f)*
thankless • *adj* vanþakklátur
thanks • *n* takk *(n)* • *interj* takk, takk fyrir, þakka þér
the • *art* -inn *(m)*, -in *(f)*, -ið *(n)*, -nir, -nar, -in • *adv* því + comp., því + comp.
theater • *n* leikhús *(n)*
theft • *n* þjófnaður *(m)*
theme • *n* stef *(n)*, tema *(n)*, þema *(n)*
then • *adv* þá
thence • *adv* þaðan
theosophy • *n* guðspeki *(f)*
there • *adv* þarna, þar, það, þangað
thermodynamics • *n* varmafræði
thermometer • *n* hitamælir
thermosphere • *n* hitahvolf *(n)*
thesaurus • *n* hugtakaorðabók
they • *pron* þeir, þær, þau
thicket • *n* kjarr *(n)*
thief • *n* þjófur
thieving • *adj* stelvís
thigh • *n* læri *(n)*
thimble • *n* fingurbjörg *(f)*
thin • *v* þynna, mjókka • *adj* þunnur, mjór
think • *v* hugsa, finnast, halda
third • *n* þriðji *(m)*, þriðja *(n)*, þriðjungur *(m)*, þríund *(f)* • *adj* þriðji *(m)*, þriðja *(n)*
thirst • *n* þorsti
thirsty • *adj* þyrstur
thirtieth • *adj* þrítugasta
this • *pron* þessi, þetta, það
thither • *adv* þangað
thorax • *n* brjóst *(n)*, brjóstkassi *(m)*, brjósthol *(n)*, frambolur *(m)*

thorium • *n* þórín
thorny • *adj* þyrnóttur *(m)*
thorough • *adj* ítarlegur *(m)*
thorp • *n* þorp *(n)*
thou • *pron* þú
though • *conj* þó, þótt
thought • *n* hugmynd *(f)*, hugsun *(f)*
thousandth • *adj* þúsundasti
thread • *v* þræða • *n* þráður *(m)*, spjallþráður *(m)*
three-dimensional • *adj* þrívíður
thresh • *v* þreskja
thrice • *adv* þrisvar, þrívegis
throaty • *adj* hás, rámur
thromboembolism • *n* segarek *(n)*
thrombus • *n* blóðkökkur *(m)*
throne • *n* hásæti
throw • *v* kasta, fleygja, henda, varpa,
verpa
thrush • *n* þröstur *(m)*
thulium • *n* túlín
thumb • *n* þumall *(m)*, þumalfingur *(m)*
thunder • *n* þruma *(f)*
thunderstorm • *n* þrumuveður *(n)*
thyme • *n* timjan *(n)*
thymine • *n* týmín *(n)*
tick • *n* blóðmaur *(m)*
ticket • *n* farmiði *(m)*
tickle • *v* kitla
ticklish • *adj* kitlinn
tie • *n* jafntefli *(n)*, band *(n)*
tight • *adj* þrengdur, þröngur, þéttur *(m)*,
þétt *(n)* • *adv* rótt
tights • *n* sokkabuxur
timber • *n* viður *(m)*, timbur *(n)* • *interj*
timbur
timbre • *n* hljómblær *(m)*, tónblær *(m)*
time • *v* mæla tímann á, tímamæla, tímasetja, tímastilla • *n* tími *(m)*, tíð *(f)*,
afplánunartími *(m)*
times • *prep* sinnum
tin • *n* tin *(n)*
tine • *n* tönn *(f)*
tip • *n* þjórfé *(n)*
tired • *adj* þreyttur
tissue • *n* vefur *(m)*
titanium • *n* títan *(n)*
tithe • *n* tíundi *(m)*, tíund *(f)*
to • *prep* til
toad • *n* karta
toaster • *n* brauðrist *(f)*
tobacco • *n* tóbak
toccata • *n* tokkata *(f)*
today • *adv* í dag
toe • *n* tá *(f)*
toenail • *n* tánögl *(f)*
together • *adv* saman

toilet • *n* snyrting *(f)*, klósett *(n)*, baðherbergi *(n)*, salerni *(n)*, vatnssalerni *(n)*, skítastaður *(m)*, skítapleis *(n)*
token • *n* tóki *(m)*
tom • *n* högni *(m)*
tomato • *n* tómatjurt *(f)*, tómatur *(m)*, tómati *(m)*
tombola • *n* tombóla *(f)*, hlutavelta *(f)*
tome • *n* bindi *(n)*
tomorrow • *n* morgundagur *(m)* • *adv* á
morgun
toner • *n* prentduft *(n)*, andlitsvatn *(n)*
tongs • *n* töng *(f)*
tongue • *n* tunga *(f)*, tunga á skó *(f)*, skótunga *(f)*
tonight • *n* í kvöld • *adv* í kvöld, í nótt
tooth • *n* tönn *(f)*
toothache • *n* tannpína *(f)*
toothbrush • *n* tannbursti *(m)*
topaz • *n* tópas *(m)*
torch • *n* kyndill *(m)*
torment • *n* kvöl
torpedo • *n* tundurskeyti *(n)*
torrential • *adj* straumharður *(m)*, fossandi *(m)*, helli-, flaumur *(m)*
tortoise • *n* landskjaldbaka *(f)*, skjaldbaka
(f)
touch • *v* snerta
towel • *n* handklæði *(n)*
tower • *n* turn *(m)*
town • *n* bær *(m)*
township • *n* bæjarfélag *(n)*, sveitarfélag
(n)
toy • *n* leikfang *(m)*
trace • *n* spor *(n)*
track • *n* lag *(n)*
tractor • *n* dráttarvél *(f)*
trade • *v* skipta • *n* viðskipti, verslun *(f)*,
kaup, skipti, iðn *(f)*
trademark • *n* vörumerki *(n)*
tradition • *n* hefð
tragic • *adj* sorglegur
trailer • *n* stikla *(f)*
train • *n* lest *(f)*
traitor • *n* svikari *(m)*
tram • *n* sporvagn *(m)*
trampoline • *n* trampólín *(n)*
transcendental • *adj* torræður *(m)*
transcontinental • *adj* sem fer þvert yfir
meginland, sem liggur þvert yfir meginland
transcription • *n* hjóðfræðileg umritun
transgression • *n* brot *(n)*, afbrot *(n)*, lögbrot *(n)*, áflæði *(n)*
transistor • *n* smári *(m)*
transitive • *adj* gegnvirkur
translate • *v* þýða

translation • *n* þýðing *(f)*, hliðrun *(f)*
translator • *n* þýðandi *(m)*
transliteration • *n* umritun *(f)*
transparent • *adj* gagnsær, gegnsær
transpose • *n* bylta *(f)*, bylt fylki *(n)*
transubstantiation • *n* ummyndun *(f)*,
myndbreyting *(f)*, eðlisbreyting *(f)*, gjörbreyting *(f)*, eðlisbreytingarkenningin *(f)*
trapdoor • *n* hleri *(m)*, fallhleri *(m)*, hlemmur *(m)*
travel • *v* ferðast
traveled • *adj* fjölfarinn, víðförull
trawler • *n* togari
treadmill • *n* hlaupabretti *(n)*
treason • *n* landráð, svik, föðurlandssvik
treatise • *n* fræðileg ritgerð *(f)*
tree • *n* tré
triangle • *n* þríhyrningur *(m)*, þríhorn *(n)*
tribe • *n* ættkvísl *(f)*
trichotillomania • *n* hárreitisýki
trichotomy • *n* þríflokkun *(f)*
trident • *n* þríforkur *(m)*
trigram • *n* þrístæða *(f)*
trilingual • *adj* þrítyngdur
trill • *n* trilla *(f)*, sveifluhljóð *(n)*
trilogy • *n* þríleikur *(m)*, trílógía *(f)*
trinity • *n* þríeyki *(n)*, þrenning *(f)*
trip • *v* trippa • *n* ferð, för, reisa
triplet • *n* þríburi *(m)*, tríóla *(f)*
tripod • *n* þrífótur *(m)*
trivial • *adj* augljós *(m)*
troll • *n* tröll *(n)*, þurs *(m)*
trombone • *n* básúna *(f)*
tropopause • *n* veðrahvörf
troposphere • *n* veðrahvolf *(n)*
trot • *v* brokka • *n* brokk *(n)*
trout • *n* silungur *(m)*
truck • *n* flutningsbíll
true • *adj* sannur
truffle • *n* jarðkeppur
trumpet • *v* spila, trompet, leika, básúna

• *n* trompet *(m)*
trunk • *n* koffort *(n)*, skott *(n)*
trustee • *n* fjárhaldsmaður *(m)*
truth • *n* sannleikur *(m)*, sannindi
tuba • *n* túba *(f)*
tuberculosis • *n* berklar
tugboat • *n* dráttarbátur *(m)*
tulle • *n* tjull *(n)*
tumble • *v* velta
tumor • *n* æxli *(n)*, hnútur *(m)*
tundra • *n* freðmýri *(f)*, túndra *(f)*
tungsten • *n* þungsteinn
tunnel • *n* göng, undirgöng
turban • *n* vefjarhöttur *(m)*, túrban *(m)*
turd • *n* kúkur *(m)*, sparð *(n)*, tyrðill *(m)*
tureen • *n* súpuskál *(f)*
turf • *n* torf *(n)*, torfa *(f)*
turkey • *n* kalkúnn
turmeric • *n* túrmerik *(n)*
turn • *v* snúa, beygja
turnip • *n* næpa *(f)*
turtle • *n* skjaldbaka
turtleneck • *n* rúllukragi *(m)*, rúllukragapeysa *(f)*
twelfth • *adj* tólfta
twentieth • *adj* tuttugasta
twice • *adv* tvisvar, tvívegis
twig • *n* kvistur *(m)*
twilight • *n* ljósaskipti *(f)*, húm *(n)*,
rökkur *(m)*
twin • *n* tvíburi *(m)*
tympanum • *n* gaflflötur *(m)*
type • *n* tegund *(f)*, gerð *(f)*, kyn *(n)*, sort
(f), týpa *(f)*, tag *(n)*
typewriter • *n* ritvél *(f)*, ritari *(m)*, vélritari *(m)*
typhoon • *n* fellibylur *(m)*
typical • *adj* dæmigerður *(m)*, týpískur
(m)
tyre • *n* dekk *(n)*

U

udder • *n* júgur *(n)*
ultimatum • *n* úrslitakostir
umbrage • *v* skyggja, veita forsælu •
n gremja *(f)*, skapraun *(f)*, skuggi *(m)*,
forsæla *(f)*
umbrella • *n* regnhlíf *(f)*
unary • *adj* einstæður *(m)*
unassuming • *adj* lítillátur *(m)*
unavailable • *adj* ekki í boði, ófáanlegur
unavoidable • *adj* óumflýjanlegur
unbegun • *adj* óhafinn

uncanny • *adj* óhugnanlegur, dularfullur,
undarlegur, kynlegur
uncle • *n* föðurbróðir *(m)*, móðurbróðir
(m)
unconscious • *adj* meðvitundarlaus
undemocratic • *adj* ólýðræðislegur
under • *prep* undir
underachiever • *n* fúx *(m)*, bekkjarlalli
(m)
underground • *adv* neðanjarðar
understand • *v* skilja, skiljast

underwear • *n* nærföt
underworld • *n* undirheimar
undoing • *n* banabiti *(m)*
undoubtedly • *adv* eflaust, efalaust, vafalaust, ugglaust
undress • *n* klæðaleysi *(n)*
unemployed • *adj* atvinnulaus
unemployment • *n* atvinnuleysi
unfair • *adj* ósanngjarn *(m)*
unfinished • *adj* ókláraður, ólokinn
unfortunately • *adv* þvunicameral • *adj* með einni deild
unicorn • *n* einhyrningur *(m)*
unicycle • *n* einhjól *(n)*
unilaterally • *adv* einhliða
union • *n* sammengi
unit • *n* eind *(f)*
universe • *n* alheimur *(m)*
university • *n* háskóli
unjust • *adj* ranglátur
unknown • *n* óþekkt stærð *(f)* • *adj* óþekktur *(m)*, ókunnur *(m)*
unleaded • *adj* blylaust
unless • *conj* nema
unmarried • *adj* ógiftur, ókvæntur
unobtainable • *adj* ófáanlegur
unobtrusive • *adj* látlaus *(m)*
unpardonable • *adj* ófyrirgefanlegur *(m)*
unreal • *adj* óraunverulegur, ímyndaður
unreliable • *adj* óáreiðanlegur *(m)*

until • *prep* þangað til, fyrr en, uns, þar til
untranslatable • *adj* óþýðanlegur
unusually • *adv* óvenjulega
unvoiced • *adj* ósagður, ótjáður
unwarranted • *adj* ástæðulaus *(m)*, óréttmætur *(m)*, óréttlætanlegur *(m)*, óafsakanlegur *(m)*
unworthy • *adj* óverðugur
upstart • *n* uppskafningur *(m)*
uranium • *n* úran *(n)*
urethra • *n* þvagrás *(f)*
urine • *n* þvag *(n)*, hland *(n)*
urn • *n* duftker *(n)*
use • *v* nota
used • *adj* notaður
useful • *adj* gagnlegur
usefulness • *n* gagnsemi *(f)*
useless • *adj* gagnslaus
user • *n* notandi *(m)*, eiturlyfjanotandi *(m)*, dópisti *(m)*, tölvunotandi *(m)*
usufruct • *n* afnotaréttur *(m)*, nýtingarréttur *(m)*
usurp • *v* hrifsa völd, taka yfir, ræna völdum
usurpation • *n* valdarán *(n)*
usurper • *n* valdaræningi *(m)*
utilitarianism • *n* nytjasfena
uvula • *n* úfur *(m)*

V

vacillate • *v* bera kápuna á báðum öxlum
vacuum • *v* ryksuga • *n* lofttæmi *(n)*, lofttóm *(n)*
vagina • *n* leggöng, skeið *(f)*, slíður *(n)*
vaginal • *adj* leggöng, skeið, slíður
valid • *adj* gildur
valkyrie • *n* valkyrja *(f)*
valley • *n* dalur *(m)*
value • *n* gildi *(n)*, mikilvægi *(n)*, gagnsemi *(f)*, verðgildi *(n)*, lengdargildi *(n)*
vampire • *n* vampíra *(f)*
vanadium • *n* vanadín
vandal • *n* skemmdarvargur *(m)*
vanilla • *n* vanillujurt *(f)*, vanilla *(f)*, vanilja *(f)*
vapor • *n* gufa *(f)*
vaporization • *n* gufumyndun *(f)*
vasectomy • *n* sáðrásarúrnám *(n)*
vasoconstriction • *n* æðaþrenging *(f)*, æðasamdráttur *(m)*
vasoconstrictor • *n* æðaþrengjandi *(m)*,

æðaþrengir *(m)*
vat • *n* ker *(n)*
vaudeville • *n* gamansýning *(f)*, fjölleikasýning *(f)*
vector • *n* vigur
vegetable • *n* grænmeti *(n)*
vegetarian • *n* grænmetisæta
vehement • *adj* ákafur *(m)*
vehicle • *n* farartæki *(n)*, ökutæki *(n)*
vein • *n* æð *(f)*
velar • *adj* uppgómmæltur
velocity • *n* hraði *(m)*
vendetta • *n* blóðhefnd
venerable • *adj* virðulegur *(m)*, æruverðugur *(m)*, virðing *(m)*
venial • *adj* fyrirgefanlegur *(m)*, afsakanlegur *(m)*
ventriloquism • *n* búktal *(n)*
ventriloquist • *n* búktalari *(m)*
veranda • *n* verönd *(f)*
verb • *n* sagnorð *(n)*, sögn *(f)*
verbatim • *adj* orðréttur *(m)*, orðrétt *(n)* •

adv orðrétt, orð fyrir orð
verdigris • *n* spanskgræna *(f)*, eirgræna *(f)*, spansgræna *(f)*
vermouth • *n* vermút *(n)*
vernacular • *n* þjóðtunga *(f)* • *adj* þjóðtungu-
versus • *prep* á móti, móti
vertebrate • *n* hryggleysingjar
vertical • *adj* lóðrétt
vertiginous • *adj* svimandi
very • *adv* mjög, ákaflega, afar, ýkja, fjarska, einkar
vest • *n* vesti *(n)*, nærbolur *(m)*
vestibule • *n* anddyri *(n)*, fordyri *(n)*, forstofa *(f)*, forgarður *(m)*, önd *(f)*, hol *(n)*
veterinarian • *n* dýralæknir *(m)*
veto • *v* beita neitunarvaldi • *n* neitunarvald *(n)*
vibraphone • *n* víbrafónn *(m)*
victory • *n* sigur *(m)*
videotape • *n* myndband *(n)*
view • *n* útsýni *(n)*
vile • *adj* viðbjóðslegur, andstyggilegur
village • *n* þorp *(n)*
vindictive • *adj* hefnigjarn *(m)*, heiftrækinn *(m)*
vindictiveness • *n* hefndarþorsti *(m)*
vinegar • *n* edik *(n)*
vineyard • *n* víngarður *(m)*
viola • *n* víóla *(f)*, lágfiðla *(f)*
violet • *n* fjólublár, fjóla *(f)*

violin • *n* fiðla *(f)*
viper • *n* höggormur *(m)*
virgin • *n* jómfrú *(f)*, hrein mey *(f)*, hreinn sveinn *(m)*
virus • *n* veira *(f)*
visa • *n* vegabréfsáritun
viscount • *n* vísigreifi *(m)*
visit • *v* heimsækja
vitamin • *n* vítamín *(n)*, fjörefni *(n)*
vocabulary • *n* orðaforði *(m)*
vocation • *n* köllun *(f)*
vodka • *n* vodka *(f)*
vogue • *n* tíska *(f)*, æði *(n)*
voice • *n* rödd *(f)*, málrómur *(m)*, rómur *(m)*, raust *(f)*
voiced • *adj* raddaður
voiceless • *adj* raddlaus, óraddaður
volcano • *n* eldfjall *(n)*, eldstöð
volleyball • *n* blak *(n)*, blakbolti *(m)*
volt • *n* volt
voltage • *n* rafspenna *(f)*, spenna *(f)*
vomit • *v* æla, gubba, spúa, spýja, kasta upp
vortex • *n* hringiða *(f)*
vote • *v* kjósa
vow • *v* strengja heit
vowel • *n* sérhljóð *(n)*, sérhljóði *(m)*
vulture • *n* gæsagammur, hrægammur *(m)*, gammur *(m)*
vulva • *n* píka, kvensköp, sköp

W

waffle • *n* vaffla *(f)*, bull *(n)*, þvaður *(n)*
wage • *n* laun • *v* heyja stríð, heyja
wail • *n* æpa
waist • *n* mitti *(n)*
waistcoat • *n* vesti *(n)*
wait • *v* bíða
waiter • *n* þjónn *(m)*
wake • *n* kjölfar *(n)*, slóð *(f)*
walk • *v* ganga, labba
wall • *v* múra • *n* múr *(m)*, veggur *(m)*
wallet • *n* veski *(n)*, seðlaveski *(n)*, budda *(f)*
wallflower • *n* gulltoppur *(m)*, veggjaskraut *(n)*, bekkjarrós *(f)*
walnut • *n* valhneta *(f)*
walrus • *n* rostungur *(m)*
wan • *adj* fölur
wandering • *n* vapp
want • *v* vilja
wanted • *adj* eftirlýstur

war • *n* stríð *(n)*, styrjöld *(f)*
warehouse • *n* vöruhús *(n)*, lager *(m)*, pakkhús *(n)*, skemma *(f)*
warn • *v* aðvara
warning • *n* viðvörun *(f)*, aðvörun *(f)*, varnaðarorð *(n)*
wart • *n* varta *(f)*
warthog • *n* vörtusvín *(n)*
wash • *v* þvo
wasp • *n* geitungur *(m)*
watch • *n* úr *(m)*
water • *n* vatn *(n)*
waterfall • *n* foss *(m)*
waterproof • *adj* vatnsheldur
watershed • *n* vatnaskil *(n)*
watt • *n* vatt
wax • *n* vax *(n)*
way • *n* vegur *(m)*
we • *pron* við
weak • *adj* veikur

weapon • *n* vopn *(n)*
weather • *n* veður *(n)*
weave • *v* vefa
weaver • *n* vefari *(m)*
wedding • *n* gifting *(f)*
weed • *n* illgresi *(n)*, gras *(n)*
week • *n* vika *(f)*
weekend • *n* helgi *(f)*
weep • *v* gráta
weigh • *v* vega
weird • *adj* skrýtinn *(m)*, skrýtin *(f)*, skrýtið *(n)*, kynlegur *(m)*
welcome • *interj* velkominn, velkomin, velkomnir, velkomnar
well • *interj* jæja • *n* brunnur *(m)*, borhola *(f)*
werewolf • *n* varúlfur
west • *n* vestur *(n)* • *adv* vestur
western • *n* vestri *(m)*
wet • *adj* votur, blautur
whale • *n* hvalur *(m)*
whaler • *n* hvalveiðimaður *(m)*, hvalveiðiskip *(n)*, hvalbátur *(m)*, hvalveiðibátur *(m)*, hvalskip *(n)*
what • *interj* ha? • *pron* hvað
wheat • *n* hveiti *(n)*
wheel • *n* hjól *(n)*
wheelbarrow • *n* hjólbörur
wheelchair • *n* hjólastóll *(m)*
when • *adv* hvenær • *interj* takk • *conj* þegar
whence • *adv* hvaðan
where • *adv* hvar • *conj* þar sem, þangað sem
whether • *conj* hvort
whey • *n* mysa *(f)*
whippersnapper • *n* oflátungur *(m)*, merkikerti *(n)*
whirl • *v* hvirfla
whiskey • *n* viskí
whisper • *v* hvísla, hvískra, pískra, pukra
whist • *n* vist *(f)*
white • *n* hvítur • *adj* hvítur
whither • *adv* hvert
who • *pron* hver *(f)*, hvert, hvað *(n)*, sem
whole • *adj* heild, heill
wholesale • *n* heildsala *(f)*, heildverslun *(f)*
whore • *n* hóra
why • *n* ástæða • *adv* af hverju, hví • *interj* nú
wick • *n* kveikur *(m)*
wide • *adj* breiður, víður
widow • *n* ekkja *(f)*
wife • *n* eiginkona *(f)*, kona *(f)*
wig • *n* hárkolla *(f)*
wilderness • *n* óbyggðir *(f)*

willow • *n* víðir *(m)*
wilt • *v* fölna
winch • *n* vinda *(f)*
wind • *n* vindur *(m)* • *v* vinda
windmill • *n* vindmylla *(f)*
window • *n* gluggi *(m)*
windshield • *n* framrúða *(f)*
wine • *n* vín *(n)*, víndrykkur *(m)*, vín-rauður
wineskin • *n* vínbelgur *(m)*
wing • *n* vængur *(m)*, vængur, álma
wingspan • *n* vænghaf *(n)*
wink • *v* blikka • *n* blikk *(n)*
winter • *n* vetur *(m)*
wire • *n* vír *(m)*
wisdom • *n* viska *(f)*, vísdómur *(m)*
wisent • *n* evrópskur vísundur *(m)*
wish • *v* óska • *n* ósk *(f)*
wistful • *adj* angurvær, löngunarfullur *(m)*
witch • *n* norn *(f)*
with • *prep* með
without • *prep* án
wizard • *n* galdramaður *(m)*, galdrakarl *(m)*, töframaður *(m)*, vitki *(m)*
wok • *n* wok-panna *(f)*
wolf • *n* úlfur *(m)*
wolverine • *n* jarfi *(m)*
woman • *n* kona *(f)*, kvenmaður *(m)*
womanizer • *n* kvennabósi *(m)*, flagari *(m)*, slarkari *(m)*
womb • *n* leg *(n)*, móðurlíf *(n)*
wonder • *v* undra • *n* undur *(n)*, snillingur *(m)*
wonderful • *adj* yndislegur *(m)*, dásamlegur *(m)*, undursamlegur *(m)*
woodpecker • *n* spæta *(f)*
woodwind • *n* tréblásturshljóðfæri *(n)* • *adj* tréblásturshljóðfæra, tréblásara
woof • *v* voffa • *n* voff
wool • *n* ull
word • *v* orða • *n* orð *(n)*
work • *n* vinna *(f)* • *v* iðja, starfa, sýsla, vinna
worker • *n* starfsmaður *(m)*
workhorse • *n* klár *(m)*, víkingur til vinnu *(m)*, hamhleypa til vinnu *(m)*
workplace • *n* vinnustaður *(m)*
world • *n* veröld *(f)*, heimur *(m)*
worm • *n* maðkur *(m)*, ormur
wound • *v* særa, meiða • *n* sár *(n)*
wow • *interj* vá
wren • *n* músarindill
wrinkle • *n* hrukka *(f)*, korpa *(f)*
wrist • *n* úlnliður *(m)*
wristwatch • *n* armbandsúr *(n)*, úr *(n)*
write • *v* skrifa, rita, rithöfundur

writer • *n* rithöfundur *(m)*
wrong • *v* gera rangt til, beita ranglæti
• *adj* rangur, óréttur, hafa rangt fyrir sér,
hafa á röngu að standa, ranglátur, siðfer-

ðilega rangur, ósiðlegur, ósiðsamur, vera
að • *adv* rangt, vitlaust, kolvitlaust

X

xenon • *n* xenon
xenophobia • *n* útlendingahatur

xylophone • *n* sílófónn *(m)*

Y

yacht • *n* snekkja *(f)*
yak • *n* jakuxi *(m)*
yarn • *n* garn *(n)*
yawn • *v* geispa, gapa • *n* geispi *(m)*
yay • *interj* jei, vei
yeah • *adv* já
year • *n* ár
yearly • *adj* árlegur, árviss
yeast • *n* ger *(n)*
yell • *v* hrópa, öskra, gala
yellow • *v* gulna • *n* gulur *(m)* • *adj* gulur,
huglaus
yen • *n* jen *(n)*
yesterday • *n* gærdagur, gærdagurinn,

gærdagur *(m)* • *adv* í gær
yodel • *v* jóðla
yogurt • *n* jógúrt
yolk • *n* eggjarauða *(f)*, eggjablómi *(m)*
yonder • *adv* þarna
yore • *n* fyrir, langt
you • *pron* ykkur, þig, yður, þið, þú, þér,
maður, mann
young • *adj* ungur
yours • *pron* þinn, ykkar
ytterbium • *n* ytterbín
yttrium • *n* yttrín
yuck • *interj* oj

Z

zebra • *n* sebrahestur *(m)*
zee • *n* zeð *((zeth))*
zeitgeist • *n* tíðarandi *(m)*
zero • *n* núllstöð *(f)*
zinc • *n* sink

zirconium • *n* sirkon
zither • *n* sítar *(m)*
zombie • *n* uppvakningur *(m)*
zoo • *n* dýragarður *(m)*

ICELANDIC-ENGLISH

A

á • *v* listen, shit • *n* river
ábatasamur • *adj* lucrative
abbadís • *n* abbess
ábending • *n* advice • *adj* demonstrative
ábóti • *n* abbot
að • *v* shit
aðal- • *adj* cardinal
aðalatriði • *n* gist
aðalbláber • *n* bilberry
aðallega • *adv* primarily
aðalsmaður • *n* gentleman
áðan • *adv* just
aðdáanlegur • *adj* admirable
adenín • *n* adenine
aðfella • *n* asymptote
aðferð • *n* method
aðflutningur • *n* immigration
aðgætinn • *adj* provident
aðgangsorð • *n* password
aðgerð • *n* operation
aðhvarf • *n* regression
aðkilinn • *adj* separate
aðlægur • *adj* contiguous
aðleiðsla • *n* induction
aðmíráll • *n* admiral
aðskeyti • *n* affix
aðskotadýr • *n* interloper
aðstoð • *n* assistance, help • *adj* assistant
aðstoðarmaður • *n* assistant
áður • *prep* before • *adv* previously
aðvara • *v* warn
aðvörun • *n* warning
æ • *n* ash
æð • *n* vein
æðakölkun • *n* arteriosclerosis
æðardúnn • *n* eiderdown
æðarfugl • *n* eider
æðasamdráttur • *n* vasoconstriction
æðasláttur • *n* pulse
æðaþrenging • *n* vasoconstriction
æðaþrengir • *n* vasoconstrictor
æðaþrengjandi • *n* vasoconstrictor
æði • *n* vogue
æðstur • *adj* supreme
æður • *n* eider
æfing • *n* etude, study
ægir • *n* ocean, sea
æla • *v* vomit
æpa • *v* shout • *n* wail
ær • *n* ewe • *adj* mad
ærlsaleikur • *n* farce
ærumeiðandi • *adj* defamatory
æruverðugur • *adj* venerable
æsa • *v* excite

æsifregn • *n* bombshell
æsifréttablað • *n* tabloid
æsifréttaefni • *n* bombshell
æstur • *adj* hysterical
æta • *v* corrode
æti • *n* grub
ætiþistill • *n* artichoke
ætla • *v* mean, plan, purpose
ætt • *n* family
ættbálkur • *n* order
ættfræði • *n* genealogy
ættingi • *n* family, relative
ættingjar • *n* family
ættjarðarvinur • *n* patriot
ættkvísl • *n* tribe
ættland • *n* fatherland
ættmenni • *n* kin
ævintýri • *n* adventure
æxlafræði • *n* oncology
æxli • *n* tumor
af • *v* consist
afæta • *n* parasite
áfangastaður • *n* destination
áfangi • *n* leg
afar • *adv* very
afbrot • *n* transgression
áfengi • *n* alcohol
afgangur • *n* rest
afgreiðsluborð • *n* counter
afhending • *n* presentation
afhýða • *v* decorticate, husk
afi • *n* grandfather
áfir • *n* buttermilk
afklæðast • *v* strip
afkomandi • *n* descendant, progeny
afkvæmi • *n* family, progeny
áflæði • *n* transgression
aflagssögn • *n* deponent
aflát • *n* intermission
afleiðing • *n* consequence
áflog • *n* brawl
afmæli • *n* anniversary
afmælisdagur • *n* birthday
afmeyja • *v* deflower
afnotaréttur • *n* usufruct
afplánunartími • *n* time
afrit • *n* backup
afsakandi • *adj* apologetic
afsakanlegur • *adj* venial
afsakið • *interj* sorry
afskurður • *n* cut
afsláttur • *n* discount
afsprengi • *n* progeny
afsteypumót • *n* matrix

afstýra • *v* avert
aftann • *n* evening
aftur • *adv* again
afturbataskeið • *n* convalescence
afturbati • *n* convalescence
afturbeygður • *adj* reflexive
afturbeyging • *n* reflexivity
afturelding • *n* dawn
afturendi • *n* butt
afturhaldssamur • *adj* reactionary
afturhaldsseggur • *n* reactionary
afturhluti • *n* back
afturstefni • *n* sternpost
afvopna • *v* disarm
ágætlega • *adv* outstandingly
agat • *n* agate
ágerast • *v* increase
agúrka • *n* cucumber
áhersla • *n* accent, stress
áhlaup • *n* assault
áhrif • *n* influence
áhugalaus • *adj* apathetic
áhugaleysi • *n* apathy
áhugasamur • *adj* interested
áhugasvið • *n* bailiwick
áhyggja • *n* anxiety
áhyggjulaus • *adj* carefree, careless
áhyggjur • *v* sweat
aka • *v* drive
akademía • *n* academy
ákafi • *n* enthusiasm, passion
ákaflega • *adv* very
ákafur • *adj* vehement
akarn • *n* acorn
ákavíti • *n* aquavit
akkeri • *n* anchor
aktín • *n* actinium
akur • *n* field
akurhæna • *n* partridge
ákveða • *n* determinant • *v* determine
ákveðni • *n* definiteness
ákvörðun • *adj* discretionary
alæta • *n* omnivore
álands- • *adj* inshore
alba • *n* alb
albúm • *n* album
aldin • *n* fruit
aldinbori • *n* cockchafer
aldrei • *adv* never
alfa • *n* alpha
alfræðiorðabók • *n* encyclopedia
álft • *n* swan
algildi • *n* modulus
algóriþmi • *n* algorithm
algrím • *n* algorithm
algyðistrúarmaður • *n* pantheist
alheimur • *n* cosmos, universe

aligæs • *n* goose
aliönd • *n* duck
álit • *n* opinion
aljafn • *adj* congruent
aljöfnuður • *n* congruence
áll • *n* eel
allrahanda • *n* allspice, pimiento
allstaðar • *adv* everywhere
allt • *pron* everything
alltaf • *adv* always
álma • *n* wing
almætti • *n* omnipotence
almáttugur • *adj* almighty, omnipotent
álmur • *n* elm
alnánd • *n* omnipresence
álög • *n* spell
alpahúfa • *n* beret
alræmdur • *adj* notorious
altalandi • *adj* fluent
altan • *n* balcony
altari • *n* altar
alþjóðavæðing • *n* internationalization
alþjóðlegur • *adj* international
alúðlegur • *adj* cordial
alur • *n* awl
alvarlegur • *adj* serious
alviska • *n* omniscience
alvitur • *adj* omniscient
ámælisverður • *adj* reprehensible
ambassadör • *n* ambassador
amen • *adv* amen
ameríkín • *n* americium
amfetamín • *n* amphetamine
amma • *n* grandmother
amper • *n* ampere
án • *prep* without
ánamaðkur • *n* earthworm
ananas • *n* pineapple
anda • *v* breathe
andagagg • *n* quack
andarungi • *n* duckling
andasæring • *n* necromancy
andasæringamaður • *n* necromancer
andast • *v* die
anddyri • *n* vestibule
andeind • *n* antiparticle
andfélagslegur • *adj* antisocial
andfýla • *n* halitosis
andheiti • *n* antonym
andhistamín • *n* antihistamine
andhverfing • *n* converse
andi • *n* ethos
andl. • *n* object
andlag • *n* object
andlangur • *n* firmament
andlegur • *adj* platonic
andlit • *n* countenance, face

andlitsvatn • *n* toner
andmæli • *n* objection
andnifteind • *n* antineutron
andop • *n* spiracle
andræðni • *n* antonymy
andremma • *n* halitosis
andri • *n* ski
andrógen • *n* androgen
andróteind • *n* antiproton
andskotans • *interj* shit
andskoti • *n* devil
andskotinn • *n* devil • *interj* fuck
andstæðingur • *n* adversary, opponent
andstyggilegur • *adj* vile
andúð • *n* antipathy
andvaka • *n* insomnia
andvanafæddur • *adj* stillborn
andvarp • *n* sob
andvarpa • *v* sob
anekdóta • *n* anecdote
anekdótískur • *adj* anecdotal
angarögn • *n* jot
angist • *n* anxiety
angra • *v* bother
angurvær • *adj* wistful
anime • *n* anime
annar • *adj* second
annögl • *n* hangnail
ans • *n* answer
ansa • *v* answer
ansi • *adj* ruddy
Antíkristur • *n* antichrist
antímon • *n* antimony
apabrauðstré • *n* baobab
api • *n* ape, monkey
apókrýfur • *adj* apocryphal
apótek • *n* pharmacy
apótekari • *n* pharmacist
appelsína • *n* orange
appelsínugulur • *n* orange • *adj* orange
apríkósa • *n* apricot
ár • *n* oar, year
aragrúi • *n* myriad
árangur • *n* success
árásarmaður • *n* assailant
árbakki • *n* bank
árbítur • *n* breakfast
arðbær • *adj* lucrative
árdegi • *n* forenoon
arðsamur • *adj* lucrative
árekstur • *n* collision
arfgerð • *n* genotype
arfi • *n* chickweed
arfleiða • *v* bequeath
árgangur • *n* class
argon • *n* argon
ári • *n* devil

arinn • *n* fireplace
árita • *v* autograph
arka • *v* plod
arkitekt • *n* architect
árlegur • *adj* yearly
armband • *n* bracelet
armbandsúr • *n* wristwatch
armstjóri • *n* actuator
armsveiflun • *n* brachiation
armur • *n* arm
ármynni • *n* estuary
áróður • *n* propaganda
árós • *n* estuary
arsen • *n* arsenic
árstíð • *n* season
árþúsund • *n* millennium
ártíð • *n* anniversary
árviss • *adj* yearly
ás • *n* axis
ásaka • *adj* accusative
asetón • *n* acetone
asetýlen • *n* acetylene
aska • *n* ash
asni • *n* ass, asshole, donkey, idiot
aspas • *n* asparagus
ást • *n* love
ástæða • *n* why
ástæðulaus • *adj* unwarranted
ástalyf • *n* aphrodisiac
ástand • *n* state
astat • *n* astatine
ástkær • *adj* darling
ástvinamissir • *n* bereavement
atburður • *n* event
atferlisfræði • *n* ethology
atgeir • *n* halberd
athöfn • *n* ceremony
athugasemd • *n* comment
athugun • *n* study
athvarf • *n* shelter
athyglisverður • *adj* interesting
atkvæði • *adj* sesquipedalian • *n* syllable
atkvæðisréttur • *n* suffrage
atlaga • *n* squib
atóm • *n* atom
atóm- • *adj* nuclear
atómkjarni • *n* nucleus
atómsprengju- • *adj* nuclear
atriðaskrá • *n* index
átt • *n* direction
áttaviti • *n* compass
átthyrningur • *n* octagon
áttund • *n* octave, octet
áttundapartsnóta • *n* quaver
áttundi • *adj* eighth
áttundipartur • *n* quaver
átudrep • *n* gangrene

átvagl • *n* glutton
atvik • *n* event
atviksorð • *n* adverb
atvikssaga • *n* anecdote
atvikssögulegur • *adj* anecdotal
atvinna • *n* profession
atvinnulaus • *adj* unemployed
atvinnuleysi • *n* unemployment
atvinnuleysisbætur • *n* dole
atvinnulif • *n* economy
auðmýking • *n* abasement
auðmýkja • *v* abase
auðmýkt • *n* humility
auðna • *n* fortune
auðtrúa • *adj* gullible
auður • *adj* clean • *n* fortune
auðvaldsskipulag • *n* capitalism
auðvelt • *adj* easy
auga • *n* eye, eyeball
augablik • *n* minute
augabrún • *n* eyebrow
augljós • *adj* trivial
auglýsing • *n* advertisement
augnablik • *adj* fleeting • *n* moment
augnalaus • *adj* eyeless
augnaþrymill • *n* chalazion

augnblettur • *n* eyespot
augndíll • *n* eyespot
augngrugg • *n* floater
augnhár • *n* eyelash
augnknöttur • *n* eyeball
augnlækningar • *n* ophthalmology
augnlæknir • *n* ophthalmologist
augnlok • *n* eyelid
auk • *conj* plus
auka • *v* increase
auka- • *adj* extra
aukaafurð • *n* by-product
aukafyrirsögn • *n* subtitle
aukahringur • *n* epicycle
aukasól • *n* parhelion
ausa • *v* ladle • *n* ladle
austur • *n* east
ávarp • *n* speech
ávarpa • *v* talk
ávísun • *n* cheque
ávíta • *v* reprimand, scold
ávítur • *n* reproof
ávöxtur • *n* fruit
axla • *v* shoulder

B

babl • *n* babble
babla • *v* babble
bað • *n* bathe
baða • *v* bath, bathe
baðherbergi • *n* bathroom, toilet
baðkar • *n* bathtub
baðker • *n* bathtub
badminton • *n* badminton
baðsloppur • *n* bathrobe
baðstofa • *n* sauna
bæ • *interj* bye, goodbye
bæjar- • *adj* municipal
bæjarfélag • *n* township
bæjarstjóri • *n* mayor
bæki • *n* buckwheat
bækistöðvar • *n* base
bæklingur • *n* booklet, brochure
bæna • *v* pray
bænarstaður • *n* intercession
bær • *n* farm, stead, town
bæti • *n* byte
bætur • *n* recompense
bagall • *n* crosier
bak • *n* back, backside
baka • *v* bake • *n* pie
bakarí • *n* bakery

bakari • *n* baker
bakborði • *n* larboard
bakfjalir • *n* backboard
bakflæði • *n* reflux
bakgrunnur • *n* backdrop
bakhandar- • *adj* backhanded
bakhandarhögg • *n* backhand
bakhengi • *n* backdrop
bakhlið • *n* back, backside
bakkelsi • *n* pastry
bakki • *n* bank, shore
baknaga • *v* backbite
bakpoki • *n* backpack
bakrauf • *n* anus
bakskaut • *n* cathode
baksnúningur • *n* backspin
bakstur • *v* foment
baksvið • *n* backdrop, backstage
baksviðs • *adv* backstage
baktería • *n* bacillus
bakteríueyðir • *n* bactericide
bakteríur • *n* bacteria
bakteríuveira • *n* bacteriophage
baktjald • *n* backdrop
bakverkur • *n* backache
bál • *n* blaze, bonfire, conflagration, fire

baldýra • *v* embroider
ballett • *n* ballet
ballettdansmær • *n* ballerina
bana • *v* slay
banabiti • *n* undoing
banani • *n* banana
band • *n* ligament, string, tie
bandalag • *n* coalition
bandalag • *n* alliance
bandbreidd • *n* bandwidth
bandingi • *n* prisoner
bandormur • *n* tapeworm
bandstrik • *n* hyphen
bang • *n* bang
banga • *v* bang, pound
bankaútibú • *n* bank
banki • *n* bank
banna • *v* ban, forbid
bannfæring • *n* excommunication
bar • *n* bar
barátta • *n* battle
barbari • *n* barbarian
bardagafús • *adj* bellicose
bardagi • *n* battle, brawl, fight
barín • *n* barium
barkabólga • *n* laryngitis
barkakýli • *n* larynx
barkakýlisbólga • *n* laryngitis
barkakýliskvef • *n* laryngitis
barkakýlislok • *n* epiglottis
barkalok • *n* epiglottis
barksteri • *n* corticosteroid
barkur • *n* bark
barmmerki • *n* button
barmur • *n* bosom
barn • *n* child, kid
barnæska • *n* childhood
barnakennari • *n* pedagogue
barnalegur • *adj* babyish
barnapía • *n* babysitter
barnaskapur • *n* innocence
barnfóstra • *n* nurse
barningur • *n* percussion
barnshafandi • *adj* pregnant
barnsmorð • *n* infanticide
barnsmorðingi • *n* infanticide
barón • *n* baron
barónett • *n* baronet
barrtré • *n* conifer
barþjónn • *n* bartender
basalt • *n* basalt
basar • *n* bazaar
básúna • *n* trombone • *v* trumpet
bati • *n* convalescence
batterí • *n* battery
bátur • *n* boat
baud • *n* baud

baugur • *n* ring
bauja • *n* buoy
baul • *n* moo
baula • *n* barrel • *v* moo
baun • *n* bean, pea
bavían • *n* baboon
bavíana- • *adj* baboonish
bavíani • *n* baboon
bé • *n* bee
beðmi • *n* cellulose
beikon • *n* bacon
bein • *n* bone • *adj* right
beinaber • *adj* angular
beinabúr • *n* ossuary
beinahús • *n* ossuary
beinakerfið • *n* skeleton
beinaklefi • *n* ossuary
beinasni • *n* nincompoop
beingulur • *n* eggshell • *adj* eggshell
beinhvítur • *n* bone
beiningamaður • *n* beggar
beinn • *adj* right, roundabout, straight
beint • *adv* live • *adj* right
beinþynning • *n* osteoporosis
beiskjuefni • *n* alkaloid
beiskur • *adj* acid, bitter
bekkjarlalli • *n* underachiever
bekkjarrós • *n* wallflower
bekkur • *n* bench, class
belgaldin • *n* legume
belja • *n* cow
belti • *n* belt
beltisdýr • *n* armadillo
bendifingur • *n* forefinger
bendill • *n* cursor
bendir • *n* cursor, pointer
bensen • *n* benzene
bensín • *n* gasoline
bensól • *n* benzene
ber • *n* berry • *adj* naked
bera • *v* carry
berfættur • *adv* barefoot • *adj* discalced
berg • *n* cliff
bergja • *v* sip
bergkvika • *n* magma
bergmál • *n* echo
beri • *n* bearer
berja • *v* drum
berjast • *v* brawl, fight
berkelín • *n* berkelium
berklar • *n* tuberculosis
beryllín • *n* beryllium
bestur • *adj* best
betlari • *n* beggar
betri • *adj* better
betur • *adv* better
beyging • *n* declension, inflection

beygingardæmi • *n* paradigm
beygja • *v* bend, bow, turn
beygjanlegur • *adj* bendable
beygur • *n* fear
beyki • *n* beech
bíða • *v* await, wait
biðfæra • *v* spool
biðja • *v* pray
biðlari • *n* client
biðminni • *n* buffer
biðröð • *n* queue
biðtími • *n* latency
bifreið • *n* automobile, car
bifur • *n* beaver
bikar • *n* calyx, goblet
bikarblað • *n* sepal
bikkja • *n* nag
bílalest • *n* convoy, motorcade
bíll • *n* car
bílskúr • *n* garage
bílstjóri • *n* chauffeur, driver
binda • *v* bind
bindi • *n* necktie, tome
bíó • *n* cinema
bíómynd • *n* movie
bíótít • *n* biotite
birki • *n* birch
birkitré • *n* birch
birta • *v* appear
birtast • *v* appear
bísamrotta • *n* muskrat
biskup • *n* bishop
biskupsdæmi • *n* diocese
biskupskápa • *n* cope
biskupsstafur • *n* crosier
bismút • *n* bismuth
bíta • *v* bite
bitakort • *n* bitmap
biti • *n* baud, bit
bitmúli • *n* muzzle
bjálki • *n* beam
bjalla • *n* beetle, bell
bjáni • *n* fool
bjarg • *n* cliff
bjarga • *v* save
bjarnarber • *n* bramble
bjart • *adj* bright, light
bjartur • *adj* bright, light
bjóða • *v* invite
bjór • *n* beaver, beer, pediment
björgunarbátur • *n* lifeboat
björk • *n* birch
bjórkrús • *n* beer
björn • *n* bear
björt • *adj* bright, light
bjúgaldin • *n* banana
bláber • *n* blueberry

blað • *n* blade, lobe
blaðadrengur • *n* paperboy
blaðamaður • *n* journalist
blaðamennska • *n* journalism
blaðberi • *n* paperboy
blaðburðardrengur • *n* paperboy
blaðgræna • *n* chlorophyll
blaðlaukur • *n* leek
blaðlús • *n* aphid
blaðra • *v* babble • *n* balloon
blaðsíða • *n* side
blæða • *v* bleed
blæðingar • *n* menstruation
blævængur • *n* fan
bláhrafn • *n* rook
blak • *n* volleyball
blakbolti • *n* volleyball
blámaður • *n* spade
blandari • *n* blender
blár • *n* blue • *adj* blue
blásturshola • *n* blowhole, spiracle
blástursop • *n* blowhole, spiracle
blautur • *adj* wet
bleia • *n* diaper
bleikur • *adj* pink
blek • *n* ink
blekbytta • *n* inkwell
blekfiskur • *n* cuttlefish
blekking • *n* deception
blekkja • *v* befool, deceive
bless • *interj* goodbye
blessa • *v* bless
blettatígur • *n* cheetah
blettur • *n* plot
bleyða • *n* craven
bleyði • *n* cowardice
bleyja • *n* diaper
bleytukafald • *n* sleet
blíða • *n* gentleness
blika • *n* cirrostratus
blikk • *n* wink
blikka • *v* wink
blikufjaðrir • *n* cirrus
blikutrefjar • *n* cirrus
blindraletur • *n* braille
blindur • *adj* blind
blóð • *n* blood
blóðbað • *n* bloodbath
blóðeitrun • *n* sepsis
blóðhefnd • *n* vendetta
blóðkökkur • *n* thrombus
blóðlaus • *adj* anemic
blóðleysi • *n* anemia
blóðlýsa • *n* leukemia
blóðmaur • *n* tick
blóðmör • *n* pudding
blóðnasir • *n* nosebleed

blóðrauða • *n* hemoglobin
blóðrek • *n* embolism
blóðreki • *n* embolus
blöðrubólga • *n* cystitis
blöðruhálskirtill • *n* prostate
blóðskortur • *n* anemia
blóðsuga • *n* leech
blóðsýking • *n* sepsis
blóðsykursekla • *n* hypoglycemia
blóðsykurshækkun • *n* hyperglycemia
blóðsykurskortur • *n* hypoglycemia
blóðsykurslækkun • *n* hypoglycemia
blóðug • *adj* bloody
blóðvökvi • *n* plasma
blokkflauta • *n* recorder
blóm • *n* flower
blómaframleiðslu • *n* floriculture
blómkál • *n* cauliflower
blómstra • *v* flourish, flower
blómsveigur • *n* festoon
blómvöndur • *n* bouquet, nosegay, posy
blóraböggull • *n* scapegoat
blossandi • *adj* red-hot
blóta • *v* curse, swear
blý • *n* lead
blýantur • *n* pencil
blylaust • *adj* unleaded
blysbjalla • *n* firefly
bö • *interj* boo
bobblingar • *n* jug
bobblingur • *n* breast, jug
boð • *n* invite
boðberi • *n* harbinger, messenger
boðflenna • *n* interloper
boðhlaup • *n* relay
boðorð • *n* commandment
boðskapur • *n* message
böðull • *n* executioner
bofs • *n* bark
bofsa • *v* bark
bogastrengur • *n* bowstring
böggull • *n* package
bogi • *n* bow
bogmaður • *n* archer
bogna • *v* bow
boguggi • *n* bowfin
bógur • *n* bow
bók • *n* book
bókabúð • *n* bookshop
bókaherbergi • *n* study
bókahús • *n* library
bókahylla • *n* bookshelf
bókarauki • *n* appendix
bókasafn • *n* library
bókastoð • *n* bookend
bókaverslun • *n* bookshop
bókfinka • *n* chaffinch

bókhlaða • *n* library
bókhveiti • *n* buckwheat
bókmenntir • *n* literature
bóknám • *n* study
bókrolla • *n* scroll
bókstaflegur • *adj* literal
bókstafur • *n* letter
bóla • *n* pimple
bolbrynja • *n* cuirass
bólga • *n* inflammation
bolli • *n* cup
böllur • *n* scrotum
bölsýnn • *adj* pessimistic
bolti • *n* ball
bölva • *v* curse
bölvaður • *adj* ruddy
bolverk • *n* bulwark
bolvirki • *n* bulwark
bölvun • *n* curse
bóma • *n* jib
bóndalegur • *adj* bucolic
bóndi • *n* farmer, peasant
bongótromma • *n* bongo
bónus • *n* bonus
bór • *n* boron
bor • *n* drill
bora • *v* bore
borð • *n* level, table
borða • *v* eat
borðdúkur • *n* tablecloth
borði • *n* banner
borðtölva • *n* desktop
borg • *n* castle, city
borga • *v* pay
borgar- • *adj* municipal
borgari • *n* citizen
borgarísjaki • *n* iceberg
borgarstjóri • *n* mayor
borhola • *n* well
börkur • *n* bark
bot • *n* baud
botn • *n* bottom
botnfall • *n* dregs, lees, sediment
botnlag • *n* sediment
botnlangabólga • *n* appendicitis
botnlanganám • *n* appendectomy
botnlangaskurður • *n* appendectomy
botnlangatota • *n* appendix
botnlangi • *n* appendix
botnristill • *n* caecum
box • *n* box
brá • *n* eyelid
bráð • *n* prey
bráðræði • *n* precipitation
bráðum • *adv* soon
bræta • *n* altercation
bragð • *n* taste

bragða • _v_ taste
bragðast • _v_ taste
bragðgóður • _adj_ delicious
bragðskyn • _n_ gustation • _adj_ gustatory
bragfræði • _n_ prosody
bragliður • _n_ foot
brandari • _n_ funny, joke
brandur • _n_ gangrene
brasa • _v_ solder
brasmálmur • _n_ solder
brátt • _adv_ soon, suddenly
brauð • _n_ bread, loaf
brauðmylsna • _v_ bread • _n_ breadcrumb
brauðrist • _n_ toaster
braut • _n_ strip
bréf • _n_ letter, missive
bréfspjald • _n_ postcard
bregða • _v_ brandish
breiðger • _adj_ hyperbolic
breiðnefur • _n_ platypus
breiðstræti • _n_ avenue
breiður • _adj_ wide
brekka • _n_ hill
brenna • _v_ burn, singe
brennisteinn • _n_ sulfur
brennuvargur • _n_ pyromaniac
breytast • _v_ change
bridds • _n_ bridge
brigsl • _n_ taunt
brigsla • _v_ taunt
brim • _n_ surf
bringa • _n_ breast, chest
bringubein • _adj_ sternal
bringusund • _n_ breaststroke
bris • _n_ pancreas
briskirtill • _n_ pancreas
brjálæðingur • _n_ lunatic
brjósk • _n_ cartilage
brjóst • _n_ breast, thorax
brjóstahaldari • _n_ bra
brjósthol • _n_ thorax
brjóstkassi • _n_ thorax
brjóstmynd • _n_ bust
brjóstnám • _n_ mastectomy
brjóstrið • _n_ balustrade
brjóstriðssúla • _n_ baluster, banister, bannister
brjóstsviði • _n_ heartburn
brjóstvarta • _n_ nipple
broddgöltur • _n_ hedgehog
broddkúmen • _n_ cumin
broddmjólk • _n_ colostrum
broddur • _n_ colostrum, quill, stinger, stubble
bródera • _v_ embroider
bróðir • _n_ brother
bróðurdóttir • _n_ niece

bróðursonur • _n_ nephew
brokk • _n_ trot
brokka • _v_ trot
bróm • _n_ bromine
brómber • _n_ blackberry, bramble
bros • _n_ smile
brosa • _v_ smile
brot • _n_ crease, excerpt, transgression • _adj_ fractional
brothætt • _adj_ brittle
brotinn • _adj_ cracked, fractional
brottfall • _n_ apocope, elision, syncope
brottför • _n_ departure
brottnám • _n_ mastectomy
brú • _n_ bridge
brúða • _n_ doll, puppet
brúðgumi • _n_ bridegroom
brúðkaupsafmæli • _n_ anniversary
brúðkaupsferð • _n_ honeymoon
brúður • _n_ bride
brugg • _n_ scheme
bruggari • _n_ brewer
brundur • _n_ semen
brúnn • _n_ brown • _adj_ brown
brunnur • _n_ well
brydding • _n_ hem
bryðja • _v_ crunch
bryggja • _n_ pier
bryntröll • _n_ halberd
bú • _interj_ boo
búa • _v_ live
búð • _n_ shop
búðarborð • _n_ counter
búðarþjófur • _n_ shoplifter
budda • _n_ wallet
búðingur • _n_ pudding
búfé • _n_ livestock
búferlum • _v_ move
buffall • _n_ buffalo
bugast • _v_ bow
bugt • _n_ bay
búinn • _adj_ over
búktal • _n_ ventriloquism
búktalari • _n_ ventriloquist
bull • _n_ bullshit, nonsense, waffle
bulla • _n_ piston
búr • _n_ cage
burður • _n_ burden
búretta • _n_ burette
burgeis • _n_ potentate
burkni • _n_ fern
bursta • _v_ cream
bursti • _n_ brush
bústaður • _n_ residence
bútan • _n_ butane
buxnaskálm • _n_ leg
buxur • _n_ pants

bý • *n* bee
býfluga • *n* bee
býflugnabú • *n* beehive
bygg • *n* barley
bygging • *n* building, edifice, structure
byggingarklossar • *n* brick
byggingarkubbar • *n* brick
byggingarlist • *n* architecture
byggja • *v* build
býkúpa • *n* beehive
bylta • *n* transpose
bylting • *n* revolution

byrði • *n* burden
byrja • *v* begin
byrjun • *n* beginning, inception, start
byrstur • *adj* brusque
byssa • *n* gun
byssuhlaup • *n* barrel
byssukjaftur • *n* muzzle
byssukúla • *n* bullet
byssupúður • *n* gunpowder
byssustingur • *n* bayonet
bývax • *n* beeswax

C

campa • *v* camp
cantaloup-melóna • *n* cantaloupe
capsæsín • *n* capsaicin

circa • *prep* circa

D

dá • *n* coma
dáð • *n* deed
daðla • *n* date
dægur • *adj* circadian
dægurlangur • *adj* ephemeral
dæla • *n* pump
dæmi • *n* example
dæmigerður • *adj* typical
dæmisaga • *n* fable
dafna • *v* flourish
daga • *v* dawn
dagatal • *n* calendar
dagblað • *n* newspaper
dagblaðapappír • *n* newspaper
dagbók • *n* diary
dagdýr • *adj* diurnal
daglegur • *adj* daily
dagrenning • *n* dawn
dagsetning • *n* date
dagur • *n* day
dáinn • *adj* dead
dalur • *n* dale, valley
dammtafl • *n* draughts
dammur • *n* draughts
dánarafmæli • *n* anniversary
dánardægur • *n* anniversary
dánarfregn • *n* necrology
dánarskrá • *n* necrology
dánartilkynning • *n* necrology
dans • *n* dance
dansa • *v* dance, shake
dansari • *n* dancer

dánu • *n* dead
dapur • *adj* sad
dáraaldin • *n* durian
dásamlegur • *adj* wonderful
dáti • *n* soldier
dauðadá • *n* coma
dauðafælni • *n* thanatophobia
dauði • *n* death
dauðlegur • *adj* mortal
dauður • *adj* dead
dauðvona • *adj* moribund
daufur • *adj* deaf
dé • *n* dee
deig • *n* dough
deigla • *n* crucible
deila • *n* altercation
deilanlegur • *adj* divisible
deildanlegur • *adj* differentiable
deildarfall • *n* partitive
deiling • *n* division
deilir • *n* divisor
deilistofn • *n* dividend
deiluaðili • *n* belligerent
deilugjarn • *adj* bellicose, belligerent
deilurit • *n* polemic
dekk • *n* tyre
dekka • *v* mark
dekkja • *v* darken
delta • *n* delta
demantur • *n* diamond
demba • *n* shower
dením • *n* denim

depill • *n* jot
deponenssögn • *n* deponent
detta • *v* drop, fall
deyfð • *n* phlegm
deyja • *v* die
diffranlegur • *adj* differentiable
digull • *n* crucible
díki • *n* ditch, moat
dikt • *n* poem
díler • *n* dealer
díll • *n* pixel
dimma • *n* darkness • *v* dusk
dimmur • *adj* dark
dindill • *n* tail
dingull • *n* pendulum, pituitary • *adj* pituitary
díóða • *n* diode
diskó • *n* disco
diskótek • *n* disco
diskur • *n* dish, disk, plate
djákni • *n* deacon
djass • *n* jazz
djöflaþýska • *n* gibberish
djöfull • *n* devil
djöfullinn • *n* devil • *interj* fuck
djöfullsins • *interj* shit
djöfulsins • *interj* fuck
djögl • *n* juggling
djúnka • *n* junk
djúprista • *n* draught
djúpt • *adv* deeply
djús • *n* juice
döðluplóma • *n* persimmon
dögg • *n* dew
dögun • *n* dawn, sunrise
dögurður • *n* breakfast
dökkna • *v* darken
dökkur • *adj* dark
doktor • *n* doctor
dómari • *n* judge
dómbær • *n* judge
dómkirkja • *n* cathedral
dómnefnd • *n* jury
dómstóll • *n* court
dónalegur • *adj* randy
dópisti • *n* user
dörslag • *n* colander
dós • *n* can
dóttir • *n* daughter
dótturdóttir • *n* granddaughter
dótturfyrirtæki • *n* subsidiary
draga • *v* cut
dráp • *n* kill
drasl • *n* junk, litter
dráttarbátur • *n* tugboat
dráttarvél • *n* tractor
dráttur • *n* fuck

draumkenndur • *adj* dreamy
draumsóley • *n* poppy
draumur • *n* dream
dreggjar • *n* dregs, lees, sediment
dreifa • *v* distribute
dreifinn • *adj* distributive
dreifkjörnungur • *n* prokaryote
dreki • *n* dragon
drekka • *v* drink
drengur • *n* boy
drep • *n* necrosis
drepast • *v* die
dreyma • *v* dream
dreymandi • *adj* dreamy
dreyri • *n* gore
drit • *n* guano
drjóli • *n* dick
drolla • *n* queen
drómasýki • *n* narcolepsy
drómedari • *n* dromedary
dropi • *n* drop, droplet
drottna • *v* rule
drottning • *n* monarch, queen
drukkinn • *adj* drunk
drulla • *n* diarrhea
drungalegur • *adj* dreary
drykkjuskapur • *n* drunkenness
drykkur • *n* beverage, drink
dúdúfugl • *n* dodo
dúfa • *n* dove, pigeon
duft • *n* dust, powder
duftker • *n* urn
dugleysi • *n* sloth
dúkka • *n* doll
dúkönd • *n* canvasback
dularfullur • *adj* uncanny
dulinn • *adj* arcane
dulráða • *v* decipher
dulrit • *n* cipher
dulritunaraðferð • *n* cipher
dulritunarfræði • *n* cryptography
dumbrauður • *n* maroon • *adj* maroon
dúó • *n* duo
duttlungafullur • *adj* capricious
duttlungasamur • *adj* capricious
dvelja • *v* stay
dvergkráka • *n* jackdaw
dvergur • *n* dwarf
dvína • *v* dwindle
dvöl • *n* sojourn
dýflissa • *n* dungeon
dýna • *n* mattress
dyntóttur • *adj* capricious
dýr • *n* animal • *adj* dear, expensive • *v* muzzle
dyr • *n* door
dýragarður • *n* zoo

dýralæknir • *n* veterinarian
dýraríki • *n* fauna
dyrasölumaður • *n* solicitor
dýrasterkja • *n* glycogen
dyratré • *n* lintel
dýrka • *v* adore
dýrkun • *n* deification

dýrlingur • *n* saint
dýrmætur • *adj* precious
dýrslegur • *adj* animal
dýrt • *adj* dear
dysprósín • *n* dysprosium

E

eða • *conj* or
eðalsteinn • *n* stone
eðalvagn • *n* limousine
edik • *n* vinegar
eðjufiskur • *n* bowfin
eðla • *n* lizard
eðli • *n* nature
eðlisbreyting • *n* transubstantiation
eðlisbreytingarkenningin • *n* transubstantiation
eðlisfræðingur • *n* physicist
eðun • *n* disjunction
ef • *conj* if
efablandinn • *adj* hesitant
efahyggja • *n* skepticism
efalaus • *adj* indubitable
efalaust • *adv* undoubtedly
efasemd • *n* doubt
eflaust • *adv* undoubtedly
efnafræði • *n* chemistry
efnahagslíf • *n* economy
efnahagur • *n* finance
efnahvati • *n* catalyst
efnaskipti • *n* metabolism
efnatillífun • *n* chemosynthesis
efni • *n* subject
eftir • *prep* after, by, in • *v* listen
eftirfari • *n* successor
eftirför • *n* chase
eftirherma • *n* parrot
eftirköst • *n* repercussion
eftirlíking • *n* replica
eftirlýstur • *adj* wanted
eftirmæli • *n* epitaph
eftirmál • *n* repercussion
eftirmáli • *n* epilogue
eftirmiðdagur • *n* afternoon
eftirminnilegur • *adj* memorable
eftirmynd • *n* replica
eftirnafn • *n* surname
eftirréttur • *n* dessert
eftirsetning • *n* postposition
ég • *pron* me
egg • *n* blade, edge, egg, ovum
eggaldin • *n* eggplant

eggfruma • *n* egg, oocyte, ovum
egghylki • *n* cocoon
eggjablómi • *n* yolk
eggjahvíta • *n* albumen
eggjarauða • *n* yolk
eggjaskurn • *n* eggshell
eggjastokkur • *n* ovary
egglos • *n* ovulation
ei • *adv* not • *conj* not
eiði • *n* isthmus
eiður • *n* oath
eiga • *v* own
eigi • *adv* not • *conj* not
eigindlegur • *adj* qualitative
eiginhandaráritun • *n* autograph
eiginkona • *n* wife
eiginleiki • *n* property
eiginmaður • *n* husband
eign • *n* property
eignarfall • *n* genitive • *adj* genitive
eik • *n* oak
eikinn • *adj* oaken
eikitré • *n* oak
eilífð • *n* eternity
eilífur • *adj* eternal
eimbað • *n* sauna
einangrari • *n* insulator
einangri • *n* insulator
einangur • *n* insulator
eind • *n* unit
einelti • *n* bullying
einer • *n* juniper
eineygður • *adj* one-eyed
eineygur • *adj* one-eyed
einfaldlega • *adv* simply
einfaldur • *adj* easy, simple
einfeldningur • *n* nincompoop
eingerður • *adj* homogeneous
einglyrni • *n* monocle
eingyðistrú • *n* monotheism
einhalla • *adj* monotonic
einhalli • *n* monotony
einhjól • *n* unicycle
einhleyplingur • *n* bachelor
einhleypni • *n* bachelorhood**

einhliða • *adj* one-sided • *adv* unilaterally
einhver • *pron* somebody
einhverfa • *n* autism
einhyrningur • *n* unicorn
eining • *n* morpheme
einkabílstjóri • *n* chauffeur
einkamállýska • *n* idiolect
einkar • *adv* very
einkaþjónn • *n* manservant
einkirningasótt • *n* mononucleosis
einkvæður • *adj* monosyllabic
einkvæni • *adj* monogamous
einkvænis- • *adj* monogamous
einleitur • *adj* homogeneous
einliða • *n* monomer
einlífi • *n* bachelorhood
einlitna • *adj* haploid
einmálga • *adj* monolingual
einmana • *adj* lonely
einnig • *adv* also, moreover
einokunarhringur • *n* cartel
einræða • *n* soliloquy
einræði • *n* dictatorship
einræðiherra • *n* dictator
eins • *adj* congruent
einsátta • *adj* isotropic
einsemd • *n* solitude
einsetumaður • *n* hermit
einsetumunkur • *n* hermit
einshyrndur • *adj* similar
einslaga • *adj* similar
einslagaður • *adj* similar
einsleitur • *adj* homogeneous
einsmótun • *n* isomorphism
einsstaksmengi • *n* singleton
einstæðingsskapur • *n* bereavement
einstæður • *adj* monadic, unary
einsteinín • *n* einsteinium
einstökungur • *n* singleton
eintal • *n* soliloquy
eintala • *n* singular • *adj* singular
eintyngdur • *adj* monolingual
einvaldsherra • *n* monarch
einvaldur • *n* monarch
einvetni • *n* protium
eir • *n* copper
eirgræna • *n* verdigris
eistalyppa • *n* epididymis
eistnalyppa • *n* epididymis
eitilfruma • *n* lymphocyte
eitilfrumukrabbamein • *n* lymphoma
eitlaæxli • *n* lymphoma
eitlasótt • *n* mononucleosis
eitthvað • *pron* something
eitur • *n* poison
eiturlyf • *n* drug
eiturlyfjanotandi • *n* user

eiturlyfjasali • *n* dealer
ekkasog • *n* sob
ekkert • *pron* nothing
ekki • *adv* not • *interj* not • *conj* not • *n* sob
ekkja • *n* widow
él • *n* squall
elda • *v* cook
eldfælni • *n* pyrophobia
eldfjall • *n* volcano
eldflauga • *n* skyrocket
eldfluga • *n* firefly
eldheitur • *adj* red-hot
eldhús • *n* kitchen
elding • *n* lightning
eldiviður • *n* firewood
eldmóður • *n* enthusiasm
eldsneyti • *n* fuel
eldstæði • *n* fireplace
eldstöð • *n* volcano
eldsvoði • *n* blaze, conflagration
eldur • *n* fire
eldvarpa • *n* flamethrower
eldveggur • *n* firewall
elfting • *n* horsetail
elfur • *n* river
elgur • *n* moose
elri • *n* alder
elska • *n* love
elskan • *n* darling, honey
elta • *v* chase
en • *conj* but • *adv* how • *prep* than
endaþarmsop • *n* anus
endaþarmsstíll • *n* suppository
endurkast • *n* ricochet
endurkastast • *v* ricochet
endurómur • *n* echo
endurskoðandi • *n* accountant, auditor
endurtaka • *v* repeat
endurvísandi • *adj* anaphoric
engi • *n* meadow
engifer • *n* ginger
engill • *n* angel
enginn • *pron* none
engispretta • *n* grasshopper
enni • *n* forehead
ensímbót • *n* coenzyme
epli • *n* apple
epoxíð • *n* epoxy
epoxý- • *adj* epoxy
er • *conj* as • *v* is
erbín • *n* erbium
erfðafar • *n* genotype
erfðafræði • *n* genetics
erfðagervi • *n* genotype
erfðamengi • *n* genome
erfiður • *adj* difficult, hard

ergja • *v* bother
erki- • *adj* egregious
erkibiskup • *n* archbishop
erkiengill • *n* archangel
erkifjandi • *n* archenemy
erkihertogi • *n* archduke
erkióvinur • *n* archenemy
ermi • *n* sleeve
erótískur • *adj* erotic
errinn • *adj* bellicose
erta • *n* pea
espressó • *n* espresso
et. • *adj* singular
éta • *v* eat
eta • *v* eat • *n* eta
etja • *v* sic
etýða • *n* etude, study
evropín • *n* europium
ex • *n* ex

extra • *adj* extra
ey • *n* island
eyðilegging • *n* destruction
eyðileggja • *v* destroy
eyðimerkurliljuætt • *n* agave
eyðimörk • *n* desert
eyðing • *n* deletion
eyðingarlyf • *n* pesticide
eyðslukló • *n* prodigal, spendthrift
eyja • *n* island
eyjaklasi • *n* archipelago
eyjavaki • *n* insulin
eyland • *n* island
eyra • *n* ear
eyrna- • *adj* aural
eyrnalæknir • *n* aurist
eyrnalaus • *adj* earless
eyrnalokk • *n* earring

F

fábjáni • *n* nincompoop
fabrikka • *n* factory
fábrotinn • *adj* run-of-the-mill
faðir • *n* father
faðma • *v* hug
faðmlag • *n* hug
fæða • *v* feed
fæðast • *adj* nascent
fæði • *n* food, sustenance
fæðing • *n* birth
fæðingardagur • *n* birthday
fæðumauk • *n* chyme
fægiflötur • *n* facet
fær • *adj* proficient
færa • *v* bring, move
færsla • *n* map, mapping, record
fáfræði • *n* ignorance
fáfróður • *n* ignoramus
fag • *n* subject
faga • *n* bacteriophage
faggi • *n* fruit
fagnaðarlæti • *n* ovation
fagott • *n* bassoon
fagottleikari • *n* bassoonist
fagur • *adj* beautiful, fair, pulchritudinous
fagurblár • *n* azure
fagurfífill • *n* daisy
fagurfræði • *n* aesthetics
fákunnátta • *n* ignorance
falda • *v* hem
faldur • *n* hem
fálkaveiðar • *n* falconry

fálki • *n* falcon, gyrfalcon, kestrel
fall • *n* case, function
falla • *v* fall
fallbeyging • *n* declension
fallbyssa • *n* cannon, gun
fallegur • *adj* beautiful, pulchritudinous
fallhleri • *n* trapdoor
fallhlíf • *n* parachute
fallinn • *adj* fallen
fals- • *adj* quack, spurious
falsaður • *adj* spurious
falsari • *n* quack
falskur • *adj* bogus, spurious
falur • *n* halyard
fán • *n* faun
fána • *n* fauna
fangaklefi • *n* cell
fangelsa • *v* imprison, jug
fangelsi • *n* jug, prison
fangi • *n* prisoner
fáni • *n* flag, pennant
fara • *v* fare, go, part
faraldsfræði • *n* epidemiology
faraldur • *n* epidemic
faraldursfræði • *n* epidemiology
fáránlegur • *adj* preposterous
farartæki • *n* vehicle
farði • *n* makeup
fareind • *n* ion
farfi • *n* hue
farlama • *adj* decrepit
farmiði • *n* ticket
farrými • *n* class

farsi • *n* farce
farsótt • *n* epidemic
farsóttafræði • *n* epidemiology
farþegi • *n* passenger
farþjófur • *n* stowaway
farþröstur • *n* robin
fartölva • *n* laptop
fárviðri • *n* hurricane
fashani • *n* pheasant
fast • *adv* fast
fasta • *v* fast
fasteign • *n* property
fastheldinn • *adj* tenacious
fastland • *n* mainland
fastur • *adj* fast
fata • *n* bucket
fátækt • *n* poverty
fatafella • *n* stripper
fatnaður • *n* clothing, dress
fatta • *v* see
fávís • *n* ignoramus
fáviska • *n* ignorance
fáviti • *n* nincompoop
fax • *n* mane
fé • *n* money
fegra • *v* beautify
fegrunarheiti • *n* euphemism
fegurð • *n* beauty
feigur • *adj* fey
feiminn • *adj* shy
feitlaginn • *adj* corpulent
feitur • *adj* corpulent, fat
fela • *v* conceal
félag • *n* society
félagi • *n* companion, comrade, friend, member
félagsandi • *n* camaraderie
félagsmótun • *n* socialization
felast • *v* encompass
feldspat • *n* feldspar
feldur • *n* pelt
fell • *n* fell
fellibylur • *n* hurricane, typhoon
felling • *n* pleat
feminismi • *n* feminism
fenna • *v* snow
fennikka • *n* fennel
fer- • *adj* square
ferð • *n* journey, trip
ferðast • *v* fare, journey, travel
ferðatölva • *n* laptop
ferfætlingur • *n* quadruped
ferhliðungur • *n* quadrilateral
ferja • *n* ferry
ferjumaður • *n* ferryman
ferma • *v* confirm
fermín • *n* fermium

ferming • *n* confirmation
ferna • *n* carton
ferningslaga • *adj* square
ferningstala • *n* square
ferningur • *n* square
ferskja • *n* peach
ferskur • *adj* fresh
fertugasta • *adj* fortieth
festing • *n* firmament
fiðla • *n* fiddle, violin
fiðrildi • *n* butterfly
fiðurfé • *n* fowl
fífill • *n* dandelion
fífl • *n* ass, asshole, nincompoop
fíkja • *n* fig
fíkjutré • *n* ficus
fikta • *v* tamper
fílabein • *n* ivory
fílildi • *n* elephantiasis
fíll • *n* elephant
fimleikar • *n* gymnastics
fimmhyrningur • *n* pentagon
fimmta • *adj* fifth
fimmti • *adj* fifth
fimmtugasta • *adj* fiftieth
fingrafar • *n* fingerprint
fingur • *n* finger
fingurbjörg • *n* thimble
finna • *v* feel, find
finnast • *v* think
firma • *n* firm
físar • *n* bellows
fiseind • *n* neutrino
físibelgir • *n* bellows
físibelgur • *n* bellows
físir • *n* bellows
fiska • *v* fish
fiskifluga • *n* fly
fiskifræði • *n* ichthyology
fiskifræðingur • *n* ichthyologist
fiskur • *n* fish
fita • *n* fat
fitulítill • *adj* light
fitusækinn • *adj* lipophilic
fituskertur • *adj* light
fitusnauður • *adj* light
fjaðurpenni • *n* quill
fjaðurstafur • *n* quill
fjall • *n* fell, mountain
fjallageit • *n* ibex
fjandans • *interj* fuck, shit
fjandi • *n* devil
fjandinn • *n* devil • *interj* shit
fjárans • *adj* ruddy
fjárdráttur • *n* embezzlement
fjárfesting • *n* investment
fjárhagur • *n* finance

fjárhaldsmaður • *n* guardian, trustee
fjári • *n* devil • *adj* ruddy
fjárinn • *n* devil
fjárkúgun • *n* blackmail
fjarlægð • *n* distance
fjarlægja • *v* strip
fjarlægur • *adj* distant
fjarri • *adj* far
fjarska • *adv* very
fjarverandi • *adj* away
fjöður • *n* feather
fjöðurstafur • *n* calamus
fjóla • *n* violet
fjölær • *adj* perennial
fjölbreytinn • *adj* polymorphic
fjölbreytni • *n* diversity, polymorphism
fjölbreyttur • *adj* diverse
fjölbrigðni • *n* polymorphism
fjölbyrja • *adj* multiparous
fjöldaveisla • *n* banquet
fjöldi • *n* number
fjölfarinn • *adj* traveled
fjölga • *v* increase
fjölgreinafyrirtæki • *n* conglomerate
fjölgyðistrú • *n* polytheism
fjölkvæni • *adj* polygamous
fjölkvænis- • *adj* polygamous
fjölleikasýning • *n* vaudeville
fjölliða • *n* polymer
fjölmóta • *adj* polymorphic
fjölmótun • *n* polymorphism
fjölröddun • *n* polyphony
fjölskylda • *n* family
fjöltyngdur • *adj* multilingual
fjólublár • *adj* purple • *n* violet
fjölvaskipun • *n* macro
fjölvi • *n* macro
fjórðapartsnóta • *n* crotchet
fjórði • *adj* fourth
fjórðipartur • *n* crotchet
fjórðungur • *n* quarter
fjörður • *n* fjord
fjörefni • *n* vitamin
fjórhliðungur • *n* quadrilateral
fjós • *n* stable
flæða • *v* flow
flæði • *n* fluency
flækja • *n* knot
flæmingi • *n* flamingo
flagari • *n* womanizer
flagg • *n* flag
flaggdúkur • *n* bunting
flaggskip • *n* flagship
flaggstöng • *n* flagpole
flamingói • *n* flamingo
flasa • *n* dandruff
flaska • *n* bottle

flaski • *n* sliver
flatarmál • *n* area
flatbaka • *n* pizza
flatlendi • *n* plain
flatnefja • *adj* platyrrhine
flaumur • *adj* torrential
flauta • *n* flute, recorder
flautuleikari • *n* flautist
fleir- • *adj* plural
fleirtala • *n* plural
fleirtölu- • *adj* plural
fleki • *n* raft
flensa • *n* flu, influenza
flesk • *n* bacon
flétta • *v* interleave • *n* lichen
flettiorð • *n* lexeme
fleygbogi • *n* parabola
fleygja • *v* cast, throw
flík • *n* garment
flís • *n* sliver
fljót • *n* river
fljótlega • *adv* soon
fljótur • *adj* fast, quick, rapid
fló • *n* flea
flóð • *n* flood
flóðhestur • *n* hippopotamus
flog • *n* epilepsy
flogaveiki • *n* epilepsy
flói • *n* bay, gulf
flokka • *v* class, distribute, sort
flokkunarfræði • *n* taxonomy
flokkur • *n* class, flock
flóra • *n* flora
flotasveit • *n* flotilla
flotfræði • *n* rheology
flotögn • *n* floater
flóttamaður • *n* escapee
flötur • *n* facet
fluga • *n* fly
flugbraut • *n* runway
flugdreki • *n* kite
flugeldar • *n* firework
flugeldur • *n* fireworks
flugfélag • *n* airline
flughöfn • *n* airport
flugmaður • *n* pilot
flugslóði • *n* contrail
flugstjóri • *n* captain
flugstöð • *n* airport
flugtak • *n* takeoff
flugvél • *n* airplane
flugvélarslóði • *n* contrail
flugvöllur • *n* airfield, airport
flúor • *n* fluorine
flúr • *n* fluorine
flutningsbíll • *n* truck
flyðra • *n* halibut

flygilhorn • *n* flugelhorn
flýja • *v* flee
flykkjast • *v* assemble
flýtir • *n* precipitation
flytja • *v* move
flytjast • *v* move
fóarn • *n* gizzard
fóðra • *v* feed
föðurbróðir • *n* uncle
föðurland • *n* fatherland
föðurlandssvik • *n* treason
föðurlandsvinur • *n* patriot
föðursystir • *n* aunt
fógetaumdæmi • *n* bailiwick
fógeti • *n* sheriff
fokka • *n* jib
folald • *n* foal
földun • *n* convolution
foli • *n* stud
fólk • *n* people
fólksfjöldi • *n* population
fölna • *v* wilt
fólskulegur • *adj* callous
fölur • *adj* light, pale, wan
fölvi • *n* paleness, pallor
fönix • *n* phoenix
fönn • *n* snow
för • *n* trip
fordómafullur • *adj* prejudiced
fordyri • *n* vestibule
foreldri • *n* parent
forgarður • *n* vestibule
forgjöf • *n* handicap
forhúð • *n* prepuce
forhúðarostur • *n* smegma
fórinta • *n* forint
forinta • *n* forint
forjaxl • *n* bicuspid, premolar
forleikur • *n* foreplay
forliður • *n* antecedent
form • *n* format
formáli • *n* preamble
formálsorð • *n* preamble
formatta • *v* format
formengi • *n* domain
fórn • *n* sacrifice
fórna • *v* sacrifice
fornafn • *n* pronoun
fornfíll • *n* mammoth
forrit • *n* application, program
forrita • *v* program
forritari • *n* programmer
forritun • *n* programming
forsæla • *n* umbrage
forsenda • *n* premise, presupposition
forseti • *n* president
forsetning • *n* preposition

forsjáll • *adj* provident
forsmekkur • *n* taste
forsnið • *n* format
forsníða • *v* format
forstjóri • *n* president
forstofa • *n* vestibule
fortepíanó • *n* piano
fortíðarþrá • *n* nostalgia
fortóv • *n* pavement, sidewalk
forvitni • *n* curiosity
fosfór • *n* phosphorus
foss • *n* waterfall
fossandi • *adj* torrential
fóstra • *n* nurse
fóstur • *n* fetus
fósturdráp • *n* feticide
fóstureyðing • *n* abortion
föt • *n* clothes, dress
fótalaus • *adj* legless
fótaskemill • *n* footstool
fótbolti • *n* football, soccer
fótleggur • *n* leg
fötlun • *n* handicap
fótóna • *n* photon
fótskemill • *n* footstool
fótur • *n* foot, leg
frá • *prep* from
frádráttar • *adj* minus
fræ • *n* seed
fræði • *n* science, studies
fræðigrein • *n* study
fræðiiðkan • *n* study
frægð • *n* fame
fræhvíta • *n* endosperm
frændhygli • *n* nepotism
frændi • *n* cousin
fræni • *n* stigma
frænka • *n* cousin
fráfærir • *n* abductor
frakki • *n* coat, jacket
frambolur • *n* thorax
framburður • *n* pronunciation, speech
frámengi • *n* domain
framfærslufé • *n* stipend
framfall • *n* prolapse
framfarasinni • *n* progressive
framgómmæltur • *adj* palatal
framhaldsskóli • *n* gymnasium
framhlaðningur • *n* musket, muzzleloader, shotgun
framjaxl • *n* bicuspid, premolar
framkvæmd • *n* operation
framleiða • *v* produce
framrúða • *n* windshield
framsæti • *n* shotgun
framsegl • *n* jib
framsöguháttur • *n* indicative

81

framsýnn • *adj* provident
framtíð • *n* future
franki • *n* franc
fransín • *n* francium
frasi • *n* phrase
frauðplast • *n* styrofoam
frávarp • *n* projection
freðmýri • *n* tundra
fregna • *v* ask
frekna • *n* freckle
frelsa • *v* liberate
frelsi • *n* freedom, liberty
frelsingi • *n* freedman
fremdardýr • *n* primate
fremja • *v* perpetrate
fresta • *v* postpone
frestur • *n* moratorium
freta • *v* fart
frétt • *n* news
fréttablað • *n* newspaper
fréttamennska • *n* journalism
frí • *adj* away
friðarbogi • *n* rainbow
friðartími • *n* peace
friðsæll • *adj* pacific
friðþæging • *n* expiation
friður • *n* peace
frímerkjasafnari • *n* philatelist
frímerkjasöfnun • *n* philately
fískur • *adj* frisk
frístund • *n* leisure
frjáls • *adj* free
frjókorn • *n* pollen
frjónál • *n* sprout
frjósa • *v* freeze
fróa • *v* placate
froða • *n* foam, froth
fróðleikur • *n* lore
froskdýr • *n* amphibian
froskungi • *n* tadpole
froskur • *n* frog
frost • *n* frost
frostavetur • *n* frost
frúktósi • *n* fructose
frum- • *adj* primordial
fruma • *n* cell
frumbernska • *n* babyhood
frumbyggi • *n* aborigine
frumeind • *n* atom
frumeinda- • *adj* nuclear
frumeindarkjarni • *n* nucleus
frumeintak • *n* original
frumgerð • *n* prototype
frumlag • *n* subject
frumrit • *n* original
frumsenda • *n* axiom
frumsetning • *n* axiom
frumskógur • *n* jungle

frumtala • *n* cardinal
frumufræði • *n* cytology
frumukjarni • *n* nucleus
frumulíffæri • *n* organelle
frumvarp • *n* bill
frumvera • *n* protist
frygð • *n* concupiscence
frygðarauki • *n* aphrodisiac
frygðarlyf • *n* aphrodisiac
frymi • *n* protoplasm
frysta • *v* freeze
fúga • *n* fugue
fugl • *n* bird
fuglafræði • *n* ornithology
fuglahræða • *n* scarecrow
fullorðinn • *n* adult • *adj* big
fulltingi • *n* help
fulltrúi • *n* attorney, plenipotentiary
fullur • *adj* drunk, full
fullyrðing • *n* proposition
fundur • *n* find
fura • *n* pine
furstadæmi • *n* principality
fursti • *n* monarch, prince
fúskari • *n* quack
fúx • *n* underachiever
fylgifyrirbæri • *n* epiphenomenon
fylgihlutir • *n* accessory
fylgihlutur • *adj* accessory
fylgihnöttur • *n* moon
fylgisetning • *n* corollary
fylgja • *n* placenta
fylki • *n* array, matrix, state
fylking • *n* phylum
fýll • *n* fulmar
fýlustútur • *n* pout
fýlusvipur • *n* pout
fyndinn • *adj* funny
fýri • *n* pine
fyrir • *prep* by • *n* yore
fyrirbæn • *n* intercession
fyrirboði • *n* harbinger, premonition
fyrirgefa • *v* forgive
fyrirgefanlegur • *adj* venial
fyrirgefðu • *interj* sorry
fyrirgjöra • *v* loose
fyrirhyggjusamur • *adj* provident
fyrirlítanlegur • *adj* snide
fyrirlitning • *n* contempt
fyrirmiðdagur • *n* forenoon
fyrirmynd • *n* paradigm
fyrirsjáanlegur • *adj* foreseeable
fyrirtæki • *n* company, firm
fyrr • *prep* before
fyrrverandi • *n* ex
fyrstur • *adj* first
fýsn • *n* concupiscence

G

gá • *n* bark
gabba • *v* befool
gadólín • *n* gadolinium
gæfa • *n* fortune
gæfur • *adj* tame
gæfusamur • *adj* lucky
gærdagur • *n* yesterday
gærdagurinn • *n* yesterday
gæs • *n* goose
gæsagammur • *n* vulture
gáfa • *n* talent
gáfaður • *adj* intelligent
gaffall • *n* fork
gaflbrík • *n* pediment
gaflflötur • *n* tympanum
gaflhlað • *n* pediment
gáfumannaveldi • *n* meritocracy
gagga • *v* quack
gaggalagó • *interj* cock-a-doodle-doo
gagnásökun • *n* recrimination
gagnauga • *n* temple
gagnkvæði • *n* antinomy
gagnkvæmur • *adj* mutual
gagnlegt • *adj* helpful
gagnlegur • *adj* useful
gagnrýna • *v* carp, criticise
gagnsær • *adj* transparent
gagnsemi • *n* usefulness, value
gagnslaus • *adj* useless
gagnsök • *n* recrimination
gagnvegur • *n* geodesic • *adj* geodesic
gala • *v* yell
galdra- • *adj* magical
galdrakarl • *n* wizard
galdramaður • *n* mage, wizard
galdraþula • *n* spell
galeiða • *n* galley
gálgi • *n* gallows
galíon • *n* galleon
gall • *n* bile
gallblöðrubólga • *n* cholecystitis
gallín • *n* gallium
gamaldags • *adj* archaic, old-fashioned
gamall • *adj* old
gamansamur • *adj* facetious
gamansýning • *n* vaudeville
gammur • *n* vulture
ganga • *n* march • *v* walk
gangstétt • *n* pavement, sidewalk
gangtegund • *n* gait
gangur • *n* march
gangverk • *n* clockwork
gapa • *v* yawn
gardína • *n* curtain

garðrækt • *n* horticulture
garður • *n* garden
garðyrkja • *n* gardening, horticulture
garðyrkju • *adj* horticultural
garðyrkjufræði • *n* horticulture
garðyrkjufræðingur • *n* horticulturist
garðyrkjumaður • *n* horticulturist
gári • *n* budgerigar
garn • *n* yarn
gas • *n* gas
gas- • *adj* pneumatic
gáshaukur • *n* goshawk
gat • *n* hole
gata • *n* road, street
gátlisti • *n* checklist
gatnamót • *n* intersection
gaukur • *n* cuckoo
gaumlisti • *n* checklist
gaupa • *n* lynx
gaur • *n* dude
gé • *n* gee
gedda • *n* pike
geðhreinsun • *n* catharsis
geðklofi • *n* schizophrenia
geðlæknir • *n* psychiatrist
geðshræring • *n* emotion
geðsjúklingur • *n* lunatic
geðvefrænn • *adj* psychosomatic
gefa • *v* give
gegl • *n* juggling
gegn • *v* fight
gegnsær • *adj* transparent
gegnvirkur • *adj* transitive
geimfar • *n* spacecraft
geimfari • *n* astronaut
geimgrýti • *n* meteoroid
geimskip • *n* spaceship
geimsteinn • *n* meteoroid
geimur • *n* space
geiri • *n* clove
geirvarta • *n* nipple
geisja • *n* geisha
geislabaugur • *n* halo
geislalækningar • *n* radiology
geislalæknir • *n* radiologist
geislavirkur • *adj* radioactive
geisli • *n* beam, radius
geislunarfræði • *n* radiology
geislungasvæði • *adj* hypochondriac
geispa • *v* yawn
geispi • *n* yawn
geit • *n* goat
geitungur • *n* wasp
gelda • *v* sterilize

geldhani • *n* capon
geldingur • *n* eunuch
gelt • *n* bark
gelta • *v* bark
gemsa • *n* chamois
genasamsæta • *n* allele
ger • *n* yeast
gera • *v* do
gerð • *n* kind, sort, type
gerilæta • *n* bacteriophage
gerilveira • *n* bacteriophage
gerja • *v* ferment
gerlabani • *n* bactericide
gerlar • *n* bacteria
german • *n* germanium
gervihnöttur • *n* satellite
gervitungl • *n* satellite
gestgjafi • *n* host
gestrisinn • *adj* hospitable
gestur • *n* guest
geta • *v* can, guess, may, mention
getnaðarlimur • *n* penis
getnaður • *n* conception
getþótti • *adj* discretionary
gey • *n* bark
geyja • *v* bark
geymsla • *n* receptacle
gifs • *n* gypsum
gifta • *v* marry
gifting • *n* wedding
gígabæti • *n* gigabyte
gildi • *n* value
gildur • *adj* valid
gíll • *n* parhelion
gimsteinn • *n* gem, stone
gína • *n* mannequin
gír • *n* gear
gíraffi • *n* giraffe
girðing • *n* enclosure, fence
girnd • *n* concupiscence
giska • *v* guess
gisti • *n* register
gistihús • *n* hotel, inn
gítar • *n* guitar
gjalda • *v* pay
gjaldmiðill • *n* money
gjaldþrot • *n* bankruptcy
gjaldþrota • *adj* bankrupt
gjamm • *n* bark
gjamma • *v* bark
gjarna • *adv* gladly
gjarnan • *adv* gladly
gjóður • *n* osprey
gjöf • *n* gift
gjöra • *v* do
gjörbreyting • *n* transubstantiation
gjörð • *n* girth

gjóta • *v* spawn
glaðlegur • *adj* bright
glæpamaður • *n* criminal, crook
glæpur • *n* crime
glær • *adj* hyaline
glæruvængur • *n* pterygium
glæsivagn • *n* limousine
glætufluga • *n* firefly
gláka • *n* glaucoma
glápa • *v* stare
glas • *n* glass
gleði • *n* happiness, joy
gleðikona • *n* prostitute
gleðispillir • *n* spoilsport
gler • *n* glass
gleraugu • *n* spectacles
glerungur • *n* enamel
gleym-mér-ei • *n* forget-me-not
gleyma • *v* forget
gleymanleg • *adj* forgettable
gleypifruma • *n* macrophage
glitra • *v* glitter
glitur • *n* glitter
gljúfur • *n* canyon
glóbjalla • *n* firefly
glott • *n* grin
glötun • *n* perdition
gluggahleri • *n* shutter
gluggatjald • *n* curtain
gluggi • *n* window
glúkósi • *n* glucose
glundroði • *n* disorder
glýkógen • *n* glycogen
gnægð • *n* abundance
gneypur • *adj* downcast
góð • *adj* good
góða • *n* friend
góðgerðarstarfsemi • *n* charity
góðgerðarstofnun • *n* charity
góði • *n* friend
góður • *adj* good, kind
göfgun • *n* sublimation
goggur • *n* beak, bill
gögn • *n* data
göldróttur • *adj* magical
golf • *n* golf
gólf • *n* floor
golfranska • *n* gibberish
göltur • *n* boar
gómur • *n* gum
göndull • *n* dick
göng • *n* tunnel
göngulag • *n* gait
górilla • *n* gorilla
görn • *n* intestine
gort • *n* boast
gosbrunnur • *n* fountain

goshver • *n* geyser
gosi • *n* jack
got • *n* litter
gott • *adj* good
gr. • *n* article
gráblika • *n* altostratus
graðhestur • *n* stallion
gráðubogi • *n* protractor
graður • *adj* horny, randy
grædgi • *n* greed
grænkál • *n* kale
grænmeti • *n* vegetable
grænmetisæta • *n* vegetarian
grænn • *n* green • *adj* green
grænukorn • *n* chloroplast
graf • *n* plot
grafa • *n* excavator
grafít • *n* graphite
grafkyrr • *adj* motionless
grafskrift • *n* epitaph
graftarbóla • *n* pimple
graftarsótt • *n* sepsis
grámórautt • *n* dun
granaldin • *n* pineapple
granatepli • *n* pomegranate
grandaleysi • *n* innocence
grár • *n* gray • *adj* gray
gras • *n* grass, weed
grasafræði • *n* botany
grasafræðingur • *n* botanist
grasasni • *n* idiot
grasflöt • *n* meadow
grasker • *n* pumpkin
gráta • *v* cry, sob, weep
grátbiðja • *v* implore
gredda • *n* horniness
grefill • *n* spud
greftra • *v* inter
greftrun • *n* burial
greiða • *v* comb, pay
greiðslustöðvun • *n* moratorium
greifafrú • *n* countess
greifi • *n* count
greifingi • *n* badger
greifynja • *n* countess
grein • *n* article, bough, branch, subject
greina • *v* analyze
greinarmerki • *n* punctuation
greinast • *v* ramify
greind • *n* intelligence
greindarlegur • *adj* bright
greindur • *adj* bright
greining • *n* analysis, ramification
greinir • *n* article
greip • *n* grapefruit
greipaldin • *n* grapefruit
greipaldintré • *n* grapefruit

gremja • *n* umbrage
greni • *n* spruce
greni- • *n* spruce
gretta • *n* frown
gríðarstór • *adj* huge
gríma • *n* mask
grimmur • *adj* cruel
grín • *n* joke
grínast • *v* joke
grind • *n* lattice, matrix
grindverk • *n* balustrade
grip- • *adj* prehensile
gripahús • *n* stable
gripl • *n* juggling
gripla • *n* acrostic
grís • *n* piglet
gríslingur • *n* piglet
gröð • *adj* horny
gróða- • *adj* lucrative
gróðurhús • *n* greenhouse
gróðurríki • *n* flora
gróðurskáli • *n* greenhouse
gröf • *n* ditch, grave
grófgerður • *adj* bucolic
gröftur • *n* ditch, pus
grófur • *adj* randy
grön • *n* muzzle
grösugur • *adj* grassy
grund • *n* meadow
grundvallar- • *adj* cardinal
grunnflötur • *n* base
grunnsævi • *adj* inshore
grunnur • *n* foundation
grúpa • *n* group
gryfja • *n* pit
grýlukerti • *n* icicle
grýttur • *adj* stony
gúanín • *n* guanine
gubba • *v* vomit
guð • *n* god
guðleysi • *n* atheism
guðleysingi • *n* atheist
guðspeki • *n* theosophy
guðspjall • *n* gospel
guðspjallamaður • *n* evangelist
guðsþjónusta • *n* church
gufa • *n* steam, vapor
gufubað • *n* sauna
gufumyndun • *n* vaporization
Gufuskip • *n* steamship
gula • *n* jaundice
gulgrænn • *n* lime
gull • *n* gold
gullfallegur • *adj* gorgeous
gullfífill • *n* marigold
gullfiskur • *n* goldfish
gullgerðarlist • *n* alchemy

gullgerðarmaður • *n* alchemist
gullsmiður • *n* goldsmith
gulltoppur • *n* wallflower
gulna • *v* yellow
gúlpur • *n* aneurysm
gulrót • *n* carrot
gulur • *n* yellow • *adj* yellow
gúmmí • *n* rubber
gunguskapur • *n* cowardice

gúrka • *n* cucumber
guss • *n* quack
gussa • *v* quack
gustur • *n* gust
gúttaperka • *n* gutta-percha
guvernör • *n* governor
gyðja • *n* goddess
gyllinæð • *n* hemorrhoid

H

há • *n* aitch
ha • *interj* huh
ha? • *interj* what
háaloft • *n* attic, garret
háðsgrein • *n* squib
hadsjí • *n* hajj
háðslegur • *adj* derisive
háðung • *n* shame
háður • *adj* addicted
hæ • *interj* hello, hi
hæð • *n* hill, level
hæða • *v* scoff, taunt
hæðni • *n* taunt
hæðóttur • *adj* hilly
hæfileikafólk • *n* talent
hæfileikamaður • *n* talent
hæfileiki • *n* talent
hægri • *adj* right
hægt • *adv* slowly
hægur • *adj* possible
hæka • *n* haiku
hækja • *n* crutch
hæll • *n* heel
hænsn • *n* chicken
hæsi • *n* hoarseness
hætta • *v* abandon • *n* danger
hættulegur • *adj* dangerous
haf • *n* ocean, sea
hafa • *v* have, sweat
hafald • *n* heddle
haffær • *adj* seaworthy
hafmey • *n* mermaid
hafna • *v* reject
hafnabolti • *n* baseball
hafnín • *n* hafnium
haframjöl • *n* oatmeal
hafri • *n* oat
hafur • *n* buck
hagfræði • *n* economics
hagl • *n* hailstone
haglabyssa • *n* shotgun
haglél • *n* hail
hagsýni • *n* economy

hagur • *n* economy
haha • *interj* haha
haka • *n* chin
hakakross • *n* swastika
hakalega • *adv* hardly
hákarl • *n* shark
haki • *n* hook
halakarta • *n* tadpole
halastjarna • *n* comet
halda • *v* hold, stay, think
haldgóður • *adj* tenacious
háleitur • *adj* platonic
hálf- • *adj* half
hálfkák • *n* bungling
hálfleiðari • *n* semiconductor
hálfmálmur • *n* metalloid
hálfmeðvitundarleysi • *n* stupor
hálfnóta • *n* minim
hálftími • *n* half-hour
hálfviti • *n* asshole
hali • *n* tail
hallamál • *n* level
hallelúja • *n* hallelujah • *interj* hallelujah
halló • *interj* hello, hi
hálsfesti • *n* necklace
hálsmál • *n* neckline
hálsmen • *n* pendant
hálviti • *n* ass, idiot
hamagangur • *n* hullabaloo
hamar • *n* cliff, hammer, porbeagle
hamborgari • *n* hamburger
hámeri • *n* porbeagle
hamingja • *n* happiness
hamingjusamur • *adj* happy
hamstra • *v* stockpile
hamstur • *n* hamster
hanabjálki • *n* attic
hanagal • *n* crow
handaband • *n* handshake
handarbaks- • *adj* metacarpal
handarbaksleggur • *n* metacarpal
handarkriki • *n* armpit
handbók • *n* handbook

handbolti • *n* handball
handhafi • *n* bearer
handjárn • *n* manacle
handklæði • *n* towel
handleggur • *n* arm
handrið • *n* balustrade, banister, bannister
handsprengja • *n* grenade
hanga • *v* hang, swing
hann • *pron* he
hanna • *v* design
hanski • *n* glove
happdrætti • *n* lottery
hápunktur • *n* acme
hár • *n* hair • *adj* tall
hárauður • *n* cardinal • *adj* cardinal
hárbursti • *n* brush, hairbrush
harðbrjósta • *adj* callous
harðfiskur • *n* stockfish
harðfylgi • *n* perseverance
harðgeðja • *adj* callous
harðlyndur • *adj* callous
harðsoðinn • *adj* hard-boiled
harður • *adj* hard
háreyðing • *adj* depilatory
háreyðingarvara • *n* depilatory
harka • *n* austerity
hárkolla • *n* wig
hárkross • *n* reticle
harma • *v* lament
harmóníum • *n* harmonium
harpa • *n* harp
hárpípuhrif • *n* capillarity
hárpípukraftur • *n* capillarity
hárpípuverkun • *n* capillarity
hárreitisýki • *n* trichotillomania
hart • *adj* hard
hás • *adj* hoarse, throaty
hásæti • *n* throne
háseti • *n* deckhand
háskólakennari • *n* professor
háskóli • *n* university
hastarlega • *adv* suddenly
hata • *v* hate
hátalari • *n* loudspeaker, speaker
hattari • *n* hatter
hátternisfræði • *n* ethology
háttur • *n* method
hattur • *n* hat
hatur • *n* hatred
haugur • *n* mountain
haukur • *n* hawk, kestrel
haus • *n* head
hausamót • *n* fontanelle
hauskúpa • *n* skull
haust • *n* autumn
haust- • *adj* autumn

haustlegur • *adj* autumn
hausverkur • *n* headache
héðan • *adv* hence
hefð • *n* tradition
hefill • *n* plane
hefjast • *v* begin
hefla • *v* plane
hefnd • *n* revenge
hefndarþorsti • *n* vindictiveness
hefnigjarn • *adj* vindictive
hefta • *v* staple
hefti • *n* staple
hegri • *n* heron
heiðarlegur • *adj* honest
heiðblár • *n* azure
heiðhvolf • *n* stratosphere
heiði • *n* heath, moor
heiðingi • *n* atheist, heathen
heiðinn • *adj* heathen
heiðni • *n* paganism
heiðskír • *adj* cloudless
heiður • *adj* cloudless
heiðursmaður • *n* gentleman
heiftrækinn • *adj* vindictive
heigull • *n* craven
heigulsháttur • *n* cowardice
heilabólga • *n* encephalitis
heiladingull • *n* pituitary
heiladyngjubotn • *n* hypothalamus
heilagfiski • *n* halibut
heilahimnubólga • *n* meningitis
heild • *adj* whole
heilda • *v* integrate
heildsala • *n* wholesale
heildun • *n* integral
heildverslun • *n* wholesale
heili • *n* brain
heilkjörnungur • *n* eukaryote
heill • *adj* whole
heilnóta • *n* semibreve
heilsa • *v* hail • *n* health
heilsusamlegt • *adj* salubrious
heim • *n* home • *adv* home
heima • *n* home • *adv* home
heiman • *n* home
heimavinna • *n* homework
heimavist • *n* dormitory
heimild • *n* record
heimilda- • *adj* documentary
heimildamynd • *n* documentary
heimili • *n* home
heimilishjálp • *n* help
heimilisþjónn • *n* manservant
heimill • *adj* admissible
heimsækja • *v* call, visit
heimsálfa • *n* continent
heimsfaraldur • *adj* pandemic

---

heimsfræði • *n* cosmology
heimsfræðingur • *n* cosmologist
heimskur • *adj* foolish, stupid
heimsókn • *n* call
heimsslitafræði • *n* eschatology
heimsvaldastefna • *n* imperialism
heimta • *v* demand
heimþrá • *n* homesickness
heimullegur • *adj* confidential, esoteric
heimur • *n* world
heita • *v* hight, promise
heiti • *n* designation
heitinn • *adj* late
heitur • *adj* hot
hekk • *n* hedge
hekla • *v* crochet
heldur • *conj* but
helftarlömun • *n* hemiplegia
helga • *v* consecrate
helgi • *n* weekend
helgiathöfn • *n* rite
helgidagur • *n* holiday
helgisiður • *n* rite
helgiskrín • *n* reliquary
helín • *n* helium
helíum • *n* helium
heljarstökk • *n* somersault
hella • *v* pour
helli- • *adj* torrential
hellir • *n* cave
hellirigna • *v* pelt
helmingur • *n* half
hélun • *n* deposition
helvítis • *interj* fuck, shit
hempa • *n* cassock
henda • *v* happen, throw
hengill • *n* pendulum
hengimann • *n* hangman
henging • *n* hanging
hennar • *pron* hers
hentugur • *adj* convenient
heppilegur • *adj* happy
heppinn • *adj* lucky
heppni • *n* luck
hér • *adv* here
her • *n* army
hérað • *n* hundred, region
héravör • *n* harelip
herfa • *v* harrow
herfi • *n* harrow
héri • *n* hare
herkinn • *adj* hardy
herkvaðning • *n* conscription
hermaður • *n* soldier
hérmeð • *adv* hereby
hermi- • *adj* imitative
hermikráka • *n* mockingbird, parrot

hernaðaraðgerð • *n* operation
heróín • *n* heroin
herpa • *v* contract
herra • *n* gentleman, lord, mister, sir
herramaður • *n* gentleman
herramenn • *n* gentleman
herskár • *adj* bellicose, belligerent
hersli • *n* sclerosis
herstöð • *n* base
hertogadæmi • *n* duchy
hertogi • *n* duke
hervörður • *n* picket
heslihneta • *n* hazelnut
heslimús • *n* dormouse
hestbak • *n* horseback
hesthús • *n* stable
hestur • *n* horse
hetja • *n* hero
hetta • *n* hood
hey • *n* hay, haystack
heygaffall • *n* pitchfork
heyja • *v* fight, wage
heyra • *v* hear
heyrnar- • *adj* aural
heyrumst • *interj* later
heystakkur • *n* haystack
híbýli • *n* house
híena • *n* hyena
hikandi • *adj* hesitant
hilling • *n* mirage
himinblár • *n* azure
himinhvel • *n* firmament
himinhvolf • *n* firmament
himinn • *n* firmament, paradise, sky
himna • *n* membrane
himnuflæði • *n* osmosis
hín • *n* hin
hind • *n* hind
hindartré • *n* cryptomeria
hindber • *n* raspberry
hindberjum • *n* raspberry
hindrun • *n* hindrance
hindrunarhlaup • *n* steeplechase
hingað • *adv* here, hither
hingaðburður • *n* birth
hinsegin • *adj* queer
hippi • *n* hippie
hirðingi • *n* nomad
hirðingjastafur • *n* crook
hirðir • *n* herd
hirðulaus • *adj* careless
hirsi • *n* millet
hirsla • *n* receptacle
histamín • *n* histamine
hitahvolf • *n* thermosphere
hitamælir • *n* thermometer
hitasótt • *n* fever

hitastig • *n* temperature
hiti • *n* fever
hitta • *v* hit
hittast • *v* concur
hjáhringur • *n* epicycle
hjala • *v* babble
hjáleigubóndi • *n* croft
hjálmur • *n* helmet
hjálp • *n* assistance, help • *interj* help
hjálpa • *v* help
hjálparhella • *n* help
hjálparhvati • *n* coenzyme
hjálparmál • *n* metalanguage
hjálparskjöl • *n* documentation
hjálpsamur • *adj* helpful
hjalt • *n* hilt
hjarðmennska • *n* nomadism
hjarta • *adj* cardiac • *n* heart
hjartanlegur • *adj* cordial
hjartastillir • *n* defibrillator
hjásól • *n* parhelion
hjátrú • *n* superstition
hjól • *n* wheel
hjólabretti • *n* skateboard
hjólastóll • *n* wheelchair
hjólbörur • *n* wheelbarrow
hjólreiðum • *n* cycling
hjónaband • *n* marriage
hjörð • *n* flock, herd
hjörtur • *n* deer, stag
hjúkka • *n* nurse
hjúkrunarfræðingur • *n* nurse
hjúkrunarkona • *n* nurse
hlaða • *n* barn
hlaði • *n* stack
hlægilegur • *adj* laughable
hlæja • *v* laugh
hland • *n* piss, urine
hlátur • *n* laugh, laughter
hlaup • *n* barrel
hlaupa • *v* congeal, flood, run
hlaupabretti • *n* treadmill
hlé • *n* intermission
hlébarði • *n* leopard
hleifur • *n* loaf
hlemmur • *n* trapdoor
hleri • *n* shutter, trapdoor
hlíð • *n* hill
hlið • *n* edge, gate
hliðrænt • *adj* analog
hliðrun • *n* translation
hlíðskipulykkja • *n* ampersand
hlífa • *v* protect, shield
hljóð • *n* sound
hljóða • *v* sound
hljóðan • *n* phoneme
hljóðavíxl • *n* metathesis

hljóðfæraleikari • *n* instrumentalist
hljóðgerving • *n* onomatopoeia
hljóðgervingur • *n* onomatopoeia
hljóðhimna • *n* eardrum
hljóðkerfisfræði • *n* phonology
hljóðlíkingarorð • *n* onomatopoeia
hljóðnemi • *n* microphone
hljóðskipti • *n* ablaut
hljóður • *adj* quiet, silent
hljóma • *v* sound
hljómblær • *n* timbre
hljómborð • *n* keyboard
hljómfræði • *n* harmony
hljómplata • *n* record
hlóðir • *n* fireplace
hlusta • *v* listen
hlustunarpípa • *n* stethoscope
hluta • *v* divide
hlutavelta • *n* tombola
hlutfall • *n* ratio
hlutfallstala • *n* ratio
hlutgrúpa • *n* subgroup
hluti • *n* excerpt, part, piece
hlutleysi • *n* neutrality
hlutmengi • *n* subset
hlutskipti • *n* destiny
hluttekning • *n* empathy
hlutur • *n* object
hlýðinn • *adj* obedient
hlynur • *n* maple
hnakki • *n* nape
hnakkur • *n* saddle
hnallur • *n* clog
hnappaborð • *n* keyboard
hnappagat • *n* buttonhole
hnappur • *n* button, key
hné • *n* knee
hnefi • *n* fist
hnegg • *n* neigh
hneggja • *v* neigh
hneiging • *n* bow
hneppa • *v* button
hnerra • *v* sneeze
hneta • *n* nut
hnetubrjótur • *n* nutcracker
hnífaparakassi • *n* canteen
hnífur • *n* knife
hnignandi • *adj* decadent
hnísa • *n* porpoise
hnjóðsyrði • *n* jibe
hnoð • *n* doggerel
hnoða • *v* masticate
hnota • *n* nut
hnöttur • *n* sphere
hnúaleggur • *n* metacarpal
hnubbi • *n* hyrax
hnútur • *n* knot, tumor

hnýta • *v* knot
hnyttinn • *adj* funny
hof • *n* temple
höfðingi • *n* monarch, potentate
höfðingjasleikja • *n* sycophant
hófhvarf • *n* pastern
hóflaus • *adj* prodigal
hóflaust • *adj* prodigal
höfn • *n* port
höfnun • *n* repudiation
höfrungahlaup • *n* leapfrog
höfrungur • *n* dolphin
hófskegg • *n* fetlock
höfuð • *n* head
höfuð- • *adj* cardinal
höfuðborg • *n* capital
höfuðbúnaður • *n* headdress, headgear
höfuðfat • *n* hat
höfuðkúpa • *n* skull
höfuðstöðvar • *n* base
höfuðverkur • *n* headache
höfundarréttur • *n* copyright
höfundur • *n* author
hófur • *n* hoof
höggormur • *n* serpent, viper
högni • *n* tom
hógværð • *n* humility
hokkí • *n* hockey
hökt • *n* lag
hökull • *n* chasuble
hökutoppur • *n* goatee
hol • *n* vestibule
hol- • *adj* pneumatic
hola • *n* hole, pit
holdsveiki • *n* leprosy
holdvotur • *adj* drenched
holkúla • *n* bomb
hóll • *n* hill
höll • *n* palace
holmín • *n* holmium
holsepi • *n* polyp
holsjá • *n* endoscope
holsjárskoðun • *n* endoscopy
holspegill • *n* endoscope
holspeglun • *n* endoscopy
hommafælni • *n* homophobia
hommahatur • *n* homophobia
hommi • *n* homosexual
hönd • *n* hand
hönnun • *n* design
hoppa • *v* jump
hópur • *n* flock, population
hor • *n* snot
hóra • *n* ho, prostitute, whore
hörð • *adj* hard
hörfa • *v* retreat
horfa • *v* look

hörfræ • *n* linseed
horfur • *n* prognosis
hormón • *n* hormone
horn • *n* angle, horn • *adj* angular, right
hornabolti • *n* baseball
hornblendi • *n* hornblende
hornefni • *n* keratin
hornmál • *n* protractor
hornréttur • *adj* square
hörpudiskur • *n* scallop
hörpuskel • *n* scallop
hóruhús • *n* brothel
hórumangari • *n* pimp
hörund • *n* skin
hörundsdökkur • *adj* dark-skinned
hósanna • *interj* hosanna
hósta • *v* cough, expectorate
hósti • *n* cough
hótel • *n* hotel
hraðbraut • *n* highway
hraði • *n* velocity
hraðskreiður • *adj* fast
hraður • *adj* fast
hræ • *n* corpse
hræddur • *adj* frightened
hræðileg • *adj* terrible
hræðilegur • *adj* horrible
hræðsla • *n* fear
hrægammur • *n* vulture
hræking • *n* expectoration
hrækja • *v* spit
hræll • *n* reed
hræsni • *n* hypocrisy
hrafn • *n* raven
hrafntinna • *n* obsidian
hráki • *n* expectoration
hrákjötsát • *n* omophagia
hranalegur • *adj* brusque
hrár • *adj* raw
hratt • *adv* fast
hraun • *n* lava
hraustlegur • *adj* bouncing
hreðka • *n* radish
hreiður • *n* nest
hreindýr • *n* reindeer
hreinlæti • *n* hygiene
hreinn • *adj* clean, pure
hreinræktaður • *adj* purebred
hreinsa • *v* clean
hreinsunareldur • *n* purgatory
hreyfill • *n* propeller
hreyfingarlaus • *adj* motionless
hreyfingarleysis- • *adj* sedentary
hreysi • *n* hovel, shack, shanty
hreysiköttur • *n* ermine
hríma • *v* frost
hrinda • *v* push

hringekja • *n* roundabout
hringiða • *n* vortex
hringja • *v* phone, telephone
hringlaga • *adj* annular
hringtorg • *n* roundabout
hringur • *n* circle, ring
hringvöðvi • *n* sphincter
hripa • *v* jot, scrawl
hrís • *n* rice
hrísgrjón • *n* rice
hrísgrjónaakur • *n* paddy
hrísgrjónavín • *n* sake
hristingur • *n* shake
hrjóta • *v* snore
hröðun • *n* acceleration
hrogn • *n* roe
hrognkelsi • *n* lumpsucker
hrókera • *v* castle
hrókering • *n* castling
hroki • *n* hubris
hrókur • *n* rook
hrollur • *n* shudder
hróp • *n* call
hrópa • *v* call, shout, yell
hrörnandi • *adj* decadent
hrósa • *v* praise
hross • *n* horse
hrossakjöt • *n* horsemeat
hrúður • *n* scab
hrukka • *n* wrinkle
hrumur • *adj* decrepit
hrútur • *n* ram
hryðjuverkamaður • *n* terrorist
hryggð • *adj* lugubrious
hryggjarsúla • *n* spine
hryggleysingjar • *n* vertebrate
hryggur • *n* backbone, spine
hryllingur • *n* nightmare
hryssa • *n* mare
húð • *n* skin
húð- • *adj* cutaneous
húða • *v* clad
húðbeðs- • *adj* hypodermic, subcutaneous
húdd • *n* bonnet, hood
húðfeiti • *n* sebum
húðflúr • *n* tattoo
húðflúra • *v* tattoo
húðsjúkdómafræði • *n* dermatology
húðsjúkdómafræðingur • *n* dermatologist
hugarfar • *n* paradigm
hugbúnaður • *n* software
huglaus • *adj* yellow
hugmynd • *n* thought
hugmyndafræði • *n* ideology
hugrakkur • *adj* brave

hugrekki • *n* bravery, courage
hugsa • *v* think
hugsun • *n* thought
hugtak • *n* concept
hugtakaorðabók • *n* thesaurus
hulinn • *adj* arcane
hulsturblað • *n* spathe
húm • *n* dusk, twilight
húma • *v* dusk
humall • *n* hop
humar • *n* lobster
humma • *v* hem
hún • *pron* she
hunang • *n* honey
hunangsfluga • *n* bumblebee
hundapi • *n* baboon
hundgá • *n* bark
hundskamma • *v* scold
hundur • *n* dog, hound
hungraður • *adj* hungry
hungur • *n* hunger
hungursneyð • *n* famine
húnn • *n* doorknob
hunsa • *v* ignore
huppur • *n* flank
hurð • *n* door
hús • *n* edifice, house
húsasund • *n* alley
húsbóndi • *n* lord
húsfrú • *n* housewife
húsgagn • *n* furniture
húsmóðir • *n* housewife
hvað • *pron* what, who
hvaðan • *adv* whence
hvæsa • *v* hiss
hvalbátur • *n* whaler
hvalskip • *n* whaler
hvalur • *n* whale
hvalveiðibátur • *n* whaler
hvalveiðimaður • *n* whaler
hvalveiðiskip • *n* whaler
hvar • *adv* where
hvarf • *n* reaction
hvarmur • *n* eyelid
hvarvetna • *adv* everywhere
hvass • *adj* odd
hvatberi • *n* mitochondrion
hvati • *n* catalyst
hve • *adv* how
hveiti • *n* wheat
hveitibrauðsdagar • *n* honeymoon
hvekkur • *n* prostate
hvenær • *adv* when
hver • *pron* who
hverfa • *v* disappear
hverfi • *n* arrondissement, quarter
hverfull • *adj* ephemeral, fleeting

hvergi • *adv* nowhere
hvernig • *adv* how
hversdagslegur • *adj* run-of-the-mill
hversu • *adv* how
hvert • *adv* whither • *pron* who
hvetja • *v* inspire
hvetjandi • *adj* catalytic
hví • *adv* why
hvíla • *v* rest
hvíld • *n* intermission, rest
hvirfla • *v* whirl
hvískra • *v* whisper
hvísla • *v* mutter, whisper
hvissa • *v* hiss
hvítblæði • *n* leukemia
hvítkál • *n* cabbage
hvítlaukur • *n* garlic
hvítur • *n* white • *adj* white
hvolpur • *n* puppy

hvönn • *n* angelica
hvörf • *n* reaction
hvort • *conj* if, whether
hvötun • *n* catalysis
hýði • *n* peel
hýdrat • *n* hydrate
hýdríð • *n* hydride
hýdroxíð • *n* hydroxide
hylja • *v* conceal
hylki • *n* capsule
hylling • *n* ovation
hýr • *adj* bright
hyrna • *n* simplex
hyrndur • *adj* angular
hyrni • *n* keratin
hýsa • *v* host
hýsill • *n* host

Í

í • *adj* away
íbúar • *n* population
íbúð • *n* apartment
íbúi • *n* citizen, element
iðja • *v* work
iðn • *n* trade
iðnaður • *n* industry
ídrægur • *adj* hygroscopic
iðulega • *adv* often
iglur • *n* leech
íhald • *n* conservatism
íhaldssinni • *n* conservative
íhuga • *v* ponder
íkorni • *n* squirrel
íkveikjuæði • *n* pyromania
il • *n* sole
ílangur • *adj* oblong
ill • *adj* evil
illgirni • *n* malice
illgresi • *n* weed
illkvittinn • *adj* snide
illt • *adj* evil
illþýði • *n* riffraff
illur • *adj* bad, evil
ilmreynir • *n* rowan
ilmur • *n* fragrance, perfume
ilmvatn • *n* perfume
ilmviður • *n* eucalyptus
imbakassi • *n* television
imperíalismi • *n* imperialism
ímynd • *n* epitome
ímyndaður • *adj* unreal
ímyndun • *n* imagination

ímyndunarafl • *n* imagination
ímyndunarveiki • *n* hypochondria • *adj* hypochondriac
ímyndunarveikur • *adj* hypochondriac
indín • *n* indium
inflúensa • *n* flu, influenza
innblástur • *n* insufflation
innbyggður • *adj* built-in
innflytjandi • *n* immigrant
inngangsorð • *n* preamble
inngangur • *n* entrance, preamble
inniskór • *n* slipper
innkirtlafræði • *n* endocrinology
innliður • *n* mean
innræting • *n* indoctrination
innrita • *v* matriculate
innritast • *v* matriculate
innritun • *n* matriculation
innrúm • *n* matrix
innsæiskenning • *n* intuitionism
innsigla • *v* seal
innsigli • *n* seal
innspýting • *n* injection
innstunga • *n* socket
innvensl • *n* endogamy
insúlín • *n* insulin
iridín • *n* iridium
ís • *n* ice
ísbreiða • *n* glacier
ísing • *n* sleet
ísjaki • *n* floe, iceberg
ískorn • *n* sleet
ísótópur • *n* isotope

iss • *interj* pshaw
ísskápur • *n* refrigerator
ístað • *n* stirrup
ítarlegur • *adj* elaborate, thorough

íþrótt • *n* sport
íþróttahús • *n* gymnasium
ítrekun • *adj* iterative

J

já • *adv* yeah
jaðar • *n* perimeter
jáeind • *n* positron
jæja • *interj* well
jafn • *adj* even
jafna • *n* equation • *v* level
jafnaðarstefna • *n* socialism
jafnaldra • *adj* coeval
jafnaldri • *n* coeval, contemporary
jafnátta • *adj* isotropic
jafndægur • *n* equinox
jafngengur • *adj* fungible
jafnrétti • *adj* egalitarian
jafnréttissinni • *n* egalitarian
jafnréttisstefna • *n* egalitarianism
jafntefli • *n* tie
jafnvægi • *n* harmony
jakkaföt • *n* suit
jakki • *n* coat, jacket
jakuxi • *n* yak
jákvæður • *adj* plus
jarða • *v* inter
jarðarber • *n* strawberry
jarðarberjaplanta • *n* strawberry
jarðbundinn • *adj* down-to-earth
jarðepli • *n* potato
jarðfræði • *n* geology
jarðhneta • *n* peanut
jarðkeppur • *n* truffle
jarðsetja • *v* inter
jarðskjálfta- • *adj* seismic
jarðskjálftafræði • *n* seismology
jarðskjálftafræðingur • *n* seismologist
jarðskjálftamælir • *n* seismograph
jarðskjálfti • *n* earthquake
jarðsprengja • *n* mine
jarðsvín • *n* aardvark
jarðyrkja • *n* agriculture

jarðýta • *n* bulldozer
jarfi • *n* wolverine
jarl • *n* earl
jarlsfrú • *n* countess
jarm • *n* baa
jarma • *v* baa, bleat
jarmur • *n* bleat
járn • *n* iron
járna • *v* horseshoe, shoe
járnbani • *n* railway
járnbraut • *n* railway
járngata • *n* railway
járningamaður • *n* farrier
járnsmiður • *n* blacksmith
jata • *n* manger
jei • *interj* yay
jen • *n* yen
jeppi • *n* jeep
joð • *n* iodine, jay
jóðla • *v* yodel
jöfur • *n* monarch
jógúrt • *n* yogurt
jói • *n* redneck
jökull • *n* glacier
jólastjarna • *n* poinsettia
jómfrú • *n* virgin
jón • *n* ion
jóna • *n* joint
jónun • *n* ionization
jörð • *n* earth, land
jórtra • *v* ruminate
jötunn • *n* jotun
júdó • *n* judo
júgur • *n* udder
julla • *n* dinghy
júnka • *n* junk
jurt • *n* plant

K

kadmín • *n* cadmium
kæliefni • *n* coolant
kæliskápur • *n* refrigerator
kælivökvi • *n* coolant
kænn • *adj* astute

kænska • *n* guile
kær • *adj* darling, dear
kærasta • *n* girlfriend
kærasti • *n* boyfriend
kærleikur • *n* love

kærulaus • *adj* careless
kafari • *n* diver
kafbátur • *n* submarine
kaffi • *n* coffee
kaffibrúnn • *n* coffee • *adj* coffee
kaffín • *n* caffeine
kafli • *n* chapter
kajak • *n* kayak
kaka • *n* cake
kakkalakki • *n* cockroach
kakó • *n* cacao
kaktus • *n* cactus
kaldgeðja • *adj* callous
kaldlyndur • *adj* cold
kaldur • *adj* cold
kaleikur • *n* chalice
kálfur • *n* calf
kalifornín • *n* californium
kalín • *n* potassium
kalíum • *n* potassium
kalkspat • *n* calcite
kalksteinn • *n* limestone
kalkúnn • *n* turkey
kall • *n* call
kalla • *v* call
kalmusrót • *n* calamus
kalsín • *n* calcium
kalsít • *n* calcite
kameljón • *n* chameleon
kamelljón • *n* chameleon
kamfóra • *n* camphor
kampa • *v* camp
kampavín • *n* champagne
kanell • *n* cinnamon
kanill • *n* cinnamon
kaniltré • *n* cinnamon
kanína • *n* rabbit
kanna • *n* jug, pitcher
kannske • *adv* maybe
kannski • *adv* maybe
Kanslari • *n* chancellor
kantalúpmelóna • *n* cantaloupe
kantarella • *n* chanterelle
kantur • *n* edge
kápa • *n* cope
kapella • *n* chapel
kapers • *n* caper
kapsaísín • *n* capsaicin
káputapír • *n* tapir
karamella • *n* caramel
karate • *n* karate
karavella • *n* caravel
karbónat • *n* carbonate
kardináli • *n* cardinal
karfa • *n* basket
karkari • *n* carrack
karl • *n* man

karlaklósett • *n* gentleman
karlfauskur • *n* geezer
karlfugl • *n* cock
karlhormón • *n* androgen
karlmaður • *n* man
karsi • *n* cress
karta • *n* toad
kartafla • *n* potato, spud
kassi • *n* box
kasta • *v* cast, foal, throw
kastaladíki • *n* moat
kastalasíki • *n* moat
kastali • *n* castle
katóða • *n* cathode
kátur • *adj* carefree, careless
kaup • *n* salary, trade
kaupa • *v* buy
kaupandi • *n* client, customer
kaupmaður • *n* chandler
kaupsali • *n* chandler
kaupsýslumaður • *n* businessman
keðja • *n* chain
kefli • *n* spool
keila • *n* cone, cusk, pin
keilulaga • *adj* conical
keisaraviður • *n* cryptomeria
keisari • *n* emperor, monarch
kemba • *v* comb
kembiforrit • *n* debugger
kengur • *n* staple
kengúra • *n* kangaroo
kenjóttur • *adj* capricious
kenna • *v* teach
kennari • *n* pedagogue, teacher
kenninafn • *n* surname
kenning • *n* kenning
kennslubók • *n* textbook
kennslukona • *n* teacher
keppandi • *n* competitor
ker • *n* vat
keratín • *n* keratin
kerfi • *n* system
kerfill • *n* chervil
kerfiskarl • *n* bureaucrat
kertagerðarmaður • *n* chandler
kertaljós • *n* candlelight
kertasali • *n* chandler
kertastjaki • *n* candlestick
kerti • *n* candle
kerúb • *n* cherub
ketill • *n* kettle, teakettle
kettlingur • *n* kitten
keyra • *v* move
kið • *n* kid
kíkja • *v* look
kílógramm • *n* kilogram
kímlegur • *adj* doggerel

kindakjöt • *n* mutton
kínín • *n* quinine
kinn • *n* cheek
kinnalitur • *n* blush
kiosk • *n* kiosk
kirkja • *n* church
kirkjan • *n* church
kirkjufræði • *n* ecclesiology
kirkjuturn • *n* steeple
kirna • *n* churn
kirni • *n* nucleotide
kirsuber • *n* cherry
kirsuberjatré • *n* cherry
kirsuberjaviður • *n* cherry
kisa • *n* cat, pussy
kisi • *n* pussy
kísill • *n* silicon
kista • *n* chest, coffin
kistuberi • *n* bearer
kistuleggja • *v* coffin
kitla • *v* tickle
kitlinn • *adj* ticklish
kjaftæði • *n* ball, bullshit
kjaftur • *n* mouth
kjálki • *n* jaw
kjallari • *n* basement, cellar
kjánalegur • *adj* babyish
kjarkur • *n* ball, courage
kjarna- • *adj* nuclear
kjarnafrymi • *n* nucleoplasm
kjarnagerð • *n* karyotype
kjarnakorn • *n* nucleolus
kjarnasafi • *n* nucleoplasm
kjarnepli • *n* pomegranate
kjarngerð • *n* karyotype
kjarni • *n* gist, kernel, nucleus
kjarnorku- • *adj* nuclear
kjarnyrði • *n* aphorism
kjarr • *n* thicket
kjói • *n* jaeger
kjöldraga • *v* keelhaul
kjölfar • *n* wake
kjöll • *n* dress
kjölur • *n* spine
kjörbúð • *n* supermarket
kjörgildi • *n* optimum
kjörstaða • *n* optimum
kjósa • *v* vote
kjöt • *n* meat
kjötæta • *n* carnivore
kjötbolla • *n* meatball
kjötkraftur • *n* bouillon
kjuði • *n* cue
kjúka • *n* knuckle, phalanx
kjúklingur • *n* chicken
klæða • *v* array, clad, clothe, dress
klæðaleysi • *n* undress

klæðnaður • *n* clothing, dress
klæðskeri • *n* tailor
klám • *n* pornography
klámfenginn • *adj* pornographic
klapplið • *n* claque
klár • *n* workhorse
klarínett • *n* clarinet
klarínetta • *n* clarinet
klasi • *n* class
klauf • *n* hoof
klaufdýr • *n* artiodactyl
klaufskur • *adj* backhanded
klaustur • *n* monastery
klefi • *n* cell, chamber
kleggi • *n* horsefly
kleinuhringur • *n* doughnut
klementína • *n* clementine
klemmuspjald • *n* clipboard
klerkdómur • *n* ministry
klettagrefingi • *n* hyrax
klettasalat • *n* rocket
klettur • *n* cliff
klífa • *v* climb
klifra • *v* climb
klikkaður • *adj* cracked
klípa • *n* knot
klippa • *v* cut
klippur • *n* shears
kljúfa • *v* cleave
kló • *n* claw
klobba • *v* nutmeg
klof • *n* crotch
klofna • *v* split
klofvega • *adv* astride
klór • *n* chlorine, scrawl
klóróform • *n* chloroform
klórófýl • *n* chlorophyll
klósett • *n* toilet
klósigi • *n* cirrus
klossi • *n* clog, klutz
klukka • *n* bell, clock
klukkan • *adv* o'clock
klukkuspil • *n* glockenspiel
klukkustund • *n* hour
klukkutími • *n* hour
klukkuverk • *n* clockwork
klunnalegur • *adj* awkward, backhanded
klúsaður • *adj* stilted
knattspyrna • *n* soccer
kné • *n* knee
knébeyging • *n* genuflection
knéfall • *n* genuflection
knéfiðla • *n* cello
knús • *n* hug
knúsa • *v* hug
kóbalt • *n* cobalt
koddi • *n* pillow

kóensím • *n* coenzyme
kofaþorp • *n* shantytown
koffín • *n* caffeine
koffíneitrun • *n* caffeinism
koffort • *n* trunk
kofi • *n* hovel, shack, shanty
köfnunarefni • *n* nitrogen
kofti • *n* helicopter
kokkur • *n* chef, cook
kókoshneta • *n* coconut
koks • *n* coke
kol • *n* coal
kolbrandur • *n* gangrene
kolefni • *n* carbon
kólesteról • *n* cholesterol
kólfur • *n* corncob, pendulum
koli • *n* plaice
kólibrífugl • *n* hummingbird
kolkrabbi • *n* octopus
kollhnís • *n* somersault
kollsigla • *v* capsize
köllun • *n* vocation
kollur • *n* stool
kölski • *n* devil
kolvatnsefni • *n* hydrocarbon
kolvetni • *n* carbohydrate, hydrocarbon
kolvetnisgas • *n* acetylene
kolvitlaust • *adv* wrong
koma • *n* arrival, coming • *v* come
komma • *n* comma
kommóða • *n* chest
kommúnismi • *n* communism
kompás • *n* compass
kona • *n* wife, woman
köngull • *n* cone
könguló • *n* spider
kónguló • *n* spider
kóngur • *n* king
koníak • *n* cognac
kónískur • *adj* conical
könnun • *n* study
konsúlat • *n* consulate
konsúll • *n* consul
kontrafagott • *n* contrabassoon
konungdæmi • *n* monarchy
konunglegur • *adj* royal
konungsdæmi • *n* kingdom
konungsríki • *n* kingdom, monarchy
konungsveldi • *n* kingdom
konungur • *n* king, monarch
kór • *n* choir
körfubolti • *n* basketball
körfuknattleikur • *n* basketball
kórkápa • *n* cope
korn • *n* mote
kornabarn • *n* baby
kornhæna • *n* quail

kóróna • *n* crown • *adj* crown
korpa • *n* wrinkle
kort • *n* map, postcard
kortagerðarmaður • *n* cartographer
kortið • *n* card
kortleggja • *v* plot
korvetta • *n* corvette
kósínus • *n* cosine
kosning • *n* election
kosningaréttur • *n* suffrage
koss • *n* kiss
kossasótt • *n* mononucleosis
kostur • *n* plus
köttur • *n* cat
krá • *n* bar, inn, pub
krabbadýr • *n* crustacean
krabbamein • *n* cancer
krabbi • *n* cancer, crab
kraftaverk • *n* miracle
kraftmikill • *adj* powerful
kragi • *n* collar
kráka • *n* crow
krakki • *n* kid
kramari • *n* chandler
krani • *n* crane
krap • *n* slush
kraparigning • *n* sleet
krassa • *v* scrawl
krefja • *v* demand
krem • *n* cream
kremaður • *adj* cream
kremja • *v* masticate
Kreppa • *n* depression
kreppa • *n* crisis
kringumstæður • *n* circumstance
krisma • *n* chrism
krít • *n* chalk
krítarsteinn • *n* chalk
kröftugur • *adj* powerful
kröfuganga • *n* march
króka- • *adj* roundabout
krókaleið • *n* roundabout
krókódíll • *n* crocodile
krókóttur • *adj* roundabout
krókstafur • *n* crosier
krókur • *n* hook
krókvegur • *n* roundabout
króm • *n* chromium
krónhjörtur • *n* deer
kross • *n* cross
krossfesta • *v* crucify
krossfiskur • *n* starfish
krosshaus • *n* crosshead
krossliður • *adj* sacral
krot • *n* scrawl
krota • *v* scrawl
krukka • *n* jar

krumpinn • *adj* despondent
krúna • *n* crown
krús • *n* jug
krybba • *n* cricket
krydd • *n* spice
kryfja • *v* dissect
krýna • *v* crown
krýólít • *n* cryolite
krypton • *n* krypton
kú • *n* cue
kúabjalla • *n* cowbell
kubbur • *n* cube
kúbein • *n* crow, crowbar
kuðungur • *n* cochlea
kúka • *v* shit
kúkur • *n* turd
kúla • *n* ball, bubble, bullet
kúlomb • *n* coulomb
kumpáni • *n* companion
kunnátta • *n* knowledge
kúnni • *n* client
kunningi • *n* friend
kúnst • *n* art
kunta • *n* cunt, pussy
kúpling • *n* clutch
kúrín • *n* curium
kurr • *v* coo • *n* coo
kurteis • *adj* polite
kústur • *n* broom
kútter • *n* sailboat
kvæði • *n* poem
kvæna • *v* marry
kvarði • *n* gauge
kvarki • *n* quark
kvarnarsteinn • *n* millstone
kvars • *n* quartz
kvarta • *v* carp
kveða • *n* foot
kveðinn • *adj* doggerel
kveðja • *n* greeting
kveðskapur • *n* doggerel
kvef • *n* cold
kvefslím • *n* phlegm
kveikja • *v* light, solder
kveikur • *n* wick
kveisa • *n* colic
kveld • *n* evening
kven- • *adj* distaff
kvenhatari • *n* misogynist
kvenhatur • *n* misogyny
kvenmaður • *n* woman
kvennabósi • *n* womanizer
kvennabúr • *n* harem
kvensjúkdómafræði • *n* gynecology
kvensjúkdómur • *adj* gynecological
kvensköp • *n* vulva
kví • *n* pen

kviðdómandi • *n* juror
kviðdómari • *n* juror
kviðdómur • *n* jury
kvíði • *n* anxiety
kvíga • *n* heifer
kvik- • *adj* dynamic
kvikasilfur • *n* mercury
kviklegur • *adj* dynamic
kvikmynd • *n* movie
kvikmyndahús • *n* cinema
kvikmyndatexti • *n* subtitle
kvikur • *adj* fast, quick
kvilli • *n* disorder
kvíslast • *v* ramify
kvíslun • *n* ramification
kvistur • *n* twig
kvöð • *n* duty
kvöl • *n* agony, torment
kvöld • *n* evening
kvöldmatur • *n* dinner
kýklópi • *n* cyclops
kýklópur • *n* cyclops
kylfa • *n* bat
kýli • *n* abscess
kyn • *n* gender, sex, type
kynæsandi • *adj* sexy
kyndill • *n* torch
kynfruma • *n* gamete
kynhvöt • *adj* antaphrodisiac
kynjalyf • *n* panacea
kynjamismunun • *n* sexism
kynlaus • *adj* asexual, epicene • *n* epicene
kynlegur • *adj* uncanny, weird
kynmök • *n* fuck
kynnir • *n* host
kynorkuaukandi • *adj* aphrodisiac
kynorkulyf • *n* aphrodisiac
kynþáttablöndun • *n* miscegenation
kynþáttafordómar • *n* racism • *adj* racist
kynþáttahatari • *n* racist
kynþáttahatur • *n* racism • *adj* racist
kynþáttahroki • *n* racism, racist • *adj* racist
kynþáttahyggja • *n* racism • *adj* racist
kynþáttarembingur • *n* racism
kynþáttastefna • *n* racism
kynþokkafullur • *adj* sexy
kýr • *n* cow
kyrr • *adj* pacific
kyrr- • *adj* static
kyrrabelti • *n* doldrums
kyrrlátur • *adj* pacific
kyrrlegur • *adj* static
kyrrsetu- • *adj* sedentary
kyssa • *v* kiss

L

labba • *v* walk
læða • *n* queen
læknir • *n* doctor
læknisfræði • *n* medicine
læmingi • *n* lemming
læra • *v* learn, study
lærdómur • *n* study
læri • *n* thigh
læsilegur • *adj* legible
læti • *n* panic
lævirki • *n* lark
lag • *n* song, track
lager • *n* warehouse
lágfiðla • *n* viola
lagg • *n* lag
lágmark • *n* minimum
lágský • *n* stratus
lágþrýstingur • *n* hypotension
lágþrýstisvæði • *n* low
lágur • *adj* short
lágvaxinn • *adj* short
lakk • *n* enamel
lakka • *v* enamel
lakkrís • *n* licorice
laktósi • *n* lactose
lamadýr • *n* llama
lamb • *n* lamb
lambakjöt • *n* lamb
lampaskermur • *n* lampshade
lampi • *n* lamp, lantern
lán • *n* fortune
lána • *v* lend
land • *n* country, land
landafræði • *n* geography
landamæri • *n* border
landbúnaður • *n* agriculture
landeign • *n* property
landfræði • *n* geography
landlukt • *adj* landlocked
landmæling • *n* geodesy
landmælingafræði • *n* geodesy
landráð • *n* treason
landskjaldbaka • *n* tortoise
landstjóri • *n* governor
landsvæði • *n* territory
landsvala • *n* swallow
langa • *n* ling
langferðabíll • *n* bus
langhlið • *n* hypotenuse
langt • *adv* long • *n* yore
langur • *adj* long
lánsamur • *adj* lucky
lanþan • *n* lanthanum
lárensín • *n* lawrencium

lárétt • *adj* horizontal
lás • *n* lock
lasagna • *n* lasagna
lasanja • *n* lasagna
lásbogi • *n* crossbow
látast • *v* die
látbragðsleikur • *n* pantomime
látinn • *adj* dead
látlaus • *adj* unobtrusive
lauf • *n* club, leaf
laufblað • *n* leaf
laufgræna • *n* chlorophyll
laukur • *n* onion
laumufarþegi • *n* stowaway
laumulegur • *adj* surreptitious
laun • *n* salary, wage
launa • *v* recompense
launmorðingi • *n* assassin
lausnarfé • *n* ransom
lausnargjald • *n* ransom
lávarður • *n* lord
lax • *n* salmon
laxbleikur • *adj* salmon
leður • *n* leather
leðurblaka • *n* bat
leg • *n* womb
leggja • *v* move, park
leggöng • *n* vagina • *adj* vaginal
leggur • *n* edge, leg
legill • *n* keg
legkaka • *n* placenta
legnám • *n* hysterectomy
leið • *n* path, road
leiðangur • *n* journey
leiðari • *n* conductor
leiðinlegur • *adj* boring
leiðir • *n* conductor
leiðni • *n* conductivity
leiðsögumaður • *n* leader
leifajafna • *n* congruence
leifastofn • *n* modulus
leigjandi • *n* lodger
leigubifreið • *n* taxi
leigubíll • *n* taxi
leika • *v* play, trumpet
leikaralegur • *adj* histrionic
leikari • *n* actor
leikbrúða • *n* puppet
leikdans • *n* ballet
leikfang • *n* toy
leikfimiæfing • *n* calisthenics
leikfimisalur • *n* gymnasium
leikhús • *n* theater
leikhústjald • *n* curtain

leikkona • *n* actor, actress
leiklist • *adj* histrionic
leikmaður • *n* layman
leikritaskáld • *n* playwright
leikskóli • *n* kindergarten
leikstjóri • *n* director
leikur • *n* game
leikvangur • *n* stadium
leikvölur • *n* joystick
leir • *n* clay
leirburður • *n* doggerel
leirflögur • *n* shale
leirgedda • *n* bowfin
leirrensli • *n* doggerel
leirsteinn • *n* brick, shale
leiruviðarskógur • *n* mangrove
leit • *n* search
leita • *v* hunt, look, search, seek
leki • *n* leak
lemúr • *n* lemur
lend • *adj* lumbar
lenda • *v* land
lengd • *n* length, modulus
lengdargildi • *n* value
lengdarmerki • *n* macron
lengi • *adv* long
lénsdrottinn • *n* overlord
lénsherra • *n* overlord
lénskerfi • *n* feudalism
lénsskipulag • *n* feudalism
lénsveldi • *n* feudalism
lentil • *n* lentil
lerki • *n* larch
lerkitré • *n* larch
les • *n* lexeme
lesa • *v* peruse, pick, read, study
lesandi • *n* reader
lesbía • *n* lesbian
lesblinda • *n* dyslexia • *adj* dyslexic
lesblindur • *n* dyslexic • *adj* dyslexic
lesforði • *n* lexicon
lesherbergi • *n* study
lesitín • *n* lecithin
lesning • *n* read
lessafn • *n* lexicon
lesstofa • *n* study
lest • *n* train
lestarspor • *n* railway
lestur • *n* perusal
leti • *n* sloth
letidýr • *n* sloth
létt • *adj* light
léttur • *adj* easy, light
leturborð • *n* keyboard
leturgerð • *n* font
leyfilegur • *adj* admissible
leyndarmál • *n* secret

leynilegur • *adj* backstage, confidential, secret, surreptitious • *adv* backstage
leynimakk • *n* machination
leyniorð • *n* password
leyniskytta • *n* sniper
leysa • *v* extricate
leysigeisli • *n* laser
leysingi • *n* freedman
leysir • *n* laser
leyti • *n* respect
liðband • *n* ligament
liðdýr • *n* arthropod
liði • *n* relay
liður • *n* addend
líf • *n* life
lifa • *v* live
lifandi • *adj* live
lífeðlisfræði • *n* physiology
lífefnafræði • *n* biochemistry
lífeyrir • *n* stipend
líffæri • *n* organ
líffræði • *n* biology
líffræðingur • *n* biologist
lífhimna • *n* peritoneum
lifibrauð • *n* livelihood
lífljómun • *n* bioluminescence
lífsleiði • *n* ennui
lífstykki • *n* corset
lifur • *n* liver
lífvera • *n* organism
liggja • *v* lie
lík • *n* corpse
líka • *adv* also • *v* like
líkami • *n* body
líkamsmeiðingar • *n* battery
líkamsrækt • *n* bodybuilding
líkhús • *n* morgue
líking • *n* simile
líkkista • *n* coffin
líklega • *adv* probably
líkþrá • *n* leprosy
lilja • *n* lily
limfarði • *n* smegma
limgerði • *n* hedge
limlesta • *v* maim
limmósína • *n* limousine
límonaði • *n* lemonade
limra • *n* limerick
limur • *n* penis
lína • *n* circuit, line
lind • *n* linden
lindi • *n* cummerbund
lindormur • *n* dragon
linsoðinn • *adj* soft-boiled
linur • *adj* floppy
líparít • *n* rhyolite
lípíð • *n* lipid

lirfa • *n* caterpillar, grub, larva
lirfueyðir • *n* larvicide
lirfuhýði • *n* cocoon
list • *n* art
listdans • *n* ballet
listi • *n* list
lit- • *adj* chromatic
líta • *v* look
lita • *v* color, dye
lita- • *adj* chromatic
litarefni • *n* dye
litblær • *n* hue
liþín • *n* lithium
lítið • *adv* little
lítill • *adj* little, small
lítillækkun • *n* abasement
lítillátur • *adj* unassuming
litín • *n* lithium
litir • *n* paint
litíum • *n* lithium
litningur • *n* chromosome
litur • *n* color, dye, flush, hue
litúrgískur • *adj* liturgical
ljóð • *n* poem
ljóðlist • *n* poetry
ljóðskáld • *n* poet
ljóma • *n* ember • *v* shine
ljómandi • *adj* bright
ljón • *n* lion
ljós • *n* light • *adj* light
ljósaskipti • *n* dusk, nightfall, twilight
ljósáta • *n* krill
ljósbrot • *n* refraction
ljóseind • *n* photon
ljósfræði • *n* optics
ljóshærð • *n* blond
ljóshærður • *n* blond
ljósleysa • *n* darkness
ljósmynd • *n* photograph, picture
ljósögn • *n* photon
ljósormur • *n* firefly
ljóstillífun • *n* photosynthesis
ljósvaki • *n* ether
ljúffengur • *adj* delicious
ljúfmenni • *n* gentleman
ljúfsár • *adj* bittersweet
ljúga • *v* lie
lóð • *n* plot
lóða • *v* solder
loddari • *n* quack
loðfíll • *n* mammoth
lóðmálmur • *n* solder
loðna • *n* capelin
loðningarefni • *n* solder
lóðrétt • *adj* vertical
loðskinn • *n* pelt
lóðtin • *n* solder

lóðun • *n* soldering
lof • *n* panegyric, praise
lofa • *v* promise
lófatak • *n* ovation
lofgerð • *n* panegyric
lófi • *n* palm
lofkvæði • *n* panegyric
loforð • *n* promise
lofsöngur • *n* hymn
loft • *n* air, attic, ceiling
loft- • *adj* pneumatic
lofta • *v* air
loftæðaop • *n* spiracle
loftaflfræði- • *adj* pneumatic
loftbelgur • *n* balloon
loftfylltur • *adj* pneumatic
loftknúinn • *adj* pneumatic
loftslag • *n* climate
loftsog • *n* suction
loftsteinn • *n* meteorite
lofttæmi • *n* vacuum
lofttóm • *n* vacuum
lögbrot • *n* transgression
lögfræði • *n* jurisprudence
lögfræðingur • *n* attorney, lawyer, solicitor
lögga • *n* policeman
löggusvín • *n* pig
logi • *n* flame
lögmál • *n* law
lögregla • *n* police
lögreglumaður • *n* policeman
logri • *n* logarithm • *adj* logarithmic
logsuðugas • *n* acetylene
lögun • *n* format
loka • *v* shut
lokaður • *adj* closed
lokaorð • *n* epilogue
lokari • *n* shutter
lokhljóð • *n* plosive
lokka • *v* seduce
lokkur • *n* curl, lock
lokun • *n* closure
lömun • *n* palsy, paralysis
löngun • *n* desire
löngunarfullur • *adj* wistful
loppa • *n* paw
losa • *v* extricate
lostafenginn • *adj* randy
lostafullur • *adj* randy
lostakælandi • *adj* antaphrodisiac
lostakælir • *n* antaphrodisiac
lostalaus • *adj* platonic
lostaörvandi • *adj* aphrodisiac
lostavekjandi • *adj* aphrodisiac
lostefni • *n* histamine
losti • *n* concupiscence

lottó • *n* lottery
lótus • *n* lotus
lótusblóm • *n* lotus
lúða • *n* halibut
lúffa • *n* mitten
lukka • *n* happiness, luck
lundi • *n* puffin
lundur • *n* grove
lunga • *n* lung
lunga- • *adj* pulmonary
lungna- • *adj* pulmonary
lungu • *n* lung
lús • *n* louse
lúta • *n* lute
lútesín • *n* lutetium
lútur • *n* lye
lýðræði • *n* democracy
lýður • *n* population
lýðveldi • *n* republic
lyf • *n* medicine
lyfjabúð • *n* pharmacy
lyfjafræði • *n* pharmacology

lyfjunarfræði • *n* posology
lyfleysa • *n* placebo
lyfsali • *n* pharmacist
lyfta • *n* elevator, lift
lyftiarmur • *n* jib
lygari • *n* bullshit, liar
lygi • *n* lie
lykill • *n* clef, key
lykilorð • *n* password
lykkja • *n* mesh, noose
lyklaborð • *n* keyboard
lykt • *v* smell • *n* smell
lykta • *v* smell
lyktarskyn • *n* smell
lyng • *n* heath
lýra • *n* lyre
lýsa • *v* describe, light
lýsimál • *n* metalanguage
lýsingarháttur • *n* participle
lýsingarorð • *adj* adjectival • *n* adjective

M

maðkur • *n* grub, worm
madrígal • *n* madrigal
madrígali • *n* madrigal
maður • *n* man • *pron* you
mæla • *v* talk
mæli • *n* speech
mælibogi • *n* protractor
mælifræði • *n* metrology
mænir • *n* monitor
máfur • *n* gull
magakveisa • *n* colic
magapína • *n* stomachache
magi • *n* belly, stomach
mágkona • *n* sister-in-law
magn • *n* quantity
magnesín • *n* magnesium
magnesíum • *n* magnesium
magnín • *n* magnesium
magníum • *n* magnesium
mágur • *n* brother-in-law
maískólfur • *n* corncob
majónes • *n* mayonnaise
makki • *n* mane
mál • *n* bother, language, morpheme, parlance, speech
mala • *v* babble, purr
mála • *v* paint
málafærslumaður • *n* barrister, solicitor
málaliði • *n* mercenary
málfar • *n* parlance, speech

málfræði • *n* grammar
málfræði • *n* grammar
málfræðibók • *n* grammar
málgagn • *n* organ
málglaður • *adj* talkative
málgleði • *n* talkativeness
málhæfileiki • *n* speech
málhelti • *n* alalia
malli • *n* belly
mállýska • *n* dialect
málmbróðir • *n* metalloid
málmgrýti • *n* ore
málmleysingi • *n* metalloid
málmur • *n* metal
málning • *n* paint
málrómur • *n* voice
málsháttur • *n* byword, phrase
málskipan • *n* syntax
málstaður • *n* cause
málstol • *n* aphasia
máltæki • *n* byword
máltíð • *n* meal
malurtarbrennivín • *n* absinthe
málvenja • *n* parlance
málverk • *n* painting
málvísindamaður • *n* linguist
málvísindi • *n* linguistics
mamma • *n* mother, mummy
mammút • *n* mammoth
mandla • *n* almond

mangan • *n* manganese
mangari • *n* chandler
mangó • *n* mango
máni • *n* moon
mann • *pron* you
manna • *v* man • *n* manna
mannæta • *n* cannibal
mannalæti • *n* bravado
manndráp • *n* homicide
manneskja • *n* man, person
mannfjöldi • *n* population
mannfræði • *n* anthropology
manngerður • *adj* man-made
mannkyn • *n* mankind
mannkynbætur • *n* eugenics
mannop • *n* manhole
mannorðsspjöll • *n* denigration
mannsmuga • *n* manhole
mannsöfnuður • *n* congregation
manntal • *n* census
mannúðlega • *adv* humanely
mannúðlegur • *adj* humane
mánuður • *n* month
mappa • *n* folder
marg- • *adj* plural
margendurtaka • *v* reiterate
margfætlur • *n* centipede
margföldunarandhverfa • *n* reciprocal
margföldunarumhverfa • *n* reciprocal
marghliða • *adj* multilateral
margítreka • *v* reiterate
margkvæður • *adj* sesquipedalian
margliða • *n* polynomial
marglytta • *n* jellyfish
margræður • *adj* polysemous
margvíslegur • *adj* diverse
marijúanavindlingur • *n* joint
markaðstorg • *n* agora
markaður • *n* bazaar, market
markgreifi • *n* marquess
markorð • *n* cue
markvörður • *n* goalkeeper
marmari • *n* marble
mars • *n* march
marsera • *v* march
marsering • *n* march
marsvín • *n* porpoise
martröð • *n* nightmare
mas • *n* babble
masa • *v* babble
maskari • *n* mascara
máske • *adv* maybe
máski • *adv* maybe
masókisti • *n* masochist
massaður • *adj* muscular
massi • *n* mass
mastur • *n* mast

matarlyst • *n* appetite
matarprjónn • *n* chopstick
matarréttur • *n* dish
matarveisla • *n* banquet
mathákur • *n* glutton
matreiðslu • *adj* culinary
matreiðslubók • *n* cookbook
matreiðslumaður • *n* chef
matsalur • *n* canteen
matseðill • *n* menu
matskeið • *n* tablespoon
matsölustaður • *n* restaurant
matsveinn • *n* chef
máttugur • *adj* powerful
matur • *n* food, grub, sustenance
matvæli • *n* food
matvara • *n* food
maur • *n* ant, termite
mauraæta • *n* anteater
mauraþúfa • *n* anthill
með • *adj* game • *prep* with
meðalganga • *n* intercession
meðaltal • *n* mean
meðfæddur • *adj* congenital, innate
meðganga • *n* pregnancy
meðvitundarlaus • *adj* unconscious
mee • *interj* baa
mega • *v* can, may
megabæti • *n* megabyte
megin- • *adj* cardinal
megindlegur • *adj* quantitative
meginland • *n* mainland
meginstoð • *n* backbone
meiða • *v* hurt, wound
meik • *n* foundation, makeup
mein • *n* disease
meina • *v* mean
meinafræði • *n* pathology
meindýr • *n* pest
meinfýsni • *n* malice
meinhæðið • *adj* acid
meinhæðin • *adj* acid
meinhæðinn • *adj* acid, snide
meining • *n* meaning
meinlaus • *n* innocence
meinlaust • *n* innocence
meinsæri • *n* perjury
meintur • *adj* alleged, putative
meistaraverk • *n* masterpiece
melludólgur • *n* pimp
melting • *n* digestion
men • *n* pendant
mendelevín • *n* mendelevium
mengi • *n* set
mengisbólga • *n* meningitis
mengunarmóða • *n* smog
menjar • *n* record

menning • *n* culture
menntaskóli • *n* gymnasium
menntun • *n* education
menúett • *n* minuet
mér • *pron* me
mergur • *n* marrow, matrix
meri • *n* mare
merkikerti • *n* whippersnapper
merking • *n* meaning
merkingarbær • *n* morpheme
merkingarfræðilegur • *adj* semantic
merkingarlegur • *adj* semantic
merkingarskipti • *n* metonymy
merkjamálsfræði • *n* algebra
messa • *n* church, mass • *v* mass
met • *n* record
metan • *n* methane
metanól • *n* methanol
meth • *n* ice
metýlfenídat • *n* methylphenidate
mexíkanahattur • *n* sombrero
meydómsmerki • *n* hymen
meyjarhaft • *n* hymen
miðbær • *n* downtown
miðbaugur • *n* equator
miðborg • *n* downtown
miðgildi • *n* median
miðhandar- • *adj* metacarpal
miðhandarbein • *n* metacarpal, metacarpus
miðhönd • *n* metacarpus
miðhvolf • *n* mesosphere
miðill • *n* media
miðilsgáfa • *n* medium
miðja • *v* center • *n* center
miðlungs- • *adj* run-of-the-mill
miðnætti • *n* midnight
miðnótt • *n* midnight
miðpunktur • *n* center
miðstig • *n* comparative
miðstöð • *n* center
miðsumar • *n* midsummer
miðsumarsdagur • *n* midsummer
miðtala • *n* median
mig • *pron* me
míga • *v* piss
mikill • *adj* great, large
mikilmenni • *n* prince
mikilmennskubrjálæði • *n* megalomania
mikilvægi • *n* importance, value
mikilvægur • *adj* imperative, important
míla • *n* mile
mildur • *adj* clement
milli • *n* millionaire
milliliður • *n* mean
millísekúnda • *n* millisecond

milljónamæringur • *n* millionaire
milta • *n* spleen
miltisbrandur • *n* anthrax
mín • *pron* me
minjagripur • *n* memento
minkur • *n* mink
minn • *pron* me, mine
minni • *n* memory
minning • *n* obituary
minningargrein • *n* epitaph
minningargripur • *n* memento
minnisgóður • *adj* tenacious
minnismerki • *n* monument
minnistæður • *adj* memorable
minnsta • *n* morpheme
mínus • *n* minus • *adj* minus • *conj* minus
mínusskaut • *n* cathode
mínúta • *n* minute
misátta • *adj* anisotropic
misgerð • *n* sin
misgjörð • *n* sin
mishverfur • *adj* asymmetrical
miskabætur • *n* amends
miskunnsamur • *adj* clement
mislyndur • *adj* capricious
misræmi • *n* discrepancy
missa • *v* loose
missamhverfur • *adj* asymmetrical
misskilja • *v* misunderstand
mistilteinn • *n* mistletoe
mistök • *n* error
mistur • *n* mist
mitt • *pron* me
mitti • *n* waist
mjá • *interj* meow
mjaðmargrind • *n* pelvis
mjálma • *v* meow
mjöðm • *n* hip
mjöður • *n* mead
mjög • *adv* very
mjókka • *v* thin
mjöl • *n* flour
mjólkurafurðir • *n* dairy
mjólkurbú • *n* dairy
mjólkurbúð • *n* dairy
mjólkurhristingur • *n* shake
mjónefur • *n* echidna
mjór • *adj* thin
mjúkur • *adj* soft
mö • *interj* moo
móðgun • *n* insult
móðir • *n* mother
móðurbróðir • *n* uncle
móðurlaus • *adj* motherless
móðurlaust • *adj* motherless
móðurlíf • *n* womb
móðursjúkur • *adj* hysterical

móðursýkiskast • *n* hysterics
móðursystir • *n* aunt
mögulegt • *adj* feasible
mögulegur • *adj* possible, potential
möguleiki • *n* possibility
mök • *n* fuck
moldvarpa • *n* mole
mólekúl • *n* molecule
mölur • *n* moth
mölva • *v* smash
mólýbden • *n* molybdenum
möndull • *n* axis
mont • *n* boast
möntull • *n* cloak, mantle
mör • *n* suet
mór • *n* peat
morð • *n* kill, murder
morðingi • *n* killer, murderer
mörður • *n* marten
morfem • *n* morpheme
morfín • *n* morphine
mörgæs • *n* penguin
morgundagur • *n* tomorrow
morgunfrú • *n* marigold
morgunmatur • *n* breakfast
morgunn • *n* morning
morgunsár • *n* dawn
morgunteygjur • *n* pandiculation
morgunverður • *n* breakfast
moska • *n* mosque
moskítófluga • *n* mosquito
moskusrotta • *n* muskrat
möskvi • *n* mesh
mót • *n* matrix
mótbára • *n* objection
mótetta • *n* motet
mótherji • *n* opponent
móti • *prep* versus
mótmæla • *v* object
mótor • *n* engine, motor
mótorhjól • *n* motorcycle
mótstaða • *n* resistance, resistor
motta • *n* mat, moustache
mótun • *n* modulation • *adj* nascent
mötuneyti • *n* canteen
mu • *interj* moo
múffa • *n* muff, muffin
múkki • *n* fulmar
múlasni • *n* mule
múlbinda • *v* muzzle
muldra • *v* mutter
muldur • *n* mutter
múldýr • *n* mule
múli • *n* muzzle
múll • *n* muzzle
múltuber • *n* cloudberry
múmía • *n* mummy

muna • *v* remember
munaðarleysingi • *n* orphan
munaðarleysingjahæli • *n* orphanage
mund • *n* hand
munkahetta • *n* cowl
munkur • *n* monk
munnamaga- • *adj* cardiac
munnkarfa • *n* muzzle
munnlega • *adv* orally
munnræpa • *n* logorrhea
munnur • *n* mouth, orifice
munnvatn • *n* saliva
múr • *n* wall
múra • *v* wall
múrmeldýr • *n* marmot
múrsteinn • *n* brick
mús • *n* mouse
músarbendill • *n* cursor
músarindill • *n* wren
músasmári • *n* shamrock
músík • *n* music
múskat • *n* nutmeg
musteri • *n* temple
músvákur • *n* buzzard
múta • *v* bribe • *n* bribe
mygla • *n* mold
mýgrútur • *n* myriad
mykja • *n* dung, manure
mýla • *v* muzzle
mýli • *n* muzzle
myllusteinn • *n* millstone
mynd • *n* image, movie, photo, picture, range
myndan • *n* morpheme
myndarlegur • *adj* bouncing
myndavél • *n* camera
myndband • *n* videotape
myndbreyting • *n* transubstantiation
myndefni • *n* metabolite
myndeining • *n* pixel
myndmengi • *n* range
myndun • *n* map, mapping • *adj* nascent
mynni • *n* mouth
mynnt • *n* silver
mynstur • *n* pattern
mynt • *n* coin
myntfræði • *n* numismatics
myntfræðingur • *n* numismatist
mýóglóbín • *n* myoglobin
myrða • *v* murder
mýri • *n* marsh, moor, swamp
myrkur • *n* darkness
myrkvi • *n* eclipse
myrra • *n* myrrh
mysa • *n* whey

N

náæta • *n* ghoul
nabbi • *n* pimple
náð • *n* mercy
naðra • *n* serpent
næla • *v* pin
nælon • *n* nylon
nælonsokkur • *n* nylon
næpa • *n* turnip
nærbolur • *n* vest
nærföt • *n* underwear
næring • *n* sustenance
nærri • *adj* inshore
næstsíðastur • *adj* penultimate
næstur • *adj* next
næturgali • *n* nightingale
næturkoma • *n* nightfall
nafli • *n* navel
nafn • *n* name
nafnháttur • *n* infinitive
nafnhvörf • *n* metonymy
nafnlaus • *adj* nameless
nafnorð • *n* noun
naga • *v* gnaw
nagdýr • *n* rodent
nagli • *n* nail
nágranni • *adj* neighboring
nágrenni • *n* neighborhood
náhvalur • *n* narwhal
nakinn • *adj* naked
naktur • *adj* naked
nál • *n* needle
nálgast • *v* near
nálgun • *n* approximation
nám • *n* study
náma • *n* mine
námsáætlun • *n* syllabus
námsefni • *n* study
námsgrein • *n* subject
námskeið • *n* course
námsstyrkur • *n* stipend
námumaður • *n* miner
nár • *n* corpse
nashyrningur • *n* rhinoceros
natrín • *n* sodium
natríum • *n* sodium
nátt • *n* night
náttföt • *n* pajamas
náttúra • *n* nature
nauðga • *v* rape
nauðgun • *n* rape
nauðsyn • *n* imperative
nauðsynlegur • *adj* necessary
naumlega • *adv* hardly
naut • *n* bull

nautakjöt • *n* beef
nautgripur • *n* cow
né • *conj* nor
neðanjarðar • *adv* underground
nef • *n* beak, bill, nose
nefdýr • *n* monotreme
nefna • *v* mention, name
nefnari • *n* denominator
nefnd • *n* committee
nefnilega • *adv* namely
negri • *n* boy, nigger, spade
negull • *n* clove
negulpipar • *n* allspice
nei • *n* no
neikvæður • *adj* minus
neiskaut • *n* cathode
neisti • *n* spark
neitt • *pron* nothing
neitun • *n* negation, no, repudiation
neitunarvald • *n* veto
nekt • *n* nakedness, nudity
nektardans • *n* strip
nektardansmær • *n* stripper
nema • *v* learn, take • *conj* unless
nemandi • *n* pupil, student
neodým • *n* neodymium
neon • *n* neon
neptún • *n* neptunium
nes • *n* ness
net • *n* net, network
netkorn • *n* ribosome
nettó • *adj* net
niða • *v* babble
niðji • *n* descendant
níðkvæði • *n* squib
niður • *n* babble
niðurfallssýki • *n* epilepsy
niðurgangur • *n* diarrhea
niðurlægja • *v* abase, confound
niðurlagsorð • *n* epilogue
nifl • *n* darkness
nifteind • *n* neutron
niggari • *n* spade
níggjundi • *adj* ninth
níhílismi • *n* nihilism
nikkel • *n* nickel
nióbín • *n* niobium
nirfill • *n* miser
nisti • *n* pendant
nit • *n* nit
nítrat • *n* nitrate
nítrít • *n* nitrite
nítugasta • *adj* ninetieth
nitur • *n* nitrogen

njóla • *n* night
njólubaugur • *n* rainbow
njósna • *v* spy
njósnari • *n* spy
njóta • *v* relish
nóbelín • *n* nobelium
nögl • *n* nail
nökkvar • *n* chiton
norður • *n* north
norn • *n* witch
nös • *n* nostril
nostalgía • *n* nostalgia
nóta • *n* bill
nota • *v* use
notaður • *adj* secondhand, used
notandi • *n* user
nótt • *n* night, nightfall
nú • *adv* now • *interj* why

nudd • *n* massage
nuddari • *n* masseur
núðla • *n* noodle
núkleótíð • *n* nucleotide
núllstöð • *n* zero
númer • *n* number
númera • *v* number
ný • *adj* new
nýfæddur • *adj* newborn
nýlega • *adv* recently
nýr • *adj* new
nýra • *n* kidney
nýtingarréttur • *n* usufruct
nýtinn • *adj* efficient
nytjasfena • *n* utilitarianism
nýtni • *n* economy
nýtt • *adj* new

O

ó • *interj* oh
óafsakanlegur • *adj* unwarranted
óákveðinn • *adj* hesitant
óánægja • *n* dissatisfaction
óáreiðanlegur • *adj* unreliable
óargadýr • *n* animal
óbeinn • *adj* roundabout
óbeit • *n* antipathy
óbeygjanlegur • *adj* indeclinable
óbó • *n* oboe
óbreyta • *n* invariant
óbreyttur • *adj* invariant
óbyggðir • *n* wilderness
óðagot • *n* precipitation
óðal • *n* domain
ódalíska • *n* odalisque
ódauðlegur • *adj* immortal
ódauðleiki • *n* immortality
odda- • *adj* odd
ódeilanlegur • *adj* indivisible
ódýrt • *adj* inexpensive
óeirinn • *adj* bellicose
óekta • *adj* bogus, spurious
óendanleiki • *n* infinity
ófáanlegur • *adj* unavailable, unobtainable
ofanvarp • *n* projection
ofdramb • *n* hubris
ofdyri • *n* lintel
offita • *n* obesity
oflátungur • *n* whippersnapper
ófleygur • *adj* flightless
öflugur • *adj* powerful
ofmeta • *v* overrate

ofn • *n* fire, oven
ofnæmislyf • *n* antihistamine
ofnæmisvaki • *n* allergen
ofnæmisvaldur • *n* allergen
öföndun • *n* hyperventilation
óformlegur • *adj* informal
ófrádrægur • *adj* nonnegative
ófræging • *n* denigration
ófrelsi • *n* constraint
ófreskja • *n* monster
ófriðsamur • *adj* belligerent
ófrískur • *adj* pregnant
oft • *adv* often
oftlega • *adv* often
öfuggi • *n* pervert
öfugsnúinn • *adj* backhanded
ofursamhverfa • *n* supersymmetry
ófyrirgefanlegur • *adj* unpardonable
og • *conj* and, plus
og-lykkja • *n* ampersand
ógagnsær • *adj* opaque
ógeð • *n* antipathy
ógeðslegur • *adj* disgusting
ógiftur • *adj* unmarried
ógilda • *v* rescind
ögn • *n* mote
ógrynni • *n* myriad
ogun • *n* conjunction
óhæði • *n* independence
óhafinn • *adj* unbegun
óheflaður • *adj* bucolic
óhlýðinn • *adj* disobedient
óhóflegur • *adj* excessive
óhreinn • *adj* dirty

óhrekjandi • *adj* indubitable
óhrekjanlega • *adv* indubitably
óhuggandi • *adj* inconsolable
óhugnanlegur • *adj* uncanny
oj • *interj* yuck
ójafn • *adj* odd
ójafna • *n* inequality
ójafnlitna • *adj* aneuploid
ójafnlitnun • *n* aneuploidy
okfruma • *n* zygote
okkarína • *n* ocarina
ökkli • *n* ankle
ókláraður • *adj* unfinished
ókostur • *n* minus
oktan • *n* octane
ökuljós • *n* headlight
ökumaður • *n* driver
ókunnur • *adj* unknown
ókurteis • *adj* discourteous
ókurteist • *adj* discourteous
ökutæki • *n* vehicle
ókvæni • *n* bachelorhood
ókvæntur • *adj* unmarried
ókynhneigð • *n* asexuality
öl • *n* ale, beer
ölæði • *n* drunkenness
ólæsilegur • *adj* illegible
öld • *n* century
öldungadeild • *n* senate
öldungaráðsmaður • *n* senator
öldungur • *n* elder
óléttur • *adj* pregnant
ölgerð • *n* brewery
ölgerðarhús • *n* brewery
olía • *n* oil
ólífa • *n* olive
ólivín • *n* olivine
ölkrús • *n* beer
ölmusa • *n* alms
olnbogi • *n* elbow
ólokinn • *adj* unfinished
ölstofa • *n* bar
ölvun • *n* drunkenness
ólýðræðislegur • *adj* undemocratic
ólyfseðilsskyldur • *adj* over-the-counter
óm • *n* ohm
ómennska • *n* sloth
ómögulegur • *adj* impossible
ómsjá • *n* sonar
ömurlegur • *v* suck
önd • *n* duck, vestibule
öndunarfæraslím • *n* phlegm
öndur • *n* ski
önghljóð • *n* fricative
öngstræti • *n* alley
op • *n* mouth, orifice
ópall • *n* opal

ópera • *n* opera
opinber • *adj* public
opinberun • *n* revelation
ópíum • *n* opium
ör • *adj* fast • *n* scar
óraddaður • *adj* voiceless
óráðinn • *adj* hesitant
óræður • *adj* irrational
óraunverulegur • *adj* unreal
örbylgja • *n* microwave
orð • *n* cognate, word
orða • *v* mention, word
orðabók • *n* dictionary, lexicon
orðabókafræði • *n* lexicography
orðabókargerð • *n* lexicography
orðaflaumur • *n* logorrhea
orðaforði • *n* vocabulary
orðahnippingar • *n* altercation
orðakast • *n* altercation
orðarugl • *n* anagram
orðasafn • *n* glossary, lexicon
orðasenna • *n* altercation
orðaskak • *n* altercation
orðhlutafræði • *n* morphology
orðlaus • *adj* speechless
orðrétt • *adj* verbatim • *adv* verbatim
orðréttur • *adj* verbatim
orðsifjafræði • *n* etymology
orðsifjafræðingur • *n* etymologist
orðsifjar • *n* etymology
orðskipunarfræði • *n* syntax
orðskviður • *n* aphorism
óregla • *n* drunkenness
óreglulegur • *adj* irregular
Óreiða • *n* entropy
óréttlætanlegur • *adj* unwarranted
óréttmætur • *adj* unwarranted
óréttur • *adj* wrong
organisti • *n* organist
orgel • *n* organ
orgelleikari • *n* organist
orgía • *n* orgy
orginall • *n* original
örheimur • *n* microcosm
óriganó • *n* oregano
orka • *n* energy
orki • *n* orc
örlæti • *n* benevolence
örlög • *n* destiny, fate, fortune, kismet
ormur • *n* worm
örn • *n* eagle
óró • *n* restlessness
órói • *n* anxiety, restlessness
órólegur • *adj* tense
örsmæðareikningur • *n* calculus
orsök • *n* cause
öruggur • *adj* certain

örvamælir • *n* quiver
örvasa • *adj* decrepit
örvera • *n* microbe, microorganism
öryggi • *n* safety, security
öryggis- • *adj* backup
öryggisafrit • *n* backup
ósagður • *adj* unvoiced
ósamræmi • *n* discrepancy
ósamstilltur • *adj* asynchronous
ósanngjarn • *adj* unfair
ósiðlegur • *adj* wrong
ósiðsamur • *adj* wrong
ósigrandi • *n* invincible
ósigur • *n* defeat
ósjaldan • *adv* often
ósk • *n* wish
óska • *v* wish
óskammfeilni • *n* effrontery
óskaraður • *adj* disjoint
óskemmdur • *adj* pristine
óskháttur • *n* optative
óskilgetinn • *adj* spurious
óskipulegur • *adj* haphazard
óskírlíft • *adj* incontinent
óskírlífur • *adj* incontinent
öskra • *v* shout, yell
öskrari • *n* screamer
óskrírlíf • *adj* incontinent
öskubakki • *n* ashtray
óskýr • *adj* ambiguous
osmín • *n* osmium
ósnertill • *n* asymptote

ósnortinn • *adj* pristine
óson • *n* ozone
ösp • *n* aspen
óspilltur • *adj* pristine
ostur • *n* cheese, smegma
ósveigjanlegur • *adj* inflexible
ósvífni • *n* effrontery
ósýnilegur • *adj* invisible
ósýnileiki • *n* invisibility
ótal • *n* myriad
óþægindi • *n* distress
óþekktur • *adj* nameless, unknown
óþolinmóður • *adj* impatient
óþýðanlegur • *adj* untranslatable
ótjáður • *adj* unvoiced
otur • *n* otter
ótvíræðlega • *adv* indubitably
ótvíræður • *adj* indubitable
óumflýjanlegur • *adj* unavoidable
óunninn • *adj* raw
óvarinn • *adj* naked
óvenjulega • *adv* unusually
óverðugur • *adj* unworthy
óviljandi • *adj* inadvertent
óvinur • *n* adversary, enemy
óvirðing • *n* contempt, disgrace
oxíð • *n* oxide
oxídóredúktasi • *n* oxidoreductase
öxl • *n* shoulder
öxull • *n* axle
óyndi • *n* ennui

P

pabbi • *n* daddy
paddla • *v* paddle, row
pækill • *n* brine
páfagaukur • *n* parrot
páfi • *n* pope
páfugl • *n* peacock, peafowl
páhæna • *n* peahen
pakk • *n* riffraff
pakka • *v* fold, package
pakkhús • *n* warehouse
pakki • *n* package
palata • *n* palace
palladín • *n* palladium
pant • *n* dibs
panta • *v* order
pápisti • *n* papist
pappa- • *adj* paper
pappír • *n* paper
pappírs- • *adj* paper
pappírskilja • *n* paperback

par • *n* couple, duo, pair
pára • *v* scrawl
pardusdýr • *n* panther
park • *n* park
parkera • *v* park
partí • *n* party
partur • *n* part
páskalilja • *n* narcissus
passía • *n* passion
pastínakka • *n* parsnip
pé • *n* pee
pelíkani • *n* pelican
pendúll • *n* pendulum
peningaskápur • *n* safe
peningur • *n* bread, money
penisillín • *n* penicillin
penni • *n* pen
pensill • *n* brush, paintbrush
pepsín • *n* pepsin
pera • *n* pear

perla • *n* pearl
perlumóðir • *n* mother-of-pearl
permanent • *n* permanent
perri • *n* pervert
persimónía • *n* persimmon
persóna • *n* character, person
pervert • *n* pervert
peysa • *n* sweater
pí • *n* pi
píanisti • *n* pianist
píanó • *n* piano, pianoforte
píanóleikari • *n* pianist
píka • *n* cunt, pussy, vulva
píla • *n* arrow
pílári • *n* baluster, banister, bannister, picket
pils • *n* skirt
piltur • *n* boy
pínlegur • *adj* awkward
pipar • *n* pepper
piparminta • *n* peppermint
piparrót • *n* horseradish
piparsveinn • *n* bachelor
pípetta • *n* pipette
pipra • *v* pepper
pírumpár • *n* scrawl
pískra • *v* whisper
pissa • *v* piss
pistasía • *n* pistachio
pistasíuhneta • *n* pistachio
pistasíutré • *n* pistachio
pítsa • *n* pizza
pitsa • *n* pizza
pizza • *n* pizza
pjalla • *n* pussy
plægja • *v* ear, plough
plága • *v* devil • *n* plague
plagíóklas • *n* plagioclase
plágueyðir • *n* pesticide
pláneta • *n* planet
planta • *n* plant
plast • *n* plastic
plata • *n* record
platína • *n* platinum
platónskur • *adj* platonic
plógur • *n* plough
plóma • *n* plum
plómublár • *n* plum
plómutré • *n* plum
plús • *n* plus
plúton • *n* plutonium
pöbb • *n* bar
pokabjörn • *n* koala
pokadýr • *n* marsupial
pokarotta • *n* opossum
póker • *n* poker
poki • *n* sack

pólitísk • *adj* political
pólitíska • *adj* political
póll • *n* pole
polli • *n* bollard
pollur • *n* pool, puddle
pólon • *n* polonium
pólýester • *n* polyester
pólýfónía • *n* polyphony
pólýstýren • *n* polystyrene
pólýúretan • *n* polyurethane
pönk • *n* punk
pönkari • *n* punk
pönnukaka • *n* pancake
pöntun • *n* order
poppkorn • *n* popcorn
portvín • *n* port
posi • *n* sack
pósitífur • *adj* plus
póstkort • *n* postcard
póstmódernismi • *n* postmodernism
postulín • *n* porcelain
postullegur • *adj* apostolic
potari • *n* poker
prammi • *n* barge
praseódým • *n* praseodymium
predika • *v* preach
predikun • *n* sermon
prenta • *v* print
prentari • *n* printer
prentduft • *n* toner
prests- • *adj* bucolic
prestur • *n* priest
pretta • *v* befool
prik • *n* stick
prímati • *n* primate
prins • *n* prince
prinsessa • *n* princess
prinsipp • *n* principle
prjónn • *n* chopstick
pródúsa • *v* produce
pródúsera • *v* produce
próf • *n* examination
prófarkalesari • *n* proofreader
prófessor • *n* professor
program • *n* program
prómetín • *n* promethium
própan • *n* propane
prósa • *n* prose
protaktín • *n* protactinium
prótín • *n* protium
prúðmenni • *n* gentleman
prúðmennska • *n* gentlemanliness
prumpa • *v* fart
prútta • *v* haggle
púa • *v* boo
púðli • *n* poodle
púðluhundur • *n* poodle

pukra • *v* whisper
púla • *v* slave
púls • *n* pulse
pungur • *n* scrotum
punkta • *v* jot
punktafylki • *n* bitmap
punktamynd • *n* bitmap
punktur • *n* jot, pixel
purpuralitur • *adj* purple

púrtvín • *n* port
púsl • *n* puzzle
pussa • *n* pussy
putta • *v* finger
putti • *n* finger
pylsa • *n* sausage
pýramídi • *n* pyramid
pýroxen • *n* pyroxene

R

rabarbari • *n* rhubarb
ráð • *n* advice, scheme
ráð • *n* council
ráða • *v* advise
ráða • *v* rule
ráðabrugg • *n* machination, plot
ráðagerð • *n* scheme
raddaður • *adj* voiced
raddbandakvef • *n* laryngitis
raddblær • *n* inflection
ráðdeild • *n* economy
raddlaus • *adj* voiceless
ráðgáta • *n* enigma, mystery
raðhverfa • *n* anagram
radísa • *n* radish
radíus • *n* radius
radon • *n* radon
ráðstöfun • *n* arrangement
ráðvandur • *adj* honest
rádýr • *n* deer
ræða • *n* speech
ræðismaður • *n* consul
ræðisskrifstofa • *n* consulate
ræður • *adj* rational
rægja • *v* backbite
rækja • *n* prawn, shrimp
ræna • *v* bereave, purloin
ræsa • *v* bootstrap
ræsiforrit • *n* bootstrap
rætur • *n* root
raf • *n* amber
rafeind • *n* electron
rafeindareiknir • *n* computer
rafeindatækni • *n* electronics
rafgas • *n* plasma
rafgeymir • *n* battery
rafgreining • *n* electrolysis
rafheili • *n* computer
rafhlaða • *n* battery
rafklofi • *n* electrolyte
raflausn • *n* electrolyte
rafleysa • *n* asystole
rafliði • *n* relay

rafmagn • *n* electricity
rafmagnsþéttir • *n* capacitor
rafnemi • *n* electrode
rafpóll • *n* electrode
rafrás • *n* circuit
rafreiknir • *n* computer
rafsegulfræði • *n* electromagnetism
rafskaut • *n* electrode
rafspenna • *n* voltage
rafstraumsrás • *n* circuit
rafþéttir • *n* capacitor
rafvaki • *n* electrolyte
raggeit • *n* craven
ragmennska • *n* cowardice
rakari • *n* barber
raketta • *n* skyrocket
raki • *n* damp
rakur • *adj* moist
rakvél • *n* razor
rámur • *adj* hoarse, husky, throaty
rangeygður • *adj* cross-eyed
ranglátur • *adj* unjust, wrong
rangnefni • *n* misnomer
rangstaða • *n* offside
rangstæður • *adj* offside
rangt • *adv* wrong
rangur • *adj* wrong
rannsaka • *v* delve
rannsókn • *n* study
rannsóknarefni • *n* study
rannsóknarstofa • *n* laboratory
rannsóknarstofu • *n* laboratory
rás • *n* circuit
rasismi • *n* racism
rasista- • *adj* racist
rasisti • *n* racist
rass • *n* ass, backside, butt
rassgat • *n* asshole
rasskinn • *n* buttock
rasskinnar • *n* backside
ratsjá • *n* radar
rauðbeða • *n* beetroot
rauðbrúnn • *n* maroon • *adj* maroon

rauðglóandi • *adj* red-hot
rauðleitur • *adj* reddish, ruddy
rauðrófa • *n* beetroot
rauður • *n* red • *adj* red, ruddy
raufaræðahnútur • *n* hemorrhoid
raula • *v* hum
raun • *n* fact
raunamæddur • *adj* lugubrious
raunar • *adv* really
raunverulega • *adv* really
raunveruleiki • *n* fact
raust • *n* voice
reður • *n* phallus
reðurfarði • *n* smegma
refhvörf • *n* oxymoron
refsing • *n* punishment
refur • *n* fox
reggí • *n* reggae
regla • *n* rule
reglugerð • *n* regulation
reglulegur • *adj* orderly
reglustika • *n* ruler
regn • *adj* pluvial • *n* rain
regnbogi • *n* rainbow
regndropi • *n* raindrop
regnhlíf • *n* umbrella
regnkápa • *n* raincoat
reiðhjól • *n* bicycle
reiðufé • *n* cash
reiður • *adj* angry
reikisteinn • *n* meteoroid
reikistjarna • *n* planet
reikningur • *n* account, bill
reiknirit • *n* algorithm
reiknisögn • *n* algorithm
reiknivél • *n* calculator
reiknivísi • *n* calculus
reimleiki • *n* haunting
reipi • *n* rope
reiprennandi • *adj* fluent
reisa • *v* fare • *n* trip
reisn • *n* dignity
reitur • *n* plot
reka • *v* fire
rekill • *n* driver
rekstur • *n* operation
renglulegur • *adj* gangling
renín • *n* rhenium
reníum • *n* rhenium
renna • *v* flow, slide • *n* slide
rennibekkur • *n* lathe
rennibraut • *n* slide
rennilás • *n* fly
rennilykkja • *n* noose
rennimál • *n* calipers
repjufræ • *n* rapeseed
rest • *n* rest

retróveira • *n* retrovirus
rétt • *adj* correct, right • *n* pen
réttar- • *adj* forensic
rétthyrningur • *n* rectangle
réttritun • *n* orthography
réttskeið • *n* square
réttsýnn • *adj* honest
rétttrúnaður • *n* orthodoxy
réttur • *n* dish • *adj* right
reykelsi • *n* frankincense, incense
reykháfur • *n* chimney
reykingamaður • *n* smoker
reykingar • *n* smoking
reykja • *v* smoke
reykjarmóða • *n* smog
reykur • *n* smoke
reyna • *v* experience
reyniberjatré • *n* rowan
reynir • *n* rowan
reynitré • *n* rowan
reynslulausn • *n* parole
ríða • *v* fuck
riða • *n* scrapie
riddari • *n* horse, knight
rif • *n* reef
riffill • *n* rifle
rifjárn • *n* grater
rifrildi • *n* altercation
rifta • *v* rescind
rigning • *adj* pluvial • *n* rain
ríki • *n* category, country, nation, realm, state
ríkidæmi • *n* money
ríkisborgararéttur • *n* citizenship
ríkisborgari • *n* citizen
ríkisstjóri • *n* governor
ríkisstjórn • *n* government
ríkja • *v* rule
ríkur • *adj* rich
rím • *n* rhyme
rimill • *n* baluster, banister, bannister, picket
rimlagirðing • *n* balustrade
rimlahandrið • *n* balustrade
ringlulreið • *n* pandemonium
ringulreið • *n* chaos, disorder
ris • *n* attic, garret
risaborg • *n* megalopolis
risaeðla • *n* dinosaur
rísandi • *adj* rising
risastór • *adj* huge
rishæð • *n* attic
rist • *n* instep
rita • *n* kittiwake • *v* scribe, write
ritari • *n* typewriter
ritblý • *n* graphite
rithöfundur • *n* author, writer • *v* write

ritill • *n* editor
rittáknakerfi • *n* alphabet
ritvél • *n* typewriter
rjóður • *adj* ruddy
rjómaís • *n* ice
rjómi • *n* cream
rjúpa • *n* ptarmigan
ró • *n* silence
róa • *v* paddle, placate, row
röð • *n* gamut, order, series, straight
rödd • *n* voice
roði • *adj* ruddy
ródín • *n* rhodium
roðna • *v* color
röðun • *n* arrangement
röðunarskrá • *n* index
róður • *n* rowing
rófa • *n* tail
rógbera • *v* backbite
rökhenda • *n* syllogism
rökkur • *n* dusk, twilight
rökkurbil • *n* nightfall
rökkva • *v* dusk
rökvilla • *n* fallacy
róla • *v* swing • *n* swing
rólega • *adv* deliberately, slowly
rölt • *n* stroll
rólyndi • *n* phlegm
romm • *n* rum
rómur • *n* voice
röntgenljósmyndun • *n* radiography
röntgenmynd • *n* radiograph
rós • *n* rose
röskun • *n* disorder
rostungur • *n* walrus
rót • *n* root
róta • *v* grub
róteind • *n* proton
rótt • *adv* tight

rúbidín • *n* rubidium
rúbín • *n* ruby
rúbínrauður • *adj* ruby
rúbla • *n* ruble
ruddalegur • *adj* brusque, randy
rugl • *n* ball, nonsense
rugla • *v* confound
rúgur • *n* rye
rukola • *n* rocket
rúlla • *n* roller
rúllukragapeysa • *n* turtleneck
rúllukragi • *n* turtleneck
rúllustigi • *n* escalator
rúm • *n* bed, room
rúma • *v* hold
rúmfræði • *n* geometry
rún • *n* confidant, rune
rúna • *n* confidant
rúnk • *n* masturbation
runni • *n* bush
rúsína • *n* raisin
rusl • *n* garbage, junk, litter
ruslpóstur • *n* spam
rúst • *n* ruin
rústa • *v* cream, destroy, murder
rúta • *n* bus
rúten • *n* ruthenium
rúturunni • *n* rue
ryðfrír • *adj* stainless
ryðga • *v* rust
ryðgaður • *adj* rusty
ryk • *n* dust
rykögn • *n* mote
ryksuga • *v* vacuum
rymja • *v* bray
rymur • *n* bray
rýrnun • *n* atrophy
rýtingur • *n* dagger

S

sáð • *n* semen, spermatozoon
sáðfruma • *n* spermatozoon
sáðfrumnadeyðir • *n* spermicide
sáðlát • *n* ejaculation
sáðrásarúrnám • *n* vasectomy
sáðvökvi • *n* semen
sæði • *n* semen, sperm
sæðisfruma • *n* sperm, spermatozoon
sæðiskrabbi • *n* seminoma
sækja • *v* frequent
sælilja • *n* crinoid • *adj* crinoid
særa • *v* hurt, wound
sæstjarna • *n* starfish

sætleik • *n* sweetness
sætmandla • *n* almond
sætur • *adj* cute, sugary, sweet
safamikill • *adj* juicy
safaríkur • *adj* juicy
safi • *n* juice
safír • *n* sapphire
safírblár • *adj* sapphire
safn • *n* museum
safna • *v* gather
safnrit • *n* anthology
sag • *n* sawdust
saga • *n* history, myth, saga, story, tale •

v saw
sagnbeyging • *n* conjugation
sagnfræði • *n* history
sagnorð • *n* verb
sake • *n* sake
sakkarósi • *n* sucrose
saklaus • *n* innocence
saklaust • *n* innocence
sakleysi • *n* innocence
sál • *n* soul
sala • *n* sale
sálast • *v* die
salat • *n* lettuce, salad
sáldur • *n* sieve
salerni • *n* toilet
sálfræði • *n* psychology
sálmabók • *n* hymnal
sálmur • *n* hymn, psalm
salt • *n* salt
salta • *v* salt
saltur • *adj* salt
sálumessa • *n* requiem
sama • *v* care
samaldra • *adj* coeval
samaldri • *n* coeval
saman • *adv* together
samanbuðartafla • *n* nomogram
samansetja • *v* assemble
samanstanda • *v* consist
samarín • *n* samarium
samása • *adj* coaxial, collinear
samband • *n* contact, federation, rapport
samburi • *n* litter
sameiginlegur • *adj* mutual
sameina • *v* join
sameind • *n* molecule
samfarir • *n* fuck
samfélag • *n* society
samfingrun • *n* syndactyly
samheiti • *n* synonym
samhliða • *adj* parallel
samhljóð • *n* consonant
samhljóði • *n* consonant
samhljómur • *n* harmony
samhugur • *n* concord
samhverfur • *adj* symmetrical
samkoma • *n* conjugation
samkomulag • *n* arrangement
samkomustaður • *n* agora
samkunduhús • *n* synagogue
samkynhneigð • *n* homosexuality
samkynhneigður • *n* homosexual
samkynja • *adj* homogeneous
samlægur • *adj* conterminous, contiguous
samlagning • *n* addition
samleggjandi • *n* addend

samleifa • *adj* congruent
samleifing • *n* congruence
samleitinn • *adj* convergent
samleitni • *n* convergence
samleitur • *adj* homogeneous
samliggjandi • *adj* contiguous
samlíking • *n* simile
samlína • *adj* collinear
samloka • *n* sandwich
samlyndi • *n* harmony
sammengi • *n* union
sammiðja • *adj* concentric
samnefndur • *adj* homonymous
samningur • *n* contract
samræði • *n* fuck
samræmi • *n* concord, harmony
samsæta • *n* allele, isotope
samsettur • *adj* composite, conglomerate
samsinna • *v* concur
samskeiða • *adj* concurrent
samskeyting • *n* concatenation
samsláttur • *n* percussion
samsnið • *n* congruence
samsniða • *adj* congruent
samstafa • *n* syllable
samstarf • *n* cooperation
samsteypa • *n* conglomerate
samstilltur • *adj* synchronous
samstofna • *n* cognate • *adj* cognate
samtal • *n* conversation, dialogue
samtala • *n* sum
samtáun • *n* syndactyly
samtenging • *n* conjunction, connective
samþykki • *n* consent
samþykkja • *v* consent
samtíðarmaður • *n* coeval, contemporary
samúð • *n* pity
samur • *adj* same
samúræji • *n* samurai
samvinna • *n* cooperation
samvirkni • *n* synergy
samviskusamur • *adj* conscientious
samviskusemi • *n* conscientiousness
samvísun • *n* coreference
sána • *n* sauna
sandali • *n* flip-flop, sandal
sandkassi • *n* sandbox
sandlaukur • *n* shallot
sandsteinn • *n* sandstone
sandur • *n* sand
sannarlega • *adv* really
sannindi • *n* truth
sannleikur • *n* truth
sannur • *adj* true
sápa • *n* soap
sapódilla • *n* sapodilla
sapódillaplóma • *n* sapodilla

sapódillatré • *n* sapodilla
sár • *n* injury, wound
sárabætur • *n* amends
sárasótt • *n* syphilis
sarí • *n* sari
sarklíki • *n* sarcoidosis
sársauki • *n* pain
satan • *n* devil
satt • *adj* real
sauma • *v* sew
saumaskapur • *n* needlework
saumnál • *n* needle
saumur • *n* nail
saurblað • *n* flyleaf
sebrahestur • *n* zebra
seðlaveski • *n* wallet
séður • *adj* astute
sefa • *v* placate
sefasjúkur • *adj* hysterical
segarek • *n* thromboembolism
segð • *n* expression
segja • *v* say, tell
segl • *n* sail
segull • *n* magnet
segulljós • *n* aurora
seildýr • *n* chordate
seinkun • *n* lag
seinleiki • *n* lateness
seinn • *adv* late
seinnipartur • *n* afternoon
seint • *adj* late
sekkja • *v* bag
sekkjapípa • *n* bagpipes
sekkur • *n* sack
sekúnda • *n* second
selen • *n* selenium
selja • *v* sell
seljurót • *n* celeriac
sellerí • *n* celery
selló • *n* cello
sellulósi • *n* cellulose
selur • *n* seal
sem • *pron* who
semball • *n* harpsichord
semballeikari • *n* harpsichordist
senda • *v* send
sendiboði • *n* messenger
sendibréf • *n* letter
sendiherra • *n* ambassador
sendiráð • *n* embassy
sennilega • *adv* probably
sent • *n* cent
sepi • *n* polyp
sérfróður • *n* judge
sérhljóð • *n* vowel
sérhljóði • *n* vowel
serín • *n* cerium

serótónín • *n* serotonin
sérréttur • *n* specialty
sértrúarsöfnuður • *n* sect
servíetta • *n* napkin
set • *n* sediment
setning • *n* sentence
setningafræði • *n* syntax
sexhyrningur • *n* hexagon
sexí • *adj* sexy
sextándapartsnóta • *n* semiquaver
sextándipartur • *n* semiquaver
sextugasta • *adj* sixtieth
seyða • *v* bake
seyði • *n* broth
seyta • *v* secrete
síðan • *prep* since
síðast • *adj* last
síðdegi • *n* afternoon
siðvenja • *n* custom
sífelldur • *adj* incessant
sifjaspell • *n* incest
sig • *v* dress, shit • *n* prolapse
síga • *v* prolapse
siga • *v* sic
sígaretta • *n* cigarette
sígarettustubbur • *n* butt
sígauni • *n* gypsy
sigð • *n* sickle
sigg • *n* callus, sclerosis
sigla • *v* sail
sigling • *n* sail
siglutré • *n* mast
sigra • *v* conquer, defeat
sígrænn • *adj* evergreen
sigti • *n* strainer
sigur • *n* victory
síki • *n* ditch, moat
síld • *n* herring
silfur • *n* argent, silver
silfurlitaður • *n* silver
silki • *n* silk
silkiormur • *n* silkworm
sílófónn • *n* xylophone
silungur • *n* trout
sími • *n* phone, telephone
simpansi • *n* chimpanzee
símtal • *n* bell, call
sin • *n* tendon
sinfónía • *n* symphony
sink • *n* zinc
sinnep • *n* mustard
sinnum • *prep* times
sínus • *n* sine
sínus- • *adj* sinusoidal
sínusferill • *n* sinusoid
sínuslaga • *adj* sinusoidal
sirka • *prep* circa

sirkon • *n* zirconium
síróp • *n* syrup
sísanna • *n* tautology
sítar • *n* zither
sitja • *v* sit
sitjandi • *n* backside
sítróna • *n* lemon
sítrónudrykkur • *n* lemonade
sívalningslaga • *adj* cylindrical
sjá • *v* behold, look, see
sjaldan • *adv* seldom
sjálfhverfa • *n* autism, involution
sjálfhverfur • *adj* autistic, reflexive
sjálfræði • *n* autonomy
sjálfræðisaldri • *n* age
sjálfsbani • *n* suicide
sjálfsblekking • *n* self-deception
sjálfsfróun • *n* masturbation
sjálfshól • *n* boast
sjálfsmeðaumkun • *n* self-pity
sjálfsmorð • *n* suicide
sjálfsmorðingi • *n* suicide
sjálfsstjórn • *n* autonomy
sjálfstæði • *n* independence
sjálfsvíg • *n* suicide
sjálfsvorkunn • *n* self-pity
sjálfþýða • *v* bootstrap
sjálfvirki • *n* automaton
sjálfvirkur • *adj* automatic
sjalottulaukur • *n* shallot
sjampó • *n* shampoo
sjáumst • *interj* later
sjeik • *n* shake
sjóari • *n* sailor, salt, tar
sjóher • *n* navy
sjöhyrningur • *n* heptagon
sjómaður • *n* sailor, tar
sjónarhorn • *n* angle
sjónauka • *n* telescope
sjónauki • *n* binoculars
sjónbaugur • *n* horizon
sjónblettur • *n* eyespot
sjóndeildarhringur • *n* horizon
sjónfræði • *n* optics
sjónkvarði • *n* reticle
sjónlaus • *adj* eyeless
sjónrænn • *adj* aesthetic
sjónvarp • *n* television
sjónvarpstæki • *n* television
sjoppa • *n* kiosk
sjór • *adj* marine • *n* ocean, sea
sjóræningi • *n* pirate • *adj* pirate
sjóræningjast • *v* picaroon
sjötti • *adj* sixth
sjöundi • *adj* seventh
sjóveiki • *n* seasickness
sjúkdómafræði • *n* pathology

sjúkdómur • *n* disease
sjúklingur • *n* patient
sjúkrabifreið • *n* ambulance
sjúkrabíll • *n* ambulance
sjúkrahús • *n* hospital
skaðlaus • *n* innocence
skaðlaust • *n* innocence
skaðlegur • *adj* harmful
skækja • *n* prostitute
skær • *adj* bright
skæri • *n* scissors
skæruliði • *n* guerrilla
skafgígur • *n* palimpsest
skagi • *n* peninsula
skák • *n* chess
skakkt • *adj* high
skakkur • *adj* high
skáktafl • *n* chess
skál • *n* bowl • *interj* cheers
skáld • *n* poet, skald
skáldaður • *adj* fictional
skáldkona • *n* poetess
skáldsaga • *n* novel
skáldskapur • *n* doggerel, fiction, poem
• *adj* fictional
skáli • *n* kiosk
skali • *n* gamut
skalli • *n* header
skálm • *n* leg
skalotlaukur • *n* shallot
skalottlaukur • *n* shallot
skálpur • *n* scabbard
skamma • *v* scold
skammær • *adj* ephemeral, fleeting
skammlífur • *adj* ephemeral
skammstafa • *v* abbreviate
skammstöfun • *n* abbreviation
skammt • *adj* near
skammvinnur • *adj* ephemeral
skán • *n* film
skandín • *n* scandium
skanni • *n* scanner
skap • *n* mood
skapa • *v* create
skapfesta • *n* backbone
skapraun • *n* umbrage
skápur • *n* closet
skara • *v* imbricate
skarfur • *n* cormorant
skarmengi • *n* intersection
skarphyrndur • *adj* angular
skarpskyggni • *n* acumen
skarpur • *adj* bright
skata • *n* ray, skate
skatthol • *n* escritoire
skattur • *n* tax
skaut • *n* electrode, lap

skegg • n beard, prow
skeggbroddur • n stubble
skeggjaður • adj bearded
skeið • n spoon, spoonful, vagina • adj vaginal
skeiðarfylli • n spoonful
skeifa • n horseshoe
skeita • v skateboard
skekkja • n error
skel • n shell
skemill • n footstool
skemma • v destroy • n shed, warehouse
skemmdarvargur • n vandal
skemmdarverk • n sabotage
skemmtilegur • adj funny
skemmtun • n entertainment
skera • v cut
skerfari • n sheriff
skermur • n lampshade
skerpa • n acumen
skíða • v ski
skíðamaður • n skier
skíði • n ski
skífmál • n calipers
skiki • n plot
skikkja • n cloak
skil • v see
skila • v return
skilaboð • n message
skilgreiningarmengi • n domain
skilja • v understand
skiljast • v understand
skilnaður • n divorce
skilvirkur • adj efficient
skilyrt • adj hypothetical
skilyrtur • adj hypothetical
skínandi • adj bright
skinka • n ham
skinn • n skin
skip • n ship
skipan • n arrangement
skipta • v cut, distribute, trade
skiptavinur • n customer
skipti • n trade
skipting • n division, fission
skipulag • n method
skipulegur • adj orderly
skíri • n shire
skírn • n baptism
skíta • v shit
skítapleis • n toilet
skítastaður • n toilet
skítur • n shit
skjáborð • n desktop
skjal • n document
skjalataska • n briefcase
skjaldarmerkjafræði • n heraldry

skjaldbaka • n tortoise, turtle
skjálfa • v shiver, shudder
skjálftafræði • n seismology
skjálftafræðingur • n seismologist
skjálfti • n shudder
skjár • n screen
skjól • n shelter
skjöldur • n shield
skjólstæðingur • n client
skjór • n magpie
skjóta • v shoot
skjótur • adj fast
skoða • v observe
skoðun • n study
skófatnaður • n footwear
skófla • n spade
skógur • n forest
skóhorn • n shoehorn
skokk • n jogging
skökk • adj high
skólabók • n textbook
skóli • n school
skolli • n bogey
sköllóttur • adj bald
skömm • n shame
skömmtun • n quantization
skonnorta • n schooner
sköp • n kismet, vulva
skopleikur • n farce
skopp • n ricochet
skoppa • v ricochet
skór • n shoe
skordýr • n insect
skordýraeitur • n pesticide
skordýrafræði • n entomology
skorsteinn • n chimney
skorta • v lack
skortur • n lack
skörungur • n poker
skósmiður • n cobbler
skósóli • n sole
skot • n bullet
skotapils • n kilt
skotgröf • n sap
skothylkjahólf • n magazine
skott • n tail, trunk
skottu- • adj quack
skottulækningar • n quackery
skottulæknir • n quack
skótunga • n tongue
skotvopn • n firearm, gun
skrá • n file, list, record • v scribe
skraddari • n tailor
skrækja • v shout
skrækskaði • n jay
skrafhreifinn • adj talkative
skrafhreifni • n talkativeness

skrambans • *adj* ruddy
skrambi • *adj* ruddy
skrápdýr • *n* echinoderm
skratti • *n* devil
skrattinn • *n* devil
skrauthvörf • *n* euphemism
skrautritun • *n* calligraphy
skrautskrift • *n* calligraphy
skrautyrði • *n* euphemism
skrefamælir • *n* pedometer
skrefateljari • *n* pedometer
skrefmælir • *n* pedometer
skreyta • *v* garnish
skríða • *v* crawl
skriðdreki • *n* tank
skriðdýr • *n* reptile
skriðsund • *n* crawl
skrifa • *v* scribe, write
skrifborð • *n* desk, escritoire
skrifbretti • *n* clipboard
skrifræði • *n* bureaucracy
skrifstofa • *n* office
skrifstofuveldi • *n* bureaucracy
skríll • *n* riffraff
skrípaleikur • *n* farce
skrjáf • *n* rustle
skrjáfa • *v* rustle
skröksaga • *n* myth
skrópa • *v* cut
skrúðganga • *n* parade
skrúfa • *n* screw
skrýtið • *adj* weird
skrýtin • *adj* weird
skrýtinn • *adj* weird
skuggi • *n* shadow, umbrage
skuldari • *n* debtor
skunkur • *n* skunk
skúr • *n* shack, shed, shower
skúraflákar • *n* cumulonimbus
skúraský • *n* cumulonimbus
skurðaðgerð • *n* operation
skurðgoðadýrkun • *n* idolatry
skurðlæknir • *n* surgeon
skurðmengi • *n* intersection
skurðpunktur • *n* intersection
skurður • *n* canal, cut, ditch
skutla • *v* shuttle • *n* shuttle
skutull • *n* harpoon
skutulönd • *n* pochard
skutur • *n* stern
skvetta • *n* shower
ský • *n* cloud
skyggja • *v* umbrage
skyggna • *n* slide
skyggnigáfa • *n* clairvoyance
skýjablika • *n* cirrostratus
skýjaður • *adj* cloudy

skýjafræði • *n* nephology
skýjakljúfur • *n* skyscraper
skýla • *v* shield
skylda • *n* duty
skyldmenni • *n* family, kin
skyldufræði • *n* deontology
skyldur • *adj* cognate, kin, related
skyndilega • *adv* suddenly
skyndiminni • *n* cache
skynja • *v* see
skynskiptingur • *n* idiot
skýranlegur • *adj* accountable
skyrbjúgur • *n* scurvy
skýrsla • *n* record
skyrta • *n* shirt
skyssa • *n* error
skytta • *n* shuttle
slá • *n* bar • *v* bat, hit, mow, scythe
slabb • *n* slush
slægð • *n* guile
slæmur • *adj* bad, evil
slagæð • *n* artery
slagæðargúlpur • *n* aneurysm
slagbrandur • *n* bolt
slagharpa • *n* piano
slagsmál • *n* brawl, combat
slagur • *n* fight
slagverk • *n* percussion
slanga • *n* snake, speculum
slarkari • *n* womanizer
slasa • *v* injure
slást • *v* brawl, fight
slátrari • *n* butcher
sláttarstöðvun • *n* asystole
sláttur • *n* percussion, pulse
slátur • *n* pudding
sláturhús • *n* abattoir
slaufa • *n* bow
sleði • *n* sledge, slide
slef • *n* saliva
sleikibrjóstsykur • *n* lollipop
sleikifingur • *n* forefinger
sleikipinni • *n* lollipop
sleikja • *v* lick
sleikjó • *n* lollipop
sleikjubrjóstsykur • *n* lollipop
slembi- • *adj* stochastic
slembinn • *adj* stochastic
sleppa • *v* loose
sléttur • *adj* even
sléttuúlfur • *n* coyote
slíðra • *v* sheathe
slíður • *n* vagina • *adj* vaginal
slifsi • *n* necktie
slím • *n* mucus
sljóleiki • *n* stupor
slóð • *n* wake

slöngvivaður • n lasso
sloppur • n bathrobe
slóra • v loaf, loiter
slúppa • n sloop
slydda • v sleet • n sleet
slyngur • adj astute
slys • n accident
smáatriði • n detail
smáauga • n facet
smábarnalegur • adj babyish
smábóndi • n croft
smádropi • n droplet
smækkunarending • n diminutive
smáfloti • n flotilla
smágúrka • n gherkin
smáheimur • n microcosm
smakka • v taste
smala • v assemble
smali • n assembler
smámæli • n lisp
smámunasemi • n pedantry
smán • n taunt
smána • v taunt
smánarlegur • adj egregious
smáorð • n particle
smár • adj small
smaragður • n emerald
smári • n transistor
smásmigill • n pedagogue
smásmygli • n pedantry
smástirni • n asteroid
smekkur • n bib, taste
smellinn • adj funny
smiðja • n factory
smitandi • adj contagious, infectious
smitgát • n asepsis
smjaðrari • n sycophant
smjör • n butter
smjör- • adj butyric
smjörlíki • n margarine
smokkfiskur • n squid
smokkur • n condom, squid
snær • n snow
snæri • n string
snagi • n peg
snákur • n snake
snara • v lasso • n lasso, loop
sneisafullur • adj jammed
snekkja • n yacht
snemma • adj early • adv early
snerta • v move, touch
snertill • n tangent
snerting • n contact
sneypa • v scold
snið • n cut, format, intersection
sniðmengi • n intersection
snifsi • n snip

snigill • n snail
sníkill • n parasite
sníkjudýr • n parasite
snillingur • n wonder
snípur • n clitoris
snjáldra • n shrew
snjáldurmús • n shrew
snjall • adj clever, proficient, smart
snjóa • v snow
snjóblindur • adj snow-blind
snjóflóð • n avalanche
snjóhús • n igloo
snjókarl • n snowman
snjókoma • n snow
snjókorn • n snowflake
snjór • n snow
snobb • n snob
snögglega • adv suddenly
snöggur • adj fast
snóker • n snooker
snökkt • n sob
snökta • v sob
snoppa • n muzzle
snotur • adj cute
snúa • v turn
snúningshraðamælir • n tachometer
snúra • n clothesline
snyrting • n toilet
söðulgjörð • n girth
söðull • n saddle
sofa • v sleep
sófi • n couch, sofa
söfnuður • n congregation
sög • n saw
sog • n suction
sogæðavökvi • n lymph
sögn • n verb
sogpípukraftur • n capillarity
sökka • v suck
sokkabuxur • n tights
sokkur • n sock
sökkva • v sink
söl • n dulse
sólarhringur • adj circadian
sólarlag • n sunset
sólarljós • n sunlight
sólaruppkoma • n dawn, sunrise
sólarupprás • n dawn, sunrise
sólbaugur • n ecliptic
sólblóm • n sunflower
soldán • n sultan
sóley • n buttercup
sólfall • n sunset
sólhvörf • n solstice
sóli • n sole
sólris • n dawn, sunrise
sólsetur • n sunset

sólskin • *n* sunshine
sólstingur • *n* sunstroke
sólstöður • *n* solstice
soltinn • *adj* hungry
sölumaður • *n* salesman, salesperson, solicitor
sólúr • *n* sundial
söluskáli • *n* kiosk
söluturn • *n* kiosk
sómakær • *adj* honest
sömuleiðis • *adv* likewise
sónar • *n* sonar
sonardóttir • *n* granddaughter
sónata • *n* sonata
söngkona • *n* singer
söngur • *n* song
söngvari • *n* singer
sönnun • *n* proof
sönnunarbyrði • *n* onus
sonur • *n* son
sopi • *n* sip
sópur • *n* broom
sorg • *adj* lugubrious • *n* sadness, sorrow
sorgbitinn • *adj* lugubrious
sorglegur • *adj* tragic
sori • *n* dregs
sort • *n* sort, type
sortuæxli • *n* melanoma
sósa • *n* sauce
sósíalismi • *n* socialism
sótthræðsla • *n* hypochondria
sótthreinsa • *v* sterilize
sóttsýki • *n* hypochondria
spá • *n* prognosis
spaði • *n* spade, spatula
spæll • *n* baluster, banister, bannister,
spoke
spæta • *n* woodpecker
spakmæli • *n* aphorism
spákona • *n* soothsayer
spakur • *adj* tame
spámaður • *n* prophet, soothsayer
spansgræna • *n* verdigris
spanskgræna • *n* verdigris
sparð • *n* turd
spark • *n* kick
sparka • *v* fire, kick
sparlega • *adv* sparingly
sparnaður • *n* economy
spaug • *n* joke
spauga • *v* joke
spaugsamur • *adj* facetious
spegill • *n* mirror, speculum
spegilvirkur • *adj* reflexive
spegla • *v* mirror
spékoppur • *n* dimple
speldi • *n* epiglottis, spelt

speli • *n* baluster, banister, bannister
spelt • *n* spelt
spendýr • *n* mammal
spengja • *n* bomb
spenna • *v* cock • *n* voltage
spennandi • *adj* exciting
spergilkál • *n* broccoli
spergill • *n* asparagus
spil • *n* game
spila • *v* play, trumpet
spilla • *v* rape
spilling • *n* corruption
spilltur • *adj* decadent
spínat • *n* spinach
spíra • *v* germinate • *n* spire, sprout
spírall • *n* coil
spítali • *n* hospital
spjald • *n* backboard
spjald- • *adj* sacral
spjaldbein • *adj* sacral • *n* sacrum
spjaldhryggur • *adj* sacral • *n* sacrum
spjaldliðir • *n* sacrum
spjalla • *v* converse
spjallþráður • *n* thread
spjör • *n* garment
spjót • *n* spear
spóla • *n* coil, spool
spönnuður • *n* generator
spor • *n* trace
sporbaugur • *n* ellipse
sporðdreki • *n* scorpion
sporður • *n* tail
sporjárn • *n* chisel
sporvagn • *n* tram
spotti • *n* string
sprauta • *n* hypodermic
sprengikúla • *n* bombshell
sprengistjarna • *n* supernova
sprengja • *n* bombshell • *v* explode
sprengjuleit • *n* minesweeper
springa • *v* explode
spúa • *v* spout, vomit
spúnn • *n* spoon
spurning • *n* question
spýja • *v* vomit
spyrill • *n* interviewer
spyrja • *v* ask
spyrjandi • *n* interviewer
spýta • *n* skewer, spit
staða • *n* status
staðbundinn • *adj* local
staðfesta • *v* ratify
staðreynd • *n* fact
staður • *adj* local • *n* place, stead
stærð • *n* size
stærðfræði • *n* mathematics
stærðfræðigreining • *n* analysis

stærðfræðilegur • *adj* mathematical
stærðfræðingur • *n* mathematician
stafa • *v* spell
stafabrengl • *n* anagram
stafarugl • *n* anagram
stafavíxl • *n* metathesis
stafli • *n* stack
stafrím • *n* alliteration
stafróf • *n* alphabet
stafur • *n* letter
stak • *n* element
stál • *n* steel
standa • *v* stand
standpína • *n* erection
stara • *v* stare
starf • *n* job, operation
starfa • *v* work
starfræksla • *n* operation
starfsemi • *n* operation
starfsmaður • *n* worker
starfssvið • *n* bailiwick
stari • *n* starling
staur • *n* picket
steðji • *n* anvil, incus
stef • *n* theme
stefna • *n* direction
stefnandi • *n* plaintiff
stefni • *n* stem
stefnuháður • *adj* anisotropic
stefnuhneigður • *adj* anisotropic
stefnumót • *n* date
stefnusnauður • *adj* isotropic
steindafræði • *n* mineralogy
steingervingafræði • *n* paleontology
steingervingafræðingur • *n* paleontologist
steingervingur • *n* fossil
steininn • *n* jug
steinn • *n* calculus, pebble, pit, stone
steinselja • *n* parsley
steinsteypa • *n* concrete
stél • *n* tail
stela • *v* purloin, steal
stelpa • *n* girl
stelsýki • *n* kleptomania
stelvís • *adj* thieving
steri • *n* steroid
stertur • *n* ponytail
stéttskiptingur • *n* parvenu
steypa • *n* concrete
steypast • *v* pelt, plummet
steypibað • *n* shower
stía • *n* pen
stífla • *v* clog • *n* clog, dam
stífna • *v* stiffen
stig • *n* level
stigagangur • *n* stairwell

stigahandrið • *n* banister, bannister
stigamaður • *n* highwayman
stigastærð • *n* scalar
stigi • *n* ladder, stair, stairs
stígvél • *n* boot
stígvélahanki • *n* bootstrap
stikilsber • *n* gooseberry
stikkfrí • *n* base
stikkorð • *n* cue
stikkpilla • *n* suppository
stikla • *n* preview, teaser, trailer
stiklutexti • *n* hypertext
stillanlegur • *adj* adjustable
stimpill • *n* piston, stamp
stimpla • *v* stamp
stingast • *v* plummet
stingskötur • *n* stingray
stirðkveðinn • *adj* doggerel
stírur • *n* sleep
stjaksetja • *v* impale
stjarfur • *adj* catatonic
stjarna • *n* star
stjarneðlisfræði • *n* astrophysics
stjarneðlisfræðingur • *n* astrophysicist
stjóri • *n* boss
stjórn • *n* government
stjórna • *v* rule
stjórnarskrá • *n* constitution
stjórnborði • *n* starboard
stjórnleysi • *n* anarchy
stjórnleysisstefna • *n* anarchism
stjórnmál • *n* politics
stjórnmálamaður • *n* politician
stjörnufræði • *n* astronomy
stjörnuhrap • *n* meteor
stjörnumerki • *n* asterisk, constellation
stjörnuspáfræði • *n* astrology
stjörnuspeki • *n* astrology
stjörnuþoka • *n* galaxy
stjúpa • *n* stepmother
stjúpbarn • *n* stepchild
stjúpbróðir • *n* stepbrother
stjúpdóttir • *n* stepdaughter
stjúpfaðir • *n* stepfather
stjúpi • *n* stepfather
stjúpmamma • *n* stepmother
stjúpmóðir • *n* stepmother
stjúpsonur • *n* stepson
stoð • *n* crutch
stöð • *n* station
stóð • *n* herd
stóðhestur • *n* stallion
stoðsending • *n* assist
stöðufræði • *n* statics
stöðugur • *adj* incessant
stöðvun • *n* moratorium
stofn • *n* population

stofnun • *n* foundation, institution
stokka • *v* shuffle
stökkbreyting • *n* mutation
stökkhéri • *n* hyrax
stokkönd • *n* mallard
stökkpallur • *n* springboard
stokkun • *n* shuffle
stóla • *n* stole
stóll • *n* chair
stolt • *n* pride
stöng • *n* bar, flagpole, rod
stór • *adj* great, large
stóræta • *n* macrophage
stórátfruma • *n* macrophage
stórbruni • *n* conflagration
stórhætta • *n* distress
stórkostlegur • *adj* marvelous
storkuhamur • *adj* solid
storkur • *n* stork
stórmarkaður • *n* supermarket
stormur • *n* storm
stórsameind • *n* macromolecule
stórsigla • *n* mainmast
stórskotahríð • *n* cannonade
stórveisla • *n* banquet
stórviðburður • *n* bombshell
stræti • *n* street
strætisvagn • *n* bus
strætó • *n* bus, omnibus
strákur • *n* boy
strandferðaskip • *n* coaster
strangleiki • *n* austerity
straua • *v* iron
strauja • *v* format, iron
straujárn • *n* iron
straumharður • *adj* torrential
straumrás • *n* circuit
streita • *n* stress
strengjabrúða • *n* puppet
strengur • *n* string
stress • *n* stress
streyma • *v* flow
stríð • *n* war
stríða • *v* banter
stríðni • *n* banter
strimill • *n* strip
stripp • *n* strip
strippa • *v* strip
strjúka • *v* bow
strokka • *v* churn
strokleður • *n* eraser
strompur • *n* chimney
strönd • *n* beach, coast, shore, strand
strontín • *n* strontium
strútur • *n* ostrich
stubbur • *n* butt
stúdera • *v* study

stuðlarit • *n* histogram
stuðlun • *n* alliteration
stuðningsmaður • *n* backer
stúfur • *n* frustum
stuldur • *n* larceny
stúlka • *n* girl
stunda • *v* frequent
stundum • *adv* sometimes
stungulyf • *n* hypodermic
sturta • *n* shower
stuttaralegur • *adj* brusque
stuttbuxur • *n* shorts
stuttur • *adj* short
stuttvaxinn • *adj* short
stútur • *n* pout
stykki • *n* cake, piece
stynja • *v* sob
stýrifræði • *n* cybernetics
stýrikjarni • *n* kernel
stýripinni • *n* joystick
stýristautur • *n* joystick
styrjaldaraðili • *n* belligerent
styrjöld • *n* war
styrkja • *v* corroborate
styrkur • *n* crutch, muscle, stipend
stytta • *v* abbreviate • *n* statue
stytting • *n* abbreviation, shorthand
suður • *n* south
súkkulaði • *n* chocolate
súkkulaðikökum • *n* brownie
súkrósi • *n* sucrose
súla • *n* gannet
sull • *n* piss
súlnabrjóstrið • *n* balustrade
sulta • *n* jam
sultur • *n* hunger
súlukóngur • *n* albatross
súlurit • *n* histogram
sum • *pron* some
sumar • *pron* some • *n* summer
sumir • *pron* some
summa • *n* sum
summumyndun • *n* summation
sund • *n* alley, sound, strait, swim
sundbolur • *n* swimsuit
sundföt • *n* swimsuit
sundurlægur • *adj* disjoint
sundurleitur • *adj* conglomerate
sundurliða • *v* itemize
súpuskál • *n* tureen
súr • *adj* acid, sour
súrefni • *n* oxygen
súrefnisskortur • *n* hypoxia
súrkál • *n* sauerkraut
surtur • *n* spade
sushi • *n* sushi
svæfingarlæknir • *n* anesthesiologist

svala • *n* swallow
svalir • *n* balcony
svalur • *adj* cool
svampur • *n* sponge
svangur • *adj* hungry, peckish
svanur • *n* swan
svar • *n* answer
svara • *v* answer
svartálfur • *n* goblin
svartsýnn • *adj* pessimistic
svartþröstur • *n* blackbird
svartur • *n* black • *adj* black
svartyllir • *n* elder
svefn • *n* sleep
svefndá • *n* coma
svefnherbergi • *n* bedroom
svefnhöfgi • *n* sleepiness
svefnleysi • *n* insomnia, insomniac • *adj* insomniac
svefnpurka • *n* sleepyhead
svefnsalur • *n* dormitory
svei • *interj* pshaw
sveifla • *v* brandish, flourish • *n* swing
sveiflast • *v* swing
sveifluhljóð • *n* trill
sveigja • *v* bow
sveigjanlegur • *adj* flexible
sveinn • *n* boy
sveita- • *adj* bucolic
sveitalegur • *adj* bucolic
sveitalífs- • *adj* bucolic
sveitar- • *adj* municipal
sveitarfélag • *n* municipality, township
sveitasælu- • *adj* bucolic
svelgur • *n* glutton
sveppadeyðir • *n* fungicide
sveppafræði • *n* mycology
sveppur • *n* fungus, mushroom
sverð • *n* blade, sword
sverðfiskur • *n* swordfish
sverja • *v* swear
svertingjahundur • *n* spade
sveskja • *n* prune
svið • *n* gamut, stage
svíða • *v* singe
sviðna • *v* singe
svigi • *n* parenthesis
svigna • *v* bow
svik • *n* swindle, treason
svika- • *adj* quack
svikari • *n* quack, traitor
svikinn • *adj* bogus

svíkja • *v* betray
svil • *n* milt
svili • *n* brother-in-law
svilkona • *n* sister-in-law
svimandi • *adj* vertiginous
svín • *n* pig
svínastía • *n* pigsty
svindl • *n* cheat, swindle
svindla • *v* cheat, swindle
svipbrigði • *n* expression
svipfar • *n* phenotype
svipgerð • *n* phenotype
svipta • *v* bereave, strip • *adj* bereft
svipur • *n* expression
sviss • *n* confederation
svitalyktareyðir • *n* deodorant
sviti • *n* sweat
svitna • *v* sweat
svívirðilegur • *adj* egregious
svona • *adv* so
svunta • *n* apron, counterfoil
syfja • *n* sleepiness
syfjuteygjur • *n* pandiculation
sýki • *n* disease
sýking • *n* infection
sykur • *n* sugar
sykurpúði • *n* marshmallow
sýnagóga • *n* synagogue
sýnast • *v* look
synd • *n* sin
synda • *v* swim
sýndarhugrekki • *n* bravado
sýndarmennska • *n* farce
syndga • *v* sin
syndlaus • *adj* sinless
syndugur • *adj* sinful
syngja • *v* sing
sýnisbók • *n* anthology
sýr • *n* sow
sýra • *n* acid
syrgja • *v* lament, mourn
syrja • *n* sediment
sýrustig • *n* acidity
sýsla • *v* work
sýsluhverfi • *n* arrondissement
systir • *n* sister
systkin • *n* sibling
systurdóttir • *n* niece
systursonur • *n* nephew
sýtósín • *n* cytosine
sýtosín • *n* cytosine

T

tá • *n* footpath, tau, toe
tækni • *n* technique, technology
tæknibull • *n* technobabble
tæla • *v* guile, seduce
tæma • *v* empty
tæplega • *adv* hardly
tafl • *n* game
tag • *n* type
tagl • *n* ponytail, tail
taka • *v* purloin, take
takk • *n* thanks • *interj* thanks, when
takki • *n* button, key
tákn • *n* symbol
táknið • *n* ampersand
táknrænt • *adv* symbolically
taktslag • *n* pulse
taktur • *n* bar, rhythm
tal • *n* speech
tál- • *adj* spurious
tala • *n* button, count, digit, number, speech • *v* talk
talenta • *n* talent
tálkn • *n* gill
tálma • *v* hinder
talnagrind • *n* abacus
talning • *n* count
talsmáti • *n* parlance
taminn • *adj* tame
tangens • *n* tangent
tank • *n* tank
tankur • *n* tank
tannbergsmæltur • *adj* alveolar
tannbursti • *n* brush, toothbrush
tannhjól • *n* gear
tannmæltur • *adj* dental
tannpína • *n* toothache
tannslíðurssjúkdómafræði • *n* periodontics
tánögl • *n* toenail
tantal • *n* tantalum
táp • *n* pluck
tap • *n* defeat
tappatogari • *n* corkscrew
tár • *n* tear
tar-skrá • *n* tar
táraflæði • *n* lacrimation
táraflóð • *n* lacrimation
táramyndun • *n* lacrimation
tarantúla • *n* tarantula
tárvotur • *adj* moist
tattó • *n* tattoo
tattóvera • *v* tattoo
tattú • *n* tattoo
tattúera • *v* tattoo
taug • *n* nerve
taugafræði • *n* neurology
taut • *n* mutter

tauta • *v* mutter
taxa • *v* taxi
taxi • *n* taxi
té • *n* tee
te • *n* tea
tegra • *v* integrate
tegrun • *n* integral
tegund • *n* kind, sort, type
teigur • *n* tee
teikna • *v* draw
teikning • *n* plot
teinóttur • *adj* pinstriped
teiti • *n* party
tékki • *n* cheque
teknetín • *n* technetium
telja • *v* count
teljari • *n* counter, numerator
tellúr • *n* tellurium
telpa • *n* girl
tema • *n* theme
tengdadóttir • *n* daughter-in-law
tengdamamma • *n* mother-in-law
tengdapabbi • *n* father-in-law
tengdur • *adj* related
tengi • *n* port
tengi- • *adj* associative
tengiliður • *n* contact
tengill • *n* connective
tengilykkja • *n* ampersand
tenging • *n* connective
tenginn • *adj* associative
tengisögn • *n* copula
tengsl • *n* rapport
teningur • *n* cube, die
tennis • *n* tennis
teppi • *n* carpet
terbín • *n* terbium
testósterón • *n* testosterone
textafræði • *n* philology
textaritill • *n* editor
texti • *n* subtitle, text
þá • *conj* as • *adv* then
það • *pron* it, this • *adv* there
þaðan • *adv* thence
þær • *pron* they
þætta • *v* factor
þættanlegur • *adj* composite
þágufall • *adj* dative
þak • *n* roof
þakhæð • *n* attic
þakhýsi • *n* penthouse
þakíbúð • *n* penthouse
þakinn • *adj* covered
þakklátur • *adj* grateful
þallín • *n* thallium
þangað • *adv* there, thither
þar • *adv* there

þari • *n* kelp
þarna • *adv* there, yonder
þátta • *v* factor, parse
þáttaröð • *n* season, series
þátttakandi • *n* participant
þáttur • *n* factor
þau • *pron* they
þegar • *adv* already • *conj* as, when
þegn • *n* subject
þeir • *pron* they
þekja • *v* cover
þekking • *adj* epistemic • *n* knowledge
þekkingarfræði • *n* epistemology
þekkingarleysi • *n* ignorance
þekkingarsvið • *n* bailiwick
þekkja • *v* know
þema • *n* theme
þér • *pron* you
þerna • *n* girl, tern
þessi • *pron* this
þétt • *adj* tight
þetta • *pron* this
þéttir • *n* capacitor
þéttur • *adj* narrow, tight
þeyta • *n* emulsion
þið • *pron* you
þiður • *n* capercaillie
þig • *pron* you
þing • *n* congress, parliament
þingmaður • *n* congressman
þinn • *pron* yours
þinur • *n* tensor
þjá • *v* devil
þjáður • *adj* suffering
þjáning • *n* agony, suffering
þjappa • *v* compress
þjarkafræði • *n* robotics
þjóð • *n* nation, people
þjóðaratkvæðagreiðsla • *n* plebiscite, referendum
þjóðaratkvæði • *n* plebiscite, referendum
þjóðarmorð • *n* genocide
þjóðernis- • *adj* ethnic
þjóðfélag • *n* society
þjóðhöfðingi • *n* potentate
þjóðhverfa • *n* ethnocentrism
þjóðhverfur • *adj* ethnocentric
þjóðtunga • *n* vernacular
þjóðtungu- • *adj* vernacular
þjóðvegur • *n* highway
þjófnaður • *n* larceny, theft
þjófur • *n* thief
þjónn • *n* manservant, waiter
þjónustustúlka • *n* girl
þjöppun • *n* compression
þjórfé • *n* tip
þó • *conj* though

þögn • *n* rest, silence • *interj* silence
þoka • *n* fog
þóknun • *n* recompense
þóknunarhrifslyf • *n* placebo
þokuský • *n* stratus
þolandi • *n* operand
þolfall • *n* accusative • *adj* accusative
þolgæði • *n* perseverance
þolinmóður • *adj* patient
þórín • *n* thorium
þorp • *n* thorp, village
þorpari • *n* crook
þorskur • *n* cod
þorsti • *n* thirst
þörungur • *n* alga
þótt • *conj* though
þrá • *v* long
þrá- • *adv* often
þráðkross • *n* reticle
þráður • *n* thread
þræða • *v* thread
þræla • *v* slave
þræll • *n* slave
þrálátur • *adj* incessant
þrálaus • *adj* incessant
þrautseigja • *n* perseverance
þrekvaxinn • *adj* burly
þrekvirki • *n* derring-do
þrengdur • *adj* tight
þrengingar • *n* hardship
þrenning • *n* trinity
þrep • *n* rung, stair
þrepun • *n* induction
þreskja • *v* thresh
þreykur • *n* smog
þreyttur • *adj* tired
þríburi • *n* triplet
þriðja • *n* third • *adj* third
þriðji • *adj* tertiary, third • *n* third
þriðjungur • *n* third
þríeyki • *n* trinity
þrífa • *v* clean
þríflokkun • *n* trichotomy
þríforkur • *n* trident
þrífótur • *n* tripod
þríhorn • *n* triangle
þríhyrningur • *n* triangle
þríleikur • *n* trilogy
þrístæða • *n* trigram
þrístæður • *adj* ternary
þrisvar • *adv* thrice
þrítugasta • *adj* thirtieth
þrítyngdur • *adj* trilingual
þríund • *n* third
þríunda- • *adj* ternary
þrívegis • *adv* thrice
þríviður • *adj* three-dimensional

þrjóskur • *adj* recalcitrant
þröngur • *adj* narrow, tight
þröstur • *n* thrush
þroti • *n* inflammation
þróunarkenningin • *n* evolution
þrúga • *n* grape
þruma • *n* thunder
þrumuský • *n* cumulonimbus
þrumuveður • *n* thunderstorm
þrusk • *n* rustle
þrýstilofts- • *adj* pneumatic
þú • *pron* thou, you
þumalfingur • *n* thumb
þumall • *n* thumb
þumlungur • *n* inch
þungaður • *adj* pregnant
þungavetni • *n* deuterium
þungeind • *n* baryon
þunglyndi • *n* depression, melancholy
þungsteinn • *n* tungsten
þungur • *adj* heavy
þunnur • *adj* thin
þurr • *adj* dry
þurrgufun • *n* sublimation
þurrkar • *n* drought
þurrkari • *n* dryer
þurs • *n* troll
þursabit • *n* lumbago
þúsöld • *n* millennium
þúsundasti • *adj* thousandth
þvaður • *n* waffle
þvæla • *v* babble
þvættingur • *n* bullshit
þvag • *n* urine
þvagrás • *n* urethra
þverfaglegur • *adj* interdisciplinary
þverfræðilegur • *adj* interdisciplinary
þverlamaður • *adj* paraplegic
þverlömun • *n* paraplegia
þverúðarfullur • *adj* recalcitrant
því • *conj* because
þvo • *v* wash
þvottabjörn • *n* raccoon
þvottasnúra • *n* clothesline
þýða • *v* mean, translate
þýðandi • *n* compiler, translator
þýði • *n* population
þýðing • *n* subtitle, translation
þýðingarforrit • *n* compiler
þýðingartexti • *n* subtitle
þykkskinnungur • *n* pachyderm
þykkur • *adj* fat
þynna • *v* dilute, thin
þynnka • *n* hangover
þynnt • *adj* dilute
þynntur • *adj* dilute
þyrilvængja • *n* helicopter

þyrla • *n* helicopter
þyrluvöllur • *n* heliport
þyrnililjuætt • *n* agave
þyrnóttur • *adj* thorny
þyrping • *n* crowd
þyrstur • *adj* thirsty
tí • *n* tee
tíð • *adj* frequent • *n* tense, time
tíðarandi • *n* zeitgeist
tíðatappi • *n* tampon
tíðir • *n* menstruation
tíðni • *n* frequency
tíður • *adj* frequent
tíglamynstur • *n* argyle
tígull • *n* rhombus
tigull • *n* rhombus
tígulsteinn • *n* brick
til • *v* move • *prep* to
tilbúinn • *adj* fictional, man-made, ready
tilfærsla • *n* displacement
tilfinning • *n* feeling
tilfinningalaus • *adj* callous
tilfinningar • *n* feeling
tilgáta • *n* conjecture
tilgerðarlegur • *adj* histrionic, stilted
tilhneigingu • *n* propensity
tilkynna • *v* notify
tilnefna • *v* nominate
tilraunastofa • *n* laboratory
tilvera • *n* being
tilviljanakenndur • *adj* stochastic
tilviljunarkenndur • *adj* haphazard
tilvistarsinni • *n* existentialist
tilvistarstefna • *n* existentialism
tilvitnun • *n* quotation
tímamæla • *v* time
tímarit • *n* magazine
tímasetja • *v* time
tímasetning • *n* chronology
tímastilla • *v* time
tímatal • *n* calendar, chronology
tímatalsfræði • *n* chronology
timbur • *n* timber • *interj* timber
timburmenn • *n* hangover
tími • *n* time
timjan • *n* thyme
tin • *n* tin
tinlóðun • *n* soldering
tinna • *n* flint
tíska • *n* vogue
tískuorð • *n* buzzword
títan • *n* titanium
títt • *adj* frequent • *adv* often
tittlingur • *n* bunting
títuprjónn • *n* pin
tíund • *n* tithe
tíundi • *adj* tenth • *n* tithe

tjakkur • *n* jack
tjald • *n* curtain, tent
tjalda • *v* camp
tjaldur • *n* oystercatcher
tjara • *n* tar
tjarga • *v* tar
tjörn • *n* lake, pond, tarn
tjull • *n* tulle
tóbak • *n* tobacco
töf • *n* delay, lag
tófa • *n* fox
töfraformúla • *n* panacea
töframaður • *n* wizard
töfrandi • *adj* magical
tog • *n* rope
togari • *n* trawler
tóki • *n* token
tokkata • *n* toccata
tökuorð • *n* loanword
tökuþýðing • *n* calque
tólfta • *adj* twelfth
tólg • *n* tallow
tölugildi • *n* modulus
tölusetja • *v* number
tölustærð • *n* scalar
tölustafur • *n* digit, number
tölva • *n* computer
tölvuforrit • *n* application, program
tölvumús • *n* mouse
tölvunotandi • *n* user
tölvuskjár • *n* monitor
tölvuskrá • *n* file
tölvustafur • *n* byte
tómati • *n* tomato
tómatjurt • *n* tomato
tómatur • *n* tomato
tombóla • *n* tombola
tómhyggja • *n* nihilism
tomma • *n* inch
tómstund • *n* leisure
tómur • *adj* empty
tónaróf • *n* gamut
tónaskali • *n* gamut
tónblær • *n* timbre
töng • *n* tongs
tónhæð • *n* pitch
tónleikar • *n* concert
tónlist • *n* music
tönn • *adj* dental • *n* tine, tooth
tónskáld • *n* composer
tóntegund • *n* key
tópas • *n* topaz
toppskarfur • *n* shag
toppur • *n* bang
torf • *n* peat, turf
torfa • *n* shoal, turf
torg • *n* bazaar, plaza, square

torgageigur • *n* agoraphobia
torræður • *adj* transcendental
tortíma • *v* annihilate
tossi • *n* dunce
tott • *n* fellatio
trampólín • *n* trampoline
trana • *n* crane
trappa • *n* rung, stair
tré • *n* tree
tréblásara • *adj* woodwind
tréblásturshljóðfæra • *adj* woodwind
tréblásturshljóðfæri • *n* woodwind
trefill • *n* scarf
trekt • *n* funnel
tréskór • *n* clog
trilla • *n* trill
trílógía • *n* trilogy
tríóla • *n* triplet
trippa • *v* trip
trissa • *n* pulley
trjábýll • *adj* arboreal
trjágrein • *n* bough
trjóna • *n* prow
tröð • *n* pen
troð • *n* avenue
troða • *v* cut
troðröð • *n* stack
tröll • *n* troll
tröllaldin • *n* grapefruit
tröllatré • *n* eucalyptus
tromla • *n* drum
tromma • *v* drum • *n* drum
trommari • *n* drummer
trommukjuði • *n* drumstick
trommuleikari • *n* drummer
trompet • *v* trumpet • *n* trumpet
tröppur • *n* stair
trú • *n* faith
trúarbrögð • *n* religion
trúarjátning • *n* creed
trufla • *v* annoy
truflandi • *v* annoying
trúgjarn • *adj* gullible
trúleysi • *n* atheism
trúleysingi • *n* atheist
trúnaðarmaður • *n* confidant
trúnaðarvinur • *n* confidant
trúníðingur • *n* apostate
trunta • *n* nag
tryggð • *n* fidelity
trygging • *n* bail, insurance
trýni • *n* muzzle, snout
túba • *n* tuba
tuða • *v* mutter
túlín • *n* thulium
túlkur • *n* interpreter
túndra • *n* tundra

tundurskeyti • *n* torpedo
tunga • *n* language, tongue
tungl • *n* moon
tunglfiskur • *n* sunfish
tunglvik • *n* libration
tungumál • *n* language
tunna • *n* barrel
túrban • *n* turban
túrmerik • *n* turmeric
turn • *n* tower
turnfálki • *n* kestrel
turnspíra • *n* spire
tuskast • *v* horse
tussa • *n* cunt
tútta • *n* jug
tuttugasta • *adj* twentieth
túttur • *n* jug
tvenna • *n* pair
tvenndargen • *n* allele
tvíatóma • *adj* diatomic
tvíbeind • *adj* bidirectional
tvíbendni • *n* ambivalence
tvíburi • *n* twin
tvíeyrna- • *adj* binaural
tvíheyrnar- • *adj* binaural
tvíhliða • *adj* bilateral
tvíhljóð • *n* diphthong
tvíhljóði • *n* diphthong
tvíhlustar- • *adj* binaural
tvíkynhneigð • *n* bisexuality
tvíkynjungur • *n* hermaphrodite
tvíliða • *n* binomial • *adj* binomial

tvíliðu- • *adj* binomial
tvílitna • *adj* diploid
tvíræður • *adj* backhanded
tvískauti • *n* diode
tvístæða • *n* bigram
tvístæður • *adj* binary
tvístígandi • *adj* hesitant
tvistur • *n* deuce, diode
tvisvar • *adv* twice
tvísykra • *n* disaccharide
tvítal • *n* duologue
tvítóla • *adj* hermaphrodite
tvítólaður • *adj* hermaphrodite
tvítóli • *adj* hermaphrodite
tvítyngdur • *adj* bilingual
tvíund • *n* second
tvíunda- • *adj* binary, dyadic
tvíundatölustafur • *n* bit
tvívaramæltur • *adj* bilabial
tvíveðrungur • *n* ambivalence
tvívegis • *adv* twice
tvívetni • *n* deuterium
tyggigúmmítré • *n* sapodilla
tyggja • *v* chew
týmín • *n* thymine
týna • *v* lose
týndur • *adj* lost
týpa • *n* type
týpískur • *adj* typical
typpi • *n* dick, penis
tyrðill • *n* turd

U

ú • *interj* boo
úðaefni • *n* aerosol
úði • *n* drizzle
úfur • *n* uvula
ugglaust • *adv* undoubtedly
ugla • *n* owl
úlfakreppa • *n* parhelion
úlfaldi • *n* camel
úlfur • *n* parhelion, wolf
ull • *n* wool
ullarfeiti • *n* lanolin
úlnliður • *n* wrist
umboðsmaður • *n* attorney
umbúðir • *n* bandage
umdeilanlegur • *adj* controvertible
umdeildur • *adj* controversial
umferðarhringur • *n* roundabout
umfrymi • *n* cytoplasm
umhverfa • *n* reciprocal
umhverfi • *adj* ambient • *n* nature

umkringja • *v* surround
umlykjandi • *adj* ambient
ummál • *n* circumference, perimeter
ummálsjafn • *adj* isoperimetric
ummyndun • *n* map, mapping, transubstantiation
umræðuefni • *n* subject
umritun • *n* transliteration
umsagnarliður • *n* predicate
umsagnarökfræði • *n* predicate
umskera • *v* circumcise
umskurður • *n* circumcision
umsnúningur • *n* eversion
umsögn • *n* predicate
umsókn • *n* application
umtal • *n* mention
umtalsefni • *n* subject
undanfari • *n* antecedent, harbinger • *adj*
antecedent
undantekningartilvikum • *adv* excep-

tionally
undarlegur • *adj* uncanny
undir • *prep* under
undirbúinn • *adj* ready
undirflokkur • *n* subgroup
undirfylking • *n* subphylum
undirfyrirsögn • *n* subtitle
undirgöng • *n* tunnel
undirheimar • *n* underworld
undirheiti • *n* hyponym
undirhúð • *n* hypodermis
undirlægja • *n* sycophant
undirmappa • *n* subdirectory
undirrita • *v* sign, subscribe
undirskrift • *n* signature
undirstúka • *n* hypothalamus
undirtitill • *n* subtitle
undra • *v* wonder
undralyf • *n* panacea
undraverður • *adj* astonishing, marvelous
undrun • *n* astonishment
undur • *n* wonder
undursamlegur • *adj* marvelous, wonderful
ungabarn • *n* baby
ungbarn • *n* baby
ungfrú • *n* miss
ungi • *n* litter
ungur • *adj* young
uns • *prep* until
uppáferð • *n* fuck
uppfinning • *n* invention
uppgangur • *n* expectoration
uppgerð • *n* hypocrisy
uppgerðarlegur • *adj* histrionic
uppgjafarsinni • *n* defeatist
uppgómmæltur • *adj* velar
upphaf • *n* inception, start • *adj* primordial
upphaflegur • *adj* pristine
upphrópun • *n* interjection
uppistaða • *n* backbone
uppistöðuefni • *n* matrix
upplestur • *n* dictation
upplifa • *v* experience
upploginn • *adj* fictional
upplýsingar • *n* information
uppnefna • *v* nickname
uppreisn • *n* insurrection
uppreisnarseggur • *n* discontent
upprisa • *n* resurrection
uppröðun • *n* arrangement
upprunalegur • *adj* primordial, pristine
uppsetning • *n* arrangement
uppskafningur • *n* palimpsest, parvenu, upstart

uppskrúfaður • *adj* stilted
uppskurður • *n* operation
uppsögn • *n* resignation
uppspuni • *n* myth
uppspunninn • *adj* fictional
uppstilling • *n* arrangement
upptækur • *v* confiscate
upptekinn • *adj* busy
uppþvottavél • *n* dishwasher
upptökuvél • *n* camera
upptrekktur • *adj* tense
uppvakningamaður • *n* necromancer
uppvakningur • *n* zombie
uppvaskari • *n* dishwasher
úr • *n* clock, watch, wristwatch
úran • *n* uranium
úreltur • *adj* obsolete
úrfellingarmerki • *n* apostrophe, ellipsis
úrhrak • *n* dregs
úrklippa • *n* clipping
úrkoma • *adj* pluvial • *n* precipitation
úrkynjaður • *adj* decadent
urmull • *n* myriad
úrslit • *n* final
úrslitakostir • *n* ultimatum
úrvalsstefna • *n* elitism
úrverk • *n* clockwork
uss • *interj* pshaw
útafliggjandi • *adj* supine
utandyra • *adv* outdoors
utanhúss • *adv* outdoors
útbýta • *v* distribute
útdeila • *v* distribute
útför • *n* funeral
útgangur • *n* exit
úthaf • *n* ocean, sea
útheimta • *v* demand
úthluta • *v* distribute
úthverfa • *v* evert
úthverfi • *n* suburb
úthverfing • *n* eversion
úthvolf • *n* exosphere
úti • *adv* alfresco, outdoors
útilega • *n* camping
útivistar- • *adj* outdoor
útjaðar • *n* outskirt
útkoma • *n* solution
útlægja • *v* outlaw
útlagi • *n* outlaw
útlendingahatur • *n* xenophobia
útlendingur • *n* foreigner
útnefna • *v* name
útsala • *n* sale
útsetning • *n* arrangement
útskiptanlegur • *adj* fungible
útskolun • *n* eluvium
útskúfun • *n* ostracism

útskýring • *n* explanation
útsýni • *n* view
útsynningsklakkar • *n* cumulonimbus
útvarp • *n* radio

útvarpstæki • *n* radio
útvega • *v* produce

V

vá • *n* distress • *interj* wow
vað • *n* ford
vaða • *n* shoal
vaðfugl • *n* shorebird
vændiskona • *n* prostitute
vænghaf • *n* wingspan
vængur • *n* wing
vafalaus • *adj* indubitable
vafalaust • *adv* undoubtedly
vafasamur • *adj* apocryphal, backhanded
vaffla • *n* waffle
vagga • *n* cradle
vagína • *n* pussy
vagn • *n* car, carriage
val • *n* choice
valda • *v* cause, mark
valdamaður • *n* potentate
valdamikill • *adj* powerful
valdaræningi • *n* usurper
valdarán • *n* usurpation
valdsvið • *n* bailiwick
valhnappur • *n* button
valhneta • *n* walnut
valkyrja • *n* valkyrie
valmenni • *n* gentleman
valmúi • *n* poppy
valur • *n* fallen, gyrfalcon, kestrel
vampíra • *n* vampire
vanadín • *n* vanadium
vandamál • *n* bother
vandræðalegur • *adj* abashed, awkward
vanfær • *adj* pregnant
vanhelga • *v* desecrate
vanilja • *n* vanilla
vanilla • *n* vanilla
vanillujurt • *n* vanilla
vankunnátta • *n* ignorance
vanræktur • *adj* neglected
vanþakklátur • *adj* thankless
vanþekking • *n* ignorance
vanþóknunarsvipur • *n* frown
vantrúaður • *adj* skeptical
vapp • *n* wandering
vappa • *v* rove
vara • *n* product
varabirgðir • *n* stockpile
varaforði • *n* stockpile
varalitur • *n* lipstick

varanlegur • *adj* permanent
varða • *n* cairn
varðeldur • *n* bonfire, campfire
varla • *adv* hardly
varmafræði • *n* thermodynamics
varna • *v* hinder
varnaðarorð • *n* warning
varnarleysi • *n* defenselessness
varnarmaður • *n* defender
varpa • *v* cast, throw
varta • *n* wart
varúlfur • *n* werewolf
vasaklútur • *n* handkerchief
vasaljós • *n* flashlight
vasi • *n* pocket
vaskur • *n* sink
vatn • *n* lake, water
vatnafræði • *n* hydrology
vatnakarfi • *n* carp
vatnalíffræði • *n* limnology
vatnaskil • *n* watershed
vatnsberar • *n* columbine
vatnsberi • *n* columbine
vatnsbrúsi • *n* canteen
vatnsfíkinn • *adj* hydrophilic
vatnsfræði • *n* hydrology
vatnsheldur • *adj* waterproof
vatnshöfuð • *n* hydrocephalus
vatnsklær • *n* cirrus
vatnsniður • *n* babble
vatnsrof • *n* hydrolysis
vatnssækinn • *adj* hydrophilic
vatnssalerni • *n* toilet
vatt • *n* watt
vax • *n* wax
vaxkaka • *n* honeycomb
vaxtarrækt • *n* bodybuilding
veðrahvolf • *n* troposphere
veðrahvörf • *n* tropopause
veðsetja • *v* hypothecate
veðsetning • *n* hypothecation
veður • *n* weather
veðurfarsfræði • *n* climatology
veðurfræði • *n* meteorology
veðurfræðingur • *n* meteorologist
vefa • *v* weave
vefari • *n* weaver
vefjarhöttur • *n* turban

vefstóll • *n* loom
vefsýnitaka • *n* biopsy
vefur • *n* tissue
vega • *v* weigh
vegabréf • *n* passport
vegabréfsáritun • *n* visa
vegamót • *n* intersection
vegaræningi • *n* highwayman
vegasalt • *n* seesaw
veggjakrot • *n* graffiti
veggjaskraut • *n* wallflower
veggskreyting • *n* mural
veggur • *n* wall
vegna • *adv* because • *conj* because
vegöxl • *n* shoulder
vegur • *n* road, way
vei • *interj* yay
veiða • *v* bag, fish, hunt
veiði • *n* falconry, hunt
veiðiferð • *n* hunt
veiðimaður • *n* hunter
veif • *n* semaphore
veifa • *n* pennant
veigrunarorð • *n* euphemism
veikja • *v* debilitate, dilute
veikur • *adj* dilute, ill, weak • *adv* piano
veira • *n* virus
veisla • *n* party
veitingahús • *n* restaurant
veitingasalur • *n* restaurant
veitingastaður • *n* restaurant
vél • *n* machine
véla • *v* guile
vélabrögð • *n* guile
vélarhlíf • *n* bonnet, cowl, hood
veldi • *n* realm
veldisstofn • *n* base
veldisvísir • *n* exponent, index
vélinda • *adj* esophageal
velja • *v* choose • *adj* eclectic
velkomin • *interj* welcome
velkominn • *interj* welcome
velkomnar • *interj* welcome
velkomnir • *interj* welcome
velmegun • *n* prosperity
vélmenni • *n* automaton
vélritari • *n* typewriter
velta • *v* bread, tumble
venjulegur • *adj* run-of-the-mill
venslarit • *n* nomogram
vepja • *n* lapwing
vera • *v* be, stay • *n* being
verð • *n* price
verða • *v* happen
verðbólga • *n* inflation
verðgildi • *n* value
verja • *v* defend

verk • *n* job, piece
verkefni • *n* job
verkfall • *n* strike
verkfallsvörður • *n* picket
verkfræðingur • *n* engineer
verksmiðja • *n* factory
verkur • *n* pain
vermút • *n* vermouth
vernda • *v* shield
verndari • *n* guardian
veröld • *n* world
verönd • *n* veranda
verpa • *v* throw
verri • *n* coil
verslun • *n* commerce, shop, trade
vertíð • *n* season
verufræði • *n* ontology
vesen • *n* bother
veski • *n* wallet
vessi • *n* lymph
vesti • *n* vest, waistcoat
vestri • *n* western
vestur • *n* west • *adv* west
vetni • *n* hydrogen
vetniskol • *n* hydrocarbon
vetrarbraut • *n* galaxy
vetrargarður • *n* greenhouse
vetrargrænn • *adj* evergreen
vettlingur • *n* mitten
vetur • *n* winter
víbrafónn • *n* vibraphone
við • *v* abandon, fight • *prep* by • *adj* in-shore • *pron* we
víðáttufælni • *n* agoraphobia
viðauki • *n* appendix, plus, rider
viðbein • *n* clavicle
viðbjóðslegur • *adj* disgusting, heinous, vile
viðbót • *n* addition, plus
viðdvöl • *n* sojourn
viðfang • *n* address
viðfangsefni • *n* subject
víðförull • *adj* traveled
víðir • *n* willow
viðmælandi • *n* interviewee
viðmið • *n* paradigm
viðnám • *n* resistance, resistor
viðnámstæki • *n* resistor
viðskeyti • *n* suffix
viðskiptavinur • *n* client, customer
viðskipti • *n* trade
viðstöðulaus • *adj* incessant
viðtal • *n* interview
víður • *adj* wide
viður • *n* timber
viðurværi • *n* sustenance
viðurværi • *n* livelihood

viðvörun • *n* premonition, warning
vífilengjur • *adj* roundabout
vifta • *n* fan
vígi • *n* fort
vígja • *v* marry
vigur • *n* vector
vígvöllur • *n* battlefield
vík • *n* bay, inlet
vika • *n* week
vikur • *n* pumice
vild • *adj* discretionary
vilja • *v* want
viljandi • *adv* deliberately • *adj* intentional
Villa • *n* error
villa • *n* error
vín • *n* wine
vin • *n* oasis, pasture
vina • *n* friend
vinalaus • *adj* friendless
vinalegur • *adj* friendly, kind
vinátta • *n* friendship
vináttuleikur • *n* friendly
vínbelgur • *n* wineskin
vínber • *n* grape
vinda • *n* winch • *v* wind
vindhviða • *n* gust
vindill • *n* cigar
vindmælir • *n* anemometer
vindmylla • *n* windmill
víndrykkur • *n* wine
vindubrú • *n* drawbridge
vindur • *n* wind
víngarður • *n* vineyard
vingjarnlegur • *adj* friendly
vingjarnleiki • *n* friendliness
vingull • *n* fescue
vínilmur • *n* bouquet
vinkona • *n* friend, girlfriend
vinna • *v* defeat, work • *n* job, work
vinnsla • *n* operation
vinnustaður • *n* workplace
vínrauður • *n* wine
vinsældir • *n* popularity
vinsæll • *adj* popular
vinstri • *adj* left
vinstúlka • *n* friend
vinur • *n* friend
vínviður • *n* grapevine
víóla • *n* viola
vippa • *n* flip-flop
vippurás • *n* flip-flop
vír • *n* wire
virða • *v* respect
virðast • *v* look
virðing • *n* respect • *adj* venerable
virðingarlaus • *adj* flippant

virðulegur • *adj* venerable
virðuleiki • *n* dignity
vírhefti • *n* staple
virki • *n* castle, fort, fortress, operator
virkilega • *adv* really
virkilega? • *interj* really
virkisgröf • *n* moat
virkjun • *n* activation
vísdómur • *n* wisdom
vísifingur • *n* forefinger
vísigreifi • *n* viscount
vísindamaður • *n* scientist
vísindarannsóknarmaður • *n* boffin
vísindi • *n* science
vísiputti • *n* forefinger
vísitala • *n* index
viska • *n* wisdom
viskí • *n* whiskey
viss • *adj* certain
vist • *n* whist
vista • *v* save
vistifræði • *n* ecology
vistkerfi • *n* ecosystem
vistþýðandi • *n* compiler
vísundur • *n* bison
vísvitandi • *adv* deliberately
vit • *n* acumen
vita • *v* know
vítamín • *n* vitamin
vitaturn • *n* lighthouse
viti • *n* lighthouse
vitki • *n* wizard
vitlaust • *adv* wrong
vitneskja • *n* knowledge
vitorðsmaður • *adj* accessory
vítvoðungsaldur • *n* babyhood
víxlinn • *adj* commutative
víxlveira • *n* retrovirus
voð • *n* raiment
vodka • *n* vodka
vöðvadeild • *n* sarcomere
vöðvaglóbín • *n* myoglobin
vöðvaliður • *n* sarcomere
vöðvamikill • *adj* muscular
vöðvarauði • *n* myoglobin
vöðvastæltur • *adj* muscular
vöðvi • *n* muscle • *adj* muscular
voff • *n* woof
voffa • *v* woof
vögguvísa • *n* lullaby
vogur • *n* inlet
vökvi • *n* liquid
voldugur • *adj* powerful
volt • *n* volt
völuberg • *n* conglomerate
von • *n* hope
vona • *n* hope • *v* hope

vonandi • *adv* hopefully
vonbrigði • *n* disappointment
vondur • *adj* bad, cruel, evil
vopn • *n* weapon
vopnabirgðir • *n* stockpile
vopnahlé • *n* armistice
vor • *n* spring
vör • *n* lip
vörður • *n* guard

W

waxa • *v* increase
wok-panna • *n* wok

X

xenon • *n* xenon

Y

yður • *pron* you
yfir • *prep* over
yfirborðskenndur • *adj* superficial
yfirbót • *n* expiation
yfirdraga • *v* overdraw
yfirdráttur • *n* overdraft
yfirdrepsskapur • *n* hypocrisy
yfirdrífa • *v* exaggerate
yfirfylking • *n* superphylum
yfirgefa • *v* abandon
yfirheiti • *n* hypernym
yfirhöfn • *n* overcoat
yfirlagður • *adj* premeditated
yfirmatsveinn • *n* chef
yfirráðasvæði • *n* territory
yfirregla • *n* metarule
yfirsjón • *n* sin
yfirskegg • *n* moustache
yfirskin • *n* pretext
yfirstærðfræði • *n* metamathematics

vörn • *n* defense
vörpun • *n* map, mapping
vörtubaugur • *n* areola
vörtusvín • *n* warthog
vöruhús • *n* warehouse
vörumerki • *n* trademark
vottun • *n* certification
votur • *adj* wet

yfirtónn • *n* overtone
yfirvaraskegg • *n* moustache
yfirvegað • *adv* deliberately
ygglibrún • *n* frown
ýkja • *v* exaggerate • *adv* very
ykkar • *pron* yours
ykkur • *pron* you
ýldudrep • *n* gangrene
ylliber • *n* elderberry
yllir • *n* elder
yndislegur • *adj* wonderful
yrðing • *n* proposition
yrkisefni • *n* subject
ýsa • *n* haddock
ystingur • *n* curd
ýta • *v* push
ytterbín • *n* ytterbium
yttrín • *n* yttrium

Printed in Great Britain
by Amazon

24591710R00076